MW00456998

Alla Osipenko

The Legend of Love.
Photo by Nina Alovert.

Alla Osipenko

Beauty and Resistance in Soviet Ballet

JOEL LOBENTHAL

OXFORD

UNIVERSITY PRESS

Oxford University Press is a department of the University of
Oxford. It furthers the University's objective of excellence in research,
scholarship, and education by publishing worldwide.

Oxford   New York
Auckland   Cape Town   Dar es Salaam   Hong Kong   Karachi
Kuala Lumpur   Madrid   Melbourne   Mexico City   Nairobi
New Delhi   Shanghai   Taipei   Toronto

With offices in
Argentina   Austria   Brazil   Chile   Czech Republic   France   Greece
Guatemala   Hungary   Italy   Japan   Poland   Portugal   Singapore
South Korea   Switzerland   Thailand   Turkey   Ukraine   Vietnam

Oxford is a registered trade mark of Oxford University Press
in the UK and certain other countries.

Published in the United States of America by
Oxford University Press
198 Madison Avenue, New York, NY 10016

Library of Congress Cataloging-in-Publication Data
Lobenthal, Joel.
Alla Osipenko : beauty and resistance in Soviet ballet / Joel Lobenthal.
    pages cm
Summary: "Alla Osipenko is the gripping story of one of history's greatest ballerinas, a courageous
rebel who paid the price for speaking truth to the Soviet state. A cast of characters drawn from all
sectors of Soviet and post-Perestroika society makes this biography as encyclopedic and encompassing
as a great Russian novel"— Provided by publisher.
Includes bibliographical references and index.
ISBN 978–0–19–025370–7 (hardback)
1. Osipenko, Alla Evgenyevna.   2. Ballet dancers—Russia (Federation)—Biography.   I. Title.
GV1785.O64L63 2015
792.8092—dc23
[B]
2015008481

9 8 7 6 5 4 3 2 1
Printed in the United States of America
on acid-free paper

To my aunt Dr. Lila Gordon (1932–2010), born in New York City five months before Osipenko was born in Leningrad. After my first interview with Osipenko in Hartford in January 1998, I drove down to Lila's home in Westchester. An accomplished pianist, from childhood she had nevertheless adored ballet above all other art forms. Together we watched the cassette tape Osipenko had given me. "This is the most gorgeous dancer I've ever seen in my life," was Lila's response.

Contents

PART THREE

Acknowledgments

THANKS TO RALPH Gleason for help with Wi-Fi and to Kevan Croton for computer troubleshooting.

As she has so many times, Nina Alovert generously opened up her extensive photo archives for me. Patricia Barnes and Rosemary Winckley graciously invited me to help myself to their photos of the Kirov's 1970 season in London.

In St. Petersburg, Natalia Bourmanova, Olga Rosanova, and Konstantin Balashov did extremely helpful things like arrange interviews, translate for same, and transmit archival photos. In New York, Marvin Hoshino deftly massaged some recalcitrant images.

I met Nina Baren in 1998 through Osipenko; they'd been friends in St. Petersburg. Since then she has been invaluable translator and liaison in just about everything I've done touching on Russian ballet.

I am ever-appreciative to the New York Public Library in all its manifestations, particularly the Dance Collection at the Library for the Performing Arts in Lincoln Center.

My agent Jeff Ourvan has been astute and engaged. At Oxford University Press, editor Norm Hirshy "got" the book right away, but also made some suggestions that improved it. Assistant editor Lisbeth Redfield was always helpful and responsive. Thanks to copy editor Patterson Lamb for asking the right questions. Production editor Kate Nunn is not only on top of things but patient. John Morrone provided surgical proof-reading, and Stacey Victor took the reins with enthusiasm and dispatch.

My father Joseph Lobenthal read through my entire first draft several years ago and gave it the benefit of his perspicacious parsing. My mother Shirley Lobenthal is a wonderfully obdurate stickler for prose clarity. My sister Lydia and brother Nicholas have forgiven my love of ballet, as well as other excesses, for decades now. Family and friends too numerous to mention have also been willing to learn.

And I am always grateful to the members of the Soka Gakkai International for their amazing perspective on life.

Alla Osipenko

Introduction

FIFTEEN YEARS BEFORE I met her in 1998, Alla Osipenko's name was already veiled in mystery, spoken with reverence by Soviet émigrés in New York. A prima ballerina of Leningrad's Kirov ballet during the 1950s and '60s, she was an outlaw, a dissident—politically, personally, and aesthetically.

In Soviet society, the operative word in artistic doctrine was "content," defined to mean dramatic, thematic, ideological appropriateness. After the Revolution, ballet was pressured to conform to programmatic utility. But Osipenko's movement often seemed to function abstractly, existing for its own mandate of beauty and eloquence. Ideal balletic proportions made her superlatively equipped to proclaim the beauty of ballet for ballet's sake. Her movement heeded a kinetic utility that was highly personal. "The more abstract the choreography," Gennady Smakov writes in *The Great Russian Dancers*, "the more the various facets of her personality broke through it." Choreographers had sought her out: she had been at the vanguard of ballet in her time and place.

She had been equally iconoclastic personally. Osipenko's sharp tongue and candid independence elicited frequent friction with Soviet and Kirov authorities. Osipenko was a key figure in the Soviet cultural diplomacy of the 1950s and '60s, and as well, a victim of it. She was the first generation of Kirov ballet stars to enchant Europe, winning Paris's prestigious Pavlova Prize on her initial visit there in 1956. But flouting Soviet rules for personal and political conduct soon found her all but quarantined in Russia.

From my perspective, Osipenko's mystery was deepened by the political and cultural divide existing at that time. Despite her success in Europe, in the West there was very little material available about her. But the void in the historical record where Osipenko's presence should have been was a crucial testament as well to the willed obscurity to which she had been consigned by

On tour in Holland, February 1968.
Anefo photo collection, National Archive of the Netherlands. Jac.
de Nijs / Anefo.

Soviet officialdom. Smakov's book was almost as far as we could go toward bridging the balletic divide of those years.

Thirty years ago, her émigré friends and admirers had no idea that the Soviet Union was on the verge of dissolution. But when perestroika remade the political map once again, it meant that for Osipenko, now in her mid-fifties, the gates were finally springing open. In 1988 she went to London to assist her old friend, colleague, and 1970 defector Natalia Makarova stage *La Bayadère* for the Royal Ballet. In 1989, Rudolf Nureyev, who was then artistic director of the Paris Opera Ballet, invited her to teach there where they had danced together triumphantly during the Kirov's 1961 visit, immediately before his own defection. In 1989, Osipenko moved to Italy. In 1995 she was invited to join the faculty of the Hartford Ballet school in Connecticut.

She finally had the opportunity to see the United States, and I had the chance to meet her. I was very excited at the prospect of profiling her for *Ballet Review*. Not only was I finally going to meet the legend, but I would be scoring a journalistic scoop of sorts: I would be the first American to write about her.

The legend was, of course, a woman of flesh and blood. Sixty-five when I first met her in January 1998, Osipenko remained thin as a ballerina. Her patrician features bore the weight of years and many sorrows; her blue eyes were sparkling, ironic, vulnerable. I had wondered if she would be difficult to thaw, but she had a lot on her mind and a lot she wanted to say. She let me borrow a number of her own photos during our first meeting. I was impressed above all by two pictures of her rehearsing *Swan Lake* with the Kirov in London in 1970. Here was confirmation of all that had been written about the unsurpassed beauty of Osipenko's line. She also gave me a video of herself performing various pas de deux. Her performance of the *Swan Lake* adagio alone would have been enough to establish her as one of the century's great ballerinas.

And yet, Smakov had been right: liberated from characterization, the full palette of Osipenko's movement became even more starkly displayed. On the same tape was footage of her in practice clothes, performing a stylized sequence of classroom exercises. She never moved away from the barre, never danced in the round, but watching her body stretch I felt that I was seeing the whole range of ballet's expressive possibilities demonstrated.

After five interviews with Osipenko, my *Ballet Review* article on her appeared in the Spring 1998 issue. I decided to continue interviewing her. I hoped that someday I would be able to produce a book such as this one.

I visited her successively in two modest apartments in West Hartford. The furniture was modern and impersonal: there was none of the warm patina of Russian antiques with which she had been surrounded in St. Petersburg. But her apartments were personalized with many books and many photos. She was a gracious hostess. Her little dining room table always held plentiful nibbles, and sometimes she made lunch. "I'm learning how to cook," she told me, "because I cook when you are here. I never have." There was a sizable Russian émigré community in West Hartford, and Osipenko regularly frequented the two Russian food stores there. For my part, I enjoyed introducing her to culinary novelties from a Middle Eastern specialty store on Farmington Avenue.

She taught daily at the Hartford Ballet's school and sometimes coached the company, which performed regular but infrequent seasons. She did not find most of her work especially stimulating. There were some talented dancers in the Hartford Ballet, but at the school the students were not up to the level of those with whom she'd worked in Russia. She was working for money, but when I asked her what she would be doing if she had limitless funds, she admitted, "I would work. I would teach ballet." For her, ballet is, was, and would always be a passion.

As she spoke, anger about injustices and indignities of the past would sometimes flare, and on occasion some bitterness. But never out of reach was her sense of humor. This could be wry and acerbic but was often simply droll. I was astonished when she said she had never dreamed that ballet competitions here in America were just as corrupt as anywhere else. She had arrived with the same idealized view of the United States shared by so many of the Soviet artistic elite of her generation. It seemed as if their vision of us had indeed become more romanticized in inverse proportion to the amount of anti-America disinformation disseminated by their government.

Now she was forced to grapple with the paradoxes of our own country and system. America was not simply the land of the free and the home of the brave. We began our meetings just as a national tragedy was unfolding: the persecution and eventual impeachment of President Clinton over the fact that he had lied about his affair with Monica Lewinsky. "If I spoke English I'd be defending Clinton right now," she told me. "It's nobody's damn business," she said about Clinton's indiscretions. "God forbid they would kick him out because of the scandal."

Month after month we continued our conversations in the presence of different translators. First there was Elena, a former student of hers. But the bulk was done by a professional we had somehow located named Roman. By the time Osipenko left Hartford in June 2000 we had conducted nearly forty interviews.

She was perfectly capable of criticizing with detachment the actions of her younger self. "Your tongue is your enemy," she had been told since childhood. She had certainly been her own worst enemy on more than one occasion. Rival ballerinas in the company, as well as administrators of both the Party and the Kirov, had known which buttons to push, how to provoke her so that she spoke caustic truth to power and thus reaped the whirlwind. But she made it clear that she had been at odds not only with the Soviet system but with all restrictions, beginning with familial authority.

It was Nikita Khrushchev's "thaw" of the late 1950s and early 1960s that had enabled Osipenko and her artistry to reach Western audiences. In 1998, when I first interviewed her, perestroika was allowing Russia another period of relative relaxation in state censorship—and its consequent indoctrination of the population in self-censorship. That thaw has since hardened ominously, but even then it was clear that her account of events was often the only one that could be consulted. She spoke about things that others would prefer not be talked about at all. In years to come I observed firsthand many of her colleagues and interviewed some of them. Few talked as bluntly as she. She was sardonic and often rueful about her transgressions. For me there was no doubt that she was a great woman as much as a great artist, nonetheless so for being by her own admission stubborn, opinionated, and often intractable. And for me she was all the more admirable for being able to make those admissions.

Osipenko had indulged herself; she had not always been discreet. She looked back at her sometimes outlandish indiscretions with awe at her boldness and an unclouded awareness of the price she had paid. And yet, when considering whether she would have done it all over again, she conceded that indeed she probably would have.

1

A Storied Family

DURING THE SOVIET era, Osipenko had been careful to divulge as little information as possible about her family, for the rarified manners of ballet had been to her an extension of a world she already knew. By contrast, many of her colleagues were children of peasant or working-class families, who had benefited from the class-leveling recruitment demanded by the Soviet government. But Osipenko was born on June 16, 1932, to a family that belonged to the pre-Revolutionary elite. Not only was her parents' lineage aristocratic, but many in her family had spent time living in Europe, grounds for suspicion as the grip of super-nationalism and xenophobia gained hold in the Soviet Union.

Only as perestroika began did Osipenko feel relaxed about discussing her ancestors. She was proud of them and they had remained an active context for her life. Her mother, grandmother, and great-aunt had lived with her until they died; Osipenko's four husbands had never been able to dislodge them.

But over the years there had been much conflict between her and her family, above all between Osipenko and her mother, Nina Borovikovskaya. Nina was descended from a noted eighteenth-century artist, Vladimir Borovikovsky, who painted portraits of fashionable Petersburg and court society. Nina's paternal grandfather was Alexander Borovikovsky, a senator in the Russian Duma established in 1905. He had been an advisor to Czars Alexander III and Nicholas II.

Osipenko understood the senator to have been a man of honor and progressive beliefs, who helped many, and apparently he looked for similar high standards in his colleagues. His contemporary, poet Nikolai Nekrasov, incurred his disfavor, accused by the senator of hypocrisy; Borovikovsky

Osipenko's grandfather, Alexander Borovikorsky.
Photo courtesy Alla Osipenko.

claimed that the poet's actions fell short of the noble sentiments expressed in his poetry.

Alexander himself also wrote poetry that often concerned religion. He had four children, Vera, Olga, Alexander, and Sergei. A woman named Maria Zhigacheva had been brought into the family at age sixteen as a companion and chaperone for his daughters. The younger Alexander fell in love with Maria. Osipenko never knew anything about Maria's family, only that she had been raised in a remote area.

Senator Borovikovsky bought the premises of a French photographer at 63 Nevsky Prospect so that his son Alexander could establish a business as a portraitist. He also bought a large apartment on the same floor to house the entire family. Alexander and Maria had two children: Osipenko's mother Nina was born in 1903, her brother Valentin in 1906. But Maria and Alexander remained unmarried. He was a womanizer. As an adult, Osipenko had once been given a video entitled "Athens Nights." Why did that title ring a bell, she wondered—until recalling that decades earlier she had been told of a club by that name in pre-Revolutionary Petersburg. "Athens Nights" was proverbial then for "orgies," and her grandfather had gone to the eponymous club for "a little poetry, a little kissing." Needless to say, Maria "did not like it at all."

Maria Borovikorskaya with Nina and Valentin.
Photo courtesy Alla Osipenko.

Years later, Nina told Osipenko that in 1909, when Nina was six and Valentin three, the senator called his son in and insisted that he now legitimize his union and his offspring. But Maria was angry that the idea of the marriage had come only at her father-in-law's insistence and seemingly for the benefit of her children, although she was genuinely loved by her husband's family. And so, ironically, it was the marriage that led to an irrevocable breach between Alexander and Maria. "She became just ice," said Osipenko. Photographed with her two young children, she looks stern indeed whereas her husband Alexander is hot-eyed and sybaritic.

When the Revolution came, the Borovikovskys put their jewelry and other valuables into a bank vault in roiling St. Petersburg and fled to their country estate in Ukraine, which they now shared with the local peasantry. The family remained there for six years. Army after army overran the countryside. The village was forced at intervals to barricade itself, hiding livestock, nubile women, Jews—whichever sector was to be marauded by the expected arrivals. One time a rampant battalion of Bolsheviks seized the senior Alexander and were leading him off to be executed when a delegation of peasants raced after them and saved his life by attesting that he was their friend and comrade.

Around 1924, after the civil war that followed the Revolution had finally been won by the Reds, the Borovikovskys returned to Leningrad. They found that the new regime had all but stripped them naked. The contents of their safety deposit box had been nationalized. They retained their apartment, but the government had seized the photo studio. They had no money, no jewelry. Osipenko's grandfather had no job. Initiated in 1921, the New Economic Policy now allowed a wide scale of private commercial activity. He was able to open a small photo shop in the former premises of his own photo studio, catering to the demand for passport photos.

Alexander despised the Soviets. A colleague of his had prospered by making photographic portraits of the czar's family, but after the Revolution he kept his business thriving by photographing Lenin and other Bolshevik bigwigs. "My grandfather wanted to go and kill him." He would not let his son Valentin participate in Soviet society. Instead he took over his education himself; Valentin's profession became painting Christmas decorations and puppets. Valentin was handsome in face and figure.

In Ukraine, Nina had been wooed by the sons of noble families. But Osipenko believed that her mother, snub-nosed and pretty, who continued to speak French and play the piano, suffered in the alien environment of Soviet Leningrad no less than did Alexander. Perhaps it was in the spirit of rebellion that Nina became engaged to Evgeni Osipenko, who also lived with his family in the same building. They met through mutual friends who were neighbors. Evgeni's family was descended from the upper echelons of Ukrainian society but he was an employee of the Soviet state, a police detective, although privately his views were not doctrinaire. He had a striking and dramatic appearance, with high flat cheekbones and a brooding look. Certainly, however, Alexander's disapproval of the marriage could not have come as a surprise to Nina. She and Evgeni moved out of 63 Nevsky into their own apartment, until her father forgave them and Nina returned to the Borovikovsky ménage with her husband.

Evgeni's brother Georgi was a professional actor, but Evgeni by temperament was equally a performer. The role of Sherlock Holmes suited him to perfection. When off on an investigation, Evgeni might not show up at home for two or three weeks at a time. If Nina knew where he was, she would slip away to him with a care package of food. Sometimes when a fugitive was apprehended, Evgeni and his colleagues would be given a cash bonus, which they would spend instantly in disorderly carousing, thus finding themselves locked up temporarily in a police brig, a *gauptvacht*.

The birth of his daughter Alla sent Evgeni on another celebratory bender, and so it was her grandfather Alexander who brought Osipenko home from the hospital. A relative who had emigrated had left a chaise from which the family fashioned a bed, surmounted by a canopy, for their newest arrival. But while Alexander took regular portraits of Osipenko until she was two, he could not cajole a real smile out of her. The most he could elicit was just the barest hint of one.

By this time, Alexander had found a way to palliate his rage at the Soviets: morphine, a refuge supplied by friends who worked in a hospital. Osipenko was only three when he died in 1935, but she recalled him bedridden with respiratory problems. Sunlight irritated him, probably because of his drug use, and Osipenko remembered that a large cupboard had been moved between his bed and the window. Sometimes she would go in to visit him.

"I would ask, 'Does this hurt here?' He would say, 'Yes.' I would say, 'I'm hurting here, too.'"

"Cats are hurting, dogs are hurting," her grandfather assured her, "but Alla's pain is going to go away."

The rest of the family were somewhat more sanguine than he about the Soviet government, seeing it as a continuation of monarchist absolutism. "We have lived through five czars," her grandmother and great-aunt told her: two Alexanders, one Nicholas—as well as Lenin and now Stalin.

They somehow were able to remain largely enclosed in their own niche. Many of their Old World customs, beliefs, and routines continued. Almost miraculously, their apartment was never subdivided into communal quarters. They retained their six rooms plus kitchen. Osipenko's grandmother Maria observed a quite literal detachment from the new society: she rarely left the apartment, running her household with the assistance of the same maid she'd had before the Revolution.

Apartments in their building continued to be heated by a wood stove. The courtyard was jammed with piles of logs waiting to be hauled by the super to the individual apartments. Well after World War II, merchants continued to deliver fresh dairy products to the apartment. A tankard of milk strapped on her back, a woman trudged up five flights of stairs to Maria's home. If for some reason she couldn't make it, she would send someone in her place, much to Maria's displeasure, since she was partial to a cow owned by her steady supplier.

Maria's sister Anna Grekova, who was divorced from her merchant husband, and childless, also came to live with them. While Maria was thrifty,

Anna Grekova.
Photo courtesy Alla Osipenko.

Anna was generous. She would visit the nearby farmers' market and sample produce to her heart's delight, then purchase more than Maria had authorized. She and Maria frequently squabbled about Anna's alleged profligacy.

In 1937, Osipenko's father Evgeni was working in a prison camp in Tashkent in Central Asia. For a time Nina and Alla were living there with him. As Osipenko eventually came to understand it, he was drunk one day and simply could not keep his mouth shut any longer. On horseback he charged into the marketplace, spraying the sky with bullets and mouthing imprecations against the Soviets. The next day he was in jail, and was later sentenced to five years in prison. Nina divorced him soon after. Stalin's purges were in full swing, and guilt by association was a fundament of the Soviet judicial process. Nina would have had every reason not to remain connected to a convict.

Osipenko's father was absent, yet his family was nevertheless a major influence on her. Evgeni's two brothers lived with their mother in the same bulding. Boris was an engineer. Georgi was an actor at the Alexandrinsky theater on Rossi Street, to which Osipenko was taken frequently. The repertory included the "small tragedies" of Pushkin: *Boris Godunov, The Stone Guest, Mozart and Salieri*, as well as much more recent works such as Bulgakov's *Days of the Turbins*, which dramatized the flight of the White Army after its defeat in the civil war. Bulgakov's play starred the great Nikolai Cherkasov, one of many noted actors of the day whose work she became acquainted with as a child.

Before the Revolution, her mother had auditioned for the Imperial ballet school. Nina told Alla that prospective students needed to visit the homes of leading ballerinas and show themselves prior to a vote. Nina needed eleven votes to be admitted and she had secured only ten, a disappointment that continued to fester. As an adult "she tried not to even think about ballet," Osipenko said. Nina did take her to see ballet occasionally, but as a child she went more frequently to the opera. When she was five, she and great-aunt Anna sat in the *bel étage* at the once–Imperial Mariinsky opera house—now under Communism renamed Kirov—to hear Rimsky-Korsakov's opera *Tale of Tsar Saultan*. Hysterical tears were her reaction to the Tsar's young son being unceremoniously tossed into a barrel with his mother and set adrift on the high seas. She pleaded that he be fished out. That performance ended prematurely for Osipenko when Anna escorted her from the theater.

Osipenko asked her mother if her actual father was still working in Tashkent. But neither her mother nor her grandmother wanted to talk about him, and what little they said was not complimentary. "Oh, don't ask me!" Nina said. "He was just a drunk." But great-aunt Anna was much more charitable. "Don't listen to them," she told Alla. "He was wonderful, very wise, a nice, kind man," loved by his colleagues. "Of course he drank a little after work—he was tired—but not until he passed out."

Of all the household, Osipenko was closest to Anna, who was the family conciliator, and not only concerning Evgeni. Even as a girl, Osipenko preferred to share her adventures and problems with Anna. In photos, her face, full-lipped and rather sensuous, makes her seem much more approachable than her sister Maria.

Anna ran a dressmaking business for private customers out of the apartment, assisted by two young women, Vera and Panya. Anna told Osipenko that once during a screaming argument with Nina and Maria, her father had seized Anna's sewing machine and thrown it out the window. Later he offered Anna profuse apologies, but she'd told him not to worry, she understood exactly: "It's so difficult to deal with them when they scream."

As far as Osipenko could remember, her grandmother Maria never once kissed her. Well into Osipenko's adulthood, if she fell short of expectations, Maria would refrain from a direct rebuke but would make her disapproval crystal clear with an aloof pronouncement: "Too bad, too bad, Lalasha." The reprimand still echoed in Osipenko's ears. Maria's relationship with her daughter Nina was also reserved. "We are not tender in our family," Nina told Osipenko.

Nina worked as a typist in different offices, among them the central distributor for the city's supply of firewood. She liked her job and was good at it. "She would have learned to use the Internet in one second," Osipenko said. Nina went out to work in the morning and by the time she came home in the evening Osipenko was already asleep. Sunday was her favorite day of the week because it was the one day that she could spend time with her mother. Nina took her to a restaurant on Nevsky named Krisisana, treating her to fried potatoes with meat cutlets—her favorite meal. And yet Osipenko found it difficult all her life to tell her mother what was going on in her life and what her problems were.

Like so many bourgeois Petersburg apartments, theirs had been built with both front and kitchen entrances. Intimates were instructed to ring three times. A single ring therefore signaled the approach of a stranger, and always it was possible that he was a "Finance Inspector" come to shut down the private businesses that were prohibited after the New Economic Policy was curtailed in 1928. Anna would sound an alarm to Vera, Panya, and Alla, and they would carry the bolts of fabric up to the attic until the coast was clear. (Soviet rules and regulations changed so rapidly that Anna was apparently unaware that in 1936, as Sheila Fitzpatrick reports in *Everyday Stalinism*, a number of individually owned businesses, among them dressmaking, had been re-legalized, provided that they did not distribute to the open market but worked only at the request of private clients.)

It was Anna's business that contributed most to the family's income. She outfitted her great-niece in high style. Clients customarily brought Anna three yards of fabric from which to fashion a dress, but occasionally Anna would ask them for three and a half. "I have little Alla and she needs a new dress." One summer, Osipenko went with a girlfriend, Lala, to spend the summer with Lala's family in a rustic village. After more than fifty years of separation, Osipenko was contacted again by this same Lala. "I remember when you were in our village," she told Osipenko. "You ran in your dress and I saw your underwear was made from the same fabric." Later, she would be considered the best-dressed girl in the Leningrad ballet academy.

Osipenko was close to her governess Lidia, a girl who began tending her when Osipenko was nine months old. She stayed with the family for twenty-five years, and her daughters became friends as well. But Lidia was only in her late teens when she began working for them. Told to take Osipenko out for a three-hour walk, she preferred instead to sneak her into a movie. Then they'd walk around after the film. "What a strange thing!" Maria remarked. "Lalasha walked for three hours," and in the stinging, damp city, still managed to come home pale.

The Borovikovskys did not approve when Nina's brother Valentin, now in his early thirties, fell in love with a woman older than he who had a fifteen-year-old son. Osipenko recalled Nina and Valentin storming out of a room in the Nevsky Prospect apartment. His face was bloodied. "You see what you did to me!" he screamed. But Nina was stony. For a long time he didn't live with them and was forced to fend for himself for the first time in his life. Sometimes he would appear at the service entrance of the apartment, pleading, "Lalasha, could you bring me something to eat?"

Knowledge of the purges was widespread through Soviet society, Osipenko believed, but looking back she thought that her parents' generation didn't understand or believe how one man could be responsible for so much terror. "They always were doubting, questioning themselves, 'Is he really *that* bad?'"

But like most families in the Soviet Union, the Borovikovskys were directly affected. Osipenko described Luka, Maria's half-brother, as "a professional revolutionary." He had been jailed after the February 1905 Revolution. At that time, Anna came to Senator Borovikovsky and asked for help. He bribed a prison chief who made it possible for Luka to escape. Luka was sent to Helsinki, then called Helsingfors, and given the name of someone there who would help him find refuge. He was supposed to write the information inside his cuff for easy reference, but he didn't. On the night train to Finland, officials asked for his documents and asked who he was going to see. He couldn't remember. They arrested him and, discovering that he was a fugitive, put him back in prison. Several days later, the prison chief appeared at their apartment and insisted on returning the bribe.

Luka was later freed, lived for a time in Germany, and then returned to Moscow. But Stalin had begun to cannibalize the original Bolsheviks, the true believers, veterans of the 1905 and 1917 revolutions. When several of his friends were arrested in 1937, Luka was actually upset that he had *not* been seized together with former comrades. When he was finally arrested, his daughter Valentina, Nina's cousin, told Osipenko years later that he retained his revolutionary fervor to the last. Now truth would be proven, his comrades released, slanders unmasked. It was all just a misunderstanding. But he was accused of spying for Germany and was shot. Not until years later, however, was the family able to receive confirmation of his fate.

Something of the same fervor, with perhaps a touch not just of reckless but of self-sacrificing zeal, would imprint Osipenko's later conflicts with Kirov and Communist Party officials. "Alla wanted to show the truth," a classmate at the Leningrad ballet academy would declare.

Osipenko's mother worked late, and it was Maria who would put little Alla to bed—talk and read to her. Maria invented her own story, a fable about a gray shirt imbued with magical properties. Serial installments arrived nightly and concluded with "to be continued." Sometimes Maria would lie down next to Alla and sometimes drift off in the middle of her narrative. Osipenko would shake her awake and demand to know what came next. But it was her mother who woke her every morning at seven. Most of the year her room was cold and dark; she would slip into her clothes under the blankets.

Osipenko was a tomboy who bridled at any kind of restriction. She liked small children, liked playing with them, liked being in their company. Her earliest career aspiration was either to have twelve children or to be a teacher in kindergarten. Next, she wanted to be an archaeologist and conduct excavations around the world. The family thought that she would become a world traveler, something that for a Soviet, however, was now all but impossible. But Osipenko liked to pretend that her room was Paris. She stacked up the furniture and remade the landscape throughout the whole apartment. Her elders complimented her on her rich fantasy life, but when the time had come to right the topsy-turvy room, it was "Stop traveling; you're back at home already!"

At elementary school, dance classes were offered as an elective to the students. Ballet was not the young Osipenko's choice of extracurricular enrichment, but she liked the idea of time away from her family and its strict rules, of carving out an independent life. Twice a week, therefore, she attended the ballet class. It was not love at first sight between ballet and Osipenko, nor between her and her instructor, Leonid Fimovich. Fimovich later similarly "discovered" Yuri Soloviev, and years afterward was recognized with a modest title by the Soviet government, at which time "Yura and I wrote very supportive letters," Osipenko recalled. But in his class, it had been another story: "I wanted to teach him instead of him teaching me."

"You always made me nervous," Fimovich told the adult Osipenko, "because I said one word and you answered with ten." Once he got so angry that he picked up a chair and threatened "Girl, be silent or I will kill you." Nevertheless, he recommended to Nina that she audition her daughter at the state ballet academy on Rossi Street. "He said I had a difficult character that wouldn't be so bad for ballet," she laughed in recollection.

"I failed," Nina told her; "maybe you will not fail." To be admitted, the household believed, an inside track was necessary, and they weren't about to take any chances. Anna had a customer, Irina Shashkova, whose husband was a soloist in the Kirov opera. Anna asked Shashkova to ask her husband to put in a good word for Alla. She also made a beautiful blue dress for Osipenko's audition, trimmed in chiffon and accessorized with a matching chiffon hat. When she appeared before the members of the commission for her physical exam, they instructed her to strip down to her underwear. "I was there almost naked," Osipenko told Anna when she returned home. "They didn't need your dress there!"

Somehow the nine-year-old was convinced that she would be admitted. But looking back, Osipenko didn't feel that her admittance was a foregone conclusion on her merits. Her feet were ideally balletic, but her hips were not naturally turned out, and a dispassionate assessment of raw attributes was very much part of the evaluation process. Shashkov's boost, if indeed he supplied it, may have helped, but in any case, she was admitted, immediately prior to the cataclysm that befell the Soviet Union late in June 1941. A generation of young men, celebrating high school graduation on the night of June 21, a Saturday, the Summer Solstice, woke the next morning to discover that they would soon be on the battlefield.

2

World at War

MORE THAN THREE million Axis troops attacked the USSR's western borders from the Baltic Sea in the north to the Black Sea in the south. The Kremlin was caught completely unaware: Stalin believed that the mutual non-aggression pact he had signed with the Germans in August 1939 would stand. For months, Moscow had ignored warnings from Western governments as well Soviet diplomatic attachés about the imminence of invasion.

The country's mobilization affected Osipenko's mother personally. She had fallen in love with a married colleague, Nikolai Ivanovich. Looking back, Osipenko believes that he was the love of her mother's life. She realized that when her mother told her family that she had to work in the evenings, she was actually with him. He was going to divorce his wife and marry Nina. Shortly after Russia was invaded, however, Osipenko heard them in her mother's room. Nina was crying. Nikolai would be one of more than eight million Soviet soldiers killed in combat, with almost twice as many citizens perishing as well.

A week after the invasion, schoolchildren and their mothers began to be evacuated from Leningrad, along with the staff of major cultural and technical institutions. Nina accompanied Osipenko together with the Kirov company and school when it was evacuated. The dancers as well as the older students were sent to the countryside outside the city of Perm in the Ural mountains. The younger students were settled in the city of Kostroma on the Volga, which had been sumptuously rebuilt by Catherine the Great's architects after a catastrophic fire in 1773. Wartime conditions meant a ten-day trip from Leningrad to Kostroma by train and boat. On the way, their train stopped to pick up passengers from another train that had been bombed.

Osipenko, 1934.
Photo courtesy Alla Osipenko.

Osipenko and her fellow passengers shared their food with the refugees. But she was largely oblivious to the ongoing catastrophe: for the sea leg of the trip, Osipenko and her new schoolmates played on deck happily. A starkly beautiful line of demarcation between dark blue and light green waters demonstrated where the Volga flowed into the Caspian Sea.

Two months later, after German bombs were dropped near Kostroma, Osipenko and the younger students were moved to join the rest of the ballet evacuees in the village of Palazna on the outskirts of Perm, which the Soviets had renamed Molotov. (The village was later flooded to create a reservoir.) There they rented a room in a private house while Nina found work sewing costumes for the Kirov.

In Palazna, Osipenko for the first time experienced privation, and as a result it was here that "I started to develop a character." Getting to school meant a three-kilometer walk through the forest. Frequently she ran the entire way so as not to freeze, wearing clothes she'd already outgrown. The students took ballet class in the evenings in a church that had been turned into a warehouse. Sometimes it was so cold there they would have to wear a glove on the hand resting on the barre. The pianist played in a coat and fingerless gloves.

Each evacuee was allotted a small amount of bread each day that was washed down with infusions of tasty black broth. When a horse died it was turned into cutlets for the students. Poor as their diet was, it was all but Lucullan, compared to what was endured by those remaining in Leningrad.

Food rationing in the city began mid-July. Although the Germans failed to take Leningrad in September as they had planned, nevertheless they completely encircled the city. Leningrad was to "die of starvation," Hitler declared. That objective now seemed possible because German bombs had obliterated the city's enormous food warehouses. Hundreds of thousands of people starved in Leningrad that winter. But that same autumn the "road of life" across frozen Lake Ladoga began to be constructed, allowing more Leningrad residents to be evacuated as well as some food supplies to be imported. Protected by anti-aircraft artillery on the ice and fighter planes in the air, truck convoys were nevertheless continuously strafed by German artillery and airplanes. Travel was so dangerous that the route became facetiously named the "road of death."

Among those who eventually managed to leave Leningrad on the frozen road was Osipenko's grandmother Maria, who joined Alla and Nina in Perm. But Maria's sister Anna remained in Leningrad by her own choice. She thought she would somehow be able to survive and that by staying put she could ensure that they retained their apartment.

Osipenko and her mother went to the harbor on the River Kama to meet Maria's boat. All the passengers disembarked and still they didn't see her. A heavy old woman sat with her suitcases. They were about to turn around and return home when Osipenko remarked that the old woman was wearing the same scarf as Grandmother. Lean as could be when they'd left her in Leningrad, Maria was now bloated from hunger. At home, Nina gave orders that she shouldn't be given too much to eat all at once. Nina went off to work and Osipenko went to ballet class. The owner of their house couldn't resist the urge to immediately give Maria as hearty a meal as he could supply, but it did her no harm.

One day they found a dead hen in the garbage. They had no idea whether it was diseased, but Maria fished it out and cooked it. Nina was at work in the theater. "Tell your mother if I die, don't eat the chicken," Maria instructed Alla before she turned in for the night. "Wake her up . . . see if she's alive or not," Osipenko insisted as soon as her mother got home. Maria was alive and all three festively consumed the rest of the chicken.

Also arriving in Perm in the spring of 1942 were Agrippina Vaganova, director of the school as well as the most influential figure in Soviet ballet pedagogy. With her came her pupil, the young Kirov ballerina Alla Shelest. Neither had joined the first exodus of ballet evacuees and the blockade had for a time made further evacuations impossible. All the teachers greeted Vaganova's arrival with an outdoor demonstration by each class. Osipenko was a prancing pony in a tiny display piece. She remembered hearing Vaganova ask who she was, and she remembered her teacher's response: "Alla Osipenko: a very good girl."

Choreographer Leonid Jacobson, who would later be greatly influential in Osipenko's career, was also in Perm. He was in his mid-thirties, had graduated from Rossi Street, and already had extensive experience choreographing for students. She took part in a piece he staged for the students: "Always Ready"—an exhortatory response to the ongoing conflict that echoed the slogan of the pre-Communist Party teenaged Komsomol conscripts: "Be ready!" Osipenko's neck was long and she had a habit of thrusting it forward by sticking her chin out. Jacobson approached her. "Girl, does your head move at all?" "Yes, it does," she assured him in all earnestness.

During the summers of 1942 and '43, Osipenko and her class were sent to a vacation camp in Perm for Soviet youth, the Young Pioneers. She swam, played volleyball, and practiced her high jump. Older ballet students were her counselors, and they shared problems and difficulties. For her, the traumas and shortages of wartime were eased because of their camaraderie and fellowship. Students of varied ages were happy to be invited to hospitals to dance for maimed and injured soldiers. They prepared diligently and tried their best. Among future Kirov stars a unanimity prevailed that would not survive later career struggles. "We were friends, like one team," Osipenko recalled. "War is a terrible thing, but these years were the happiest for us."

In Perm she studied for one year with Evgenia Vecheslova-Snetkova, a close associate of Vaganova. Her daughter Tatiana was a ballerina in the Kirov and would figure prominently in Osipenko's later career. But it was teacher Elizaveta Grumova who first tutored her in pointe work. It was a careful, slow progress to full facility on pointe, but for Osipenko and her fellow students, it was, she recalled, "a holiday of the soul," using the common Russian expression. Now she believed that she counted as a dancer; she had come of age.

At the end of January 1944, the Leningrad blockade was finally broken and the displaced began returning to the devastated city, which had been mercilessly bombarded by the Germans. Osipenko, her mother, and her grandmother learned that Anna was alive, but Nina's brother Valentin was dead. He hadn't been mobilized in June of 1941 because his eyesight was poor. But at some point in the siege, any ambulatory male was given a gun and pitched headlong into the fray. Certainly Valentin had never had a moment's combat training. He was among the thousands killed at Nevsky Dobrovolny on the outskirts of the city, their bodies interred in a mass grave.

Standing on Leningrad's Moscow Prospect in Victory Square, directly on the way to Pulkovo airport, is the "Monument to the Heroic Defenders of Leningrad," featuring a sculpted frieze designed by Mikhail Anikushin. Maria received a small pension honoring her son's death. When plans for the monument were announced in the late 1950s, an appeal was made for supplementary private funds, and Maria began contributing her monthly allotment. "Maria Feodorovna," an acquaintance cautioned her, "you are crazy. Why do you give your money? You know that Anikushin's wife buys diamonds with the money." Maria silenced her: "I don't even want to hear about it!"

Their apartment badly needed renovation, but money was scarce. Parts of the ceiling had collapsed, a casualty of German shelling. An instructor at the Rossi Street ballet academy made her family an offer: if they gave him two rooms, he would renovate the entire apartment. But they knew he didn't have a lot of money, whereas a certain Kunkovich told them that if they surrendered three rooms, then he would renovate everything. His offer seemed sturdier, and they accepted. They would also have less rent to pay as a result. Now their back entrance became the entrance to his apartment. Later, however, they regretted the loss of space. To make their three rooms more livable they needed to subdivide them. But no one had the will to do so; they were too attached to these rooms as they had known them for decades.

Their apartment shared a wall with an apartment where a girlfriend of Osipenko lived. Alla was five years older than she but she still enjoyed playing with younger children. Playing at her friend's place one evening, Osipenko wanted to go back to her own apartment to retrieve a particular doll. But since the door between the apartments locked with a hook on Osipenko's side, it wouldn't open no matter how hard she jerked. Instead she stepped out a window, and grasping the frame, straddled a light well to try to open one of her windows. She struggled to get it open. Finally she got in, found the doll, and was going back to her friend's. At that moment Maria walked into the room. She knew that the two girls were supposed to be in the neighboring apartment. "How on earth did you get in?" Osipenko told her what happened and Maria almost fainted. She brought her to the window and made her look down. "If somebody had called your name, you would have looked down and you'd have been finished. Do you understand what you did?" Right below those windows was a barrel filled with chlorine lime kept as rat poison. The window frame was flimsy. A month later their cat tried to do the same thing Osipenko had and was scalded.

Osipenko begged Maria not to tell Nina, who was at work. She thought back to an occasion in Perm when she slid down a hill, leading a bunch of other children. She fell and scratched herself, and later Nina whipped her with a twig switch, letting her know that she was being punished not only for her own recklessness but for encouraging her friends.

Osipenko cried all night realizing the fate that might have been hers. Finally she fell into a light sleep. All of a sudden she sensed someone nearby and her eyes popped open. "Grandma, please, don't tell Mom about it," she murmured, still half asleep. It was not Maria, however, but Nina who stood by her bedside. "What are you talking about?" Osipenko said nothing. Her mother went in to see Maria and insisted on being told what had happened. However, this time her mother didn't punish her. She simply explained again what a great risk she had taken.

Osipenko was late in learning to read: it wasn't until she was nine that she read by herself. When she was ten, she was assigned to read a story about a girl with red hair. It piqued her interest in literature, leading her to an extracurricular reading group at a club for Young Pioneers. Here she read Western authors who were condoned by the Soviets, among them Dickens, Twain, Balzac, and Harriet Beecher Stowe. Grades or credits weren't given. The teacher simply led them in discussions, free from any political cant: Young Pioneers were spared the indoctrination of the teenaged Komsomol and the adult Party.

Three years after joining the school, she was finally able to attend the hallowed ballet academy on Rossi Street, a few minutes' walk from her apartment. Crossing Nevsky Prospect into the Ekaterininsky garden, she'd walk around the colonnaded porch-front facades of the Alexandrinsky theater into Theater Street, built together with the Alexandrinsky in the 1830s by Italian architect Carlo Rossi. The facades were rhythmically punctuated with arches and semi-embedded twinned columns. Visual discipline, restraint, and harmony contextualized the studios in which she strove for those balletic virtues.

During the school's two-week winter break, Osipenko and her classmates usually went skiing. One year, she went to the school's summer camp on the Gulf of Finland. During two other summer vacations, she spent two weeks in a Young Pioneers camp in Atkak in the Crimea, to which high-achieving children were sent. There were two camp settlements, one higher in the mountains, one lower. Accompanied by several teachers, the campers walked from higher to lower through vineyards. They picked some grapes as they tramped through, but to prevent them from further pilfering they were ordered to keep their arms above their heads.

The Rossi Street school's curriculum was ambitious. Osipenko began a five-year piano course, eventually progressing to the point where she could handle something as challenging as Beethoven's *Moonlight Sonata*. Certainly it was intriguing that her piano teacher, Isaac Mileykovsky, had been Galina Ulanova's first husband. Tatiana Vecheslova, still at the peak of her career, was Osipenko's acting teacher. Vecheslova was herself a great dance actress. In class she stressed improvisational exercises. Osipenko was a boy with a dog, or a girl peering out a frosty window, tracing "I love you" on the pane. In another acting episode she waited at a train station for her boyfriend, looking metronomically into the windows of an arriving train. Vecheslova enjoyed letting the students go as far as they could. Her classes woke up their imaginations, as she developed in her pupils what Osipenko referred to as "the luggage of a dramatic actor."

3

Coming of Age

OSIPENKO WAS AWARE that she was considered unusually talented. For an annual performance given by the students in the little school theater, her teacher Lidia Tyuntina had created a piece to a Tchaikovsky waltz and assigned her the lead girl's role. In addition, performance experience at the Kirov was an integral part of the students' education, both on the opera as well as the ballet stage. Osipenko was one of six poppies dancing with six birds in the opium dream of *The Red Poppy*'s heroine Tao-Hoa, danced alternately by Kirov stars Vecheslova, Shelest, and Feya Balabina. She was a figurine page in the party entertainment in act 2 of Tchaikovsky's *Queen of Spades*, an opera she liked and had already watched many times.

A gala was held at the Kirov to celebrate the anniversary of Marius Petipa's birth. It brought a different cast for each act of *Sleeping Beauty*, which he had originally choreographed for the Mariinsky in 1890. Guests from outside the ballet company were invited to participate. In the first act, King Florestan was impersonated by Nikolai Cherkasov. The Kirov's Natalia Dudinskaya shared the role of Aurora with Marina Semyonova and Galina Ulanova, each of whom was returning from Moscow's Bolshoi to their home theater for this gala.

In act 2, Osipenko was one of eight pages in the Awakening scene, all danced by girls from the school. They had been told by their teachers that if they touched the shoes of the ballerina performing Aurora, they would be sure to someday dance Aurora themselves. The lights were down before the beginning of the Awakening scene. Ulanova was in position, lying on a couch. In the dark, all eight girls stealthily touched her talismanic foot, causing the startled ballerina to cry out.

At the Kirov in 1947, a new ballet, *A Spring Tale*, was choreographed by Fyodor Lopukhov. Here Osipenko was a dragonfly. The ballet ended with a wedding celebration, where she and an ensemble of girls had to perform no fewer than 200 waltzing balancés. "For years people remembered me in this part. They said, 'This girl is not normal.'" Apparently, she had performed with unusual zeal.

School and the theater still didn't fully satisfy her passion for theatricals. Friends who lived in small communal apartments liked coming to her place to socialize. Home theater had been a lively tradition in Russia for centuries. Osipenko and her friends wrote their own scenarios and performed them, sometimes asking their families to watch. They fantasized about being a troupe of dancers and singers, like the widely popular Beryozka or Moiseyev ensembles. Once a friend of Osipenko arrived with a log for her wood stove. "Ensemble Beryozka!" he announced, punning on the Beryozka tree, a symbol of Russian culture. On Sundays they made excursions to museums or to suburbs of Leningrad where some of the Romanovs' most lavish palaces were being restored after devastation by the Nazis.

The Hermitage was closed when Osipenko first returned to the shattered city. But when the first wing was reopened, she went with her class on a school trip. "I've been in love with it all my life." It was in the Rembrandt galleries there that she made her appearance in Alexander Sokurov's film *Russian Ark* in 2002, the final in a number of small roles she acted in Russian films beginning in the 1980s.

In the spring of 1947, Osipenko danced the first major role created for her, one of three female soloists in Vakhtang Chabukiani's *A Musical Moment*, performed to the allegro moderato from Schubert's *Six Moments Musical*. Chabukiani was already a legendary figure to the students. He had been the company's most brilliant male star during the 1930s, forging a bravura partnership with Natalia Dudinskaya. In 1941, he had returned to his native Georgia, where he danced, directed, and choreographed at the opera house in Tblisi.

Immediately before the war, he had started choreographing for the Kirov; now he was returning to create this ballet for Osipenko and two fellow soloists, Galina Kekicheva and Tatiana Isakova. They were intimidated at the thought of working with Chabukiani, but the moment he set down to work they forgot their awe. He showed what he wanted with a passion that was energizing. They worked in the "Petipa" studio in the theater, where a bust of the choreographer is exhibited.

Chabukiani's "attitude toward me was super-emotional," Osipenko said. "He liked me all his life," and the feeling was mutual. On her last trip to Georgia before his death in 1992, she went to his country house unannounced on his birthday; finding him not at home, she made do with tossing a bouquet of roses through his gates.

They first danced *A Musical Moment* in the school theater. Boris Bregvadze, later one of the Kirov's most popular leading men and a frequent partner of Osipenko, was then a senior student. "She was plump, but very beautiful," he recalled about his first sight of Osipenko on stage. "I thought she would be great."

A Musical Moment was so popular that they were soon dancing it all over the city. Once they performed at an academic society, where a bust of Stalin stood in the performance space they had been allotted. The dictator was the last thing she expected to see on stage with her, and she was so startled during the dance's finale that she blanked out. She stood frozen, while the other two girls danced and then she joined them only for the final measures.

It was around this time that Nina was involved with a man Osipenko now thinks must have been ex-military. She recalled his long officer's coat, a *galafey*, and his shaved head. Osipenko didn't like him, so much so that she told her mother that if she married him she would leave their house. In years to come, as Nina's life became more and more sublimated to her daughter's career, Osipenko realized what a mistake she had made.

Her father had been released prematurely from prison so that he could be siphoned into the army, one of the relatively few Russian soldiers to survive the war. Later she learned that during the war he'd worn a medallion in which he'd put her photo on one side, her mother's on the reverse. One day he showed up at the school in uniform, apparently displaying great panache: "Alka, there's a general waiting for you," the concierge told her. She recognized him immediately. They went for a walk and he bought her an ice cream cone, which was for her ambrosia. Even after prison and war, "my father was a merry person," Osipenko recalled. He came to dinner. Nina and he behaved cordially. He asked Nina to remarry him, and asked Alla to persuade her mother, but Nina declined. "Don't even talk about that to me. It would be the same as marrying my own brother." Soon after, Evgeni Osipenko left Leningrad, and it was years before he would become a part of Alla's life once more.

AFTER HER SUCCESS in *A Musical Moment*, Osipenko's opinion of herself was high, too high perhaps, to satisfy her teacher, Natalia Komkova, who taught one of the two intermediate level girls' classes. Komkova was a difficult personality in the classic manner of Russian ballet instructor. She was prone to yelling, throwing students out of the studio if they displeased her. Outside school, Osipenko and she got along. Indeed she was frequently at Komkova's home, because her husband was an artist who liked to sketch her. But in class, Komkova was determined to show no favoritism. Osipenko claimed that Komkova asked her to leave class more often than any other student. She was used to receiving the highest grade of 5; Komkova was her first teacher to routinely issue her a 3 or 3+, which felt like a great comedown. Komkova's ruse succeeded, for Osipenko shook off such complacency as she may have had.

Complacency of any kind or disrespect to an elder was a cardinal sin in the Leningrad ballet culture. Osipenko recalled once when she was about sixteen, she was standing with her arms folded across her chest when she saw Alexandra Vlatova, the young wife of the teacher Boris Chavrov. "Hi, good morning," she said to Vlatova. "Is that how you say, 'Good Morning'?" Vlatova screamed. "You have to stand like that when you talk to me." Ramrod straight, like a soldier at attention. "If I see you behave like that again, I give you my word you will never work in the Kirov theater!"

Most of Tyuntina's class had graduated not to Komkova's but to the parallel intermediate class taught by Elena Shiripina. Osipenko thought that Shiripina was a better teacher than Komkova. Komkova developed the dancer's expressiveness. Shirirpina's priorities were more cut and dried, but she was more meticulous in identifying technical weaknesses.

For a while, Osipenko's grades dipped in academic subjects as well as ballet, but for different reasons altogether. For academics, she had now matriculated into the "A" division, whereas before she had been part of the "B" group. The "A" students were less studious. Rather than stand out, she tried instead to deliberately downplay her readiness in class. Her academic decline aroused concern among the faculty, until it was decided that she would be sent back to academic class in the "B" division, and a concomitant improvement in her school work resulted.

In literature class she read de Musset, which started a passion for French literature. She sampled de Maupassant, Dumas, Balzac, Stendahl, and jotted down quotations. De Maupassant's *A Life* depressed her so much that after reading it she told her mother that she had decided that she was never going to get married.

Once she came to the school librarian and asked him to help her choose something interesting to read. He gave her a children's book, *Plutonia*, that was all about dinosaurs and mammals. She brought it back thinking, "What on earth did he give me? I'm already reading de Musset." She showed the book to her literature teacher, who took her back to the school library and instructed the librarian to let her take out anything she wanted.

She also availed herself of books that remained from her grandfather's library, benchmarks of Western philosophy and literature: Schopenhauer, Nietzsche, Sappho. History started to interest her. She discovered Karamzin's multi-volume history of Russia, which dated to the early 1800s. History class at school covered the same periods as did Karamzin's work, but he offered different explanations, different commentary. She began to understand how the written word manipulated.

Whatever her vow against matrimony, boys inevitably became the object of more than companionship. She and her friends began going to dances with students at the naval academy, with whom they danced "beautiful ancient dances" of the Imperial era, the Polonaise, Minuet. She liked the boys' attentions but her elders were much less enthusiastic, issuing their standard "Too bad, too bad . . ." She began asking her mother questions about her family and prowling on her own through family papers. One day she found a pre-Revolution document certifying the marriage of "the virgin Maria Zhigacheva." Noted as well were the two children to whom this particular virgin had given birth. Osipenko seized the document and wave it in front of Maria: "Why do you say, 'Too bad, too bad Lalasha'?" Maria grabbed the incriminating document out of her hands.

Choreographer Leonid Jacobson, with whom she had worked a bit in Perm, now picked her to create a new duet he was making to Tchaikovsky that was eventually titled *Meditation*. They rehearsed for over two months. This was his third attempt to choreograph to this music, and he was now finally able to bring the project to fruition. Everything in the duet had to be as if in a dream, he told her. She still couldn't move her neck entirely the way he wanted; he wished her to be more human, more vulnerable, fluid. He impressed on her that the position of the head and the neck made the greatest impression on an audience. He looked for continuation between extended leg and extended arm. She had a good extension; Zlata Bayaeva, a classmate, later recalled that people would watch class especially to see Osipenko's raised leg in ecarté. But it was gradations rather than maximum height that Jacobson was concerned with as he molded her arabesques, solo and supported, in the duet. Osipenko said "he was like Rodin," whose sculpture actually inspired a ballet by Jacobson in which she starred a decade later. Osipenko learned from Jacobson and she idolized him: "I followed Jacobson like a puppy." One day she trailed him down Nevsky Prospect. He went into the city's main bookstore, the Dom Kuniga, an Art Nouveau landmark that before the Revolution had been headquarters of the Singer Sewing Machine company. She waited outside. He came out and went on his way, while she continued to follow.

For the duet she wore a short chiffon tunic, fluttering in the breeze as she moved. It was the product of her first meeting with Simon Virsaladze, who would design many of her costumes at the Kirov. She had a crush on the handsome student who partnered her, Robert Kliaven. It was, Osipenko told me in English, "a beautiful situation."

Jacobson used her own mannerisms in the choreography as well, and *Meditation* became something of a picture of the adolescent dancer, both elegant and tentative. She danced it for many years but never again as well, she thought—never with the same lyricism, the same authenticity of emotion.

Nevertheless, the film she made of it a decade later, with the man's role now danced by the Kirov's Anatoly Nisnevich, preserves the adolescent mood she described—if by now a conscious creation of artistry rather than in any sense a self-portrait. It was perhaps fitting that this film served to introduce

Jacobson's *Meditation* with Vsevelod Oukhov.
Photo courtesy Alla Osipenko.

her to American audiences, fifty years after the creation of *Meditation*. It was shown at a seminar on Vaganova, sponsored by the Brooklyn Academy of Music in February 1998, and it enchanted the audience.

By now Nina was completely invested in Osipenko's career. Sensing her mother's need to live vicariously through her daughter gave Alla the upper hand in demanding more autonomy. "I told my mother I didn't want her near the school." But Nina's hunger to be involved was only strengthened by her daughter's denial. No sooner would she walk through the door than Nina would approach, eager for all the news of the day. "Mother, please give me a break. I'm tired. Just let me rest a little bit and I will tell you everything." It was easier to share information with Anna and Maria, who didn't pry but instead simply showered her with adoration. "You're our beauty! You're our beloved girl!" They relaxed her, and she would tell them everything: it was the elderly ladies with whom Osipenko could share her problems. If Nina came out of her room while Osipenko talked to Anna and Maria, the conversation tended to come to a halt. Nina complained about being excluded, about her loving Maria and Anna more. It wasn't true, but Nina had a sternness that was as off-putting as her eagerness.

At age sixteen, it was time for Osipenko to receive her national passport, which had been instituted in the 1930s as mandatory identification. Nina, who had now reverted to her maiden name, asked Osipenko to also use Borovikovsky on her passport. Osipenko refused. They argued and in retrospect she said that it marked the real beginning of their adult conflicts.

4

Vaganova

IN THE FALL of 1948, Osipenko reached the most exacting teacher of all: Agrippina Vaganova herself. Then sixty-nine, the great teacher led a senior girls' class at the school at 9:30 every morning, and then, also at the school, company class for the Kirov's women soloists and principal dancers shortly before noon.

Vaganova headed the school together with another outstanding teacher, Vladimir Ponomarev, but she was the strongest influence. She had been teaching at the school for two decades and had been awarded iconic status as the dominant l pedagogue in Soviet ballet. She had retired from the Imperial ballet stage in 1916; after starting to teach she had analyzed the teachings of every one of the European teachers who had dominated instruction at the school and in the Imperial Mariinsky. She learned from her friend, ex-Mariinsky prima ballerina Olga Preobrajenska, who taught at the school immediately before and after the Revolution. Indeed, until the day she died in 1951, Vaganova seemed propelled to sift, dissect, and synthesize every kinetic possibility with which she came into contact.

She produced a syllabus and a style that influenced the Soviet as well as the international ballet stage. It was strong, spacious, and also delicate. She preserved the emphases of her youth, such as the scintillating footwork inculcated by the Italian teachers. But her dancers also had a distinctive breadth that could be called quintessentially Russian. Sylistically, they preserved a golden mean of classicism. Vaganova "didn't like anything casual or overdone," ex-Kirov ballerina Ninel Kurgapkina, who graduated from Vaganova's class in 1947, recalled fifty years later. She frowned on "too much emotion or too much force, or too much accents in the acting or arms. Everything had to look easy, light, and natural."

At the end of 1917, Vaganova's common-law husband, a retired colonel and businessman, had killed himself rather than accept the new governance. Vaganova herself had never joined the Communist Party, but, inevitably, she accommodated it. She survived attacks on the school during the late 1920s that presaged a much harder cultural line to come, a scourge that had removed then-director Viktor Semenov and perhaps made her dominance possible.

In addition to her teaching, she also directed the Kirov company itself from 1931 to 1937. Yet her position remained somewhat equivocal. During the '30s, she continued to exchange letters and telegrams with celebrated former colleagues who had emigrated to the West, even extending public greetings via Western reporters. It was her association with the pre-Revolutionary ballet that apparently provided grist for her ouster as Kirov director. Ex-Kirov character dancer, choreographer, and company director Igor Belsky, who knew her in the 1940s, recalled that Vaganova's closest friends were a small circle of covert anti-Soviets.

Osipenko claimed that like Komkova, Vaganova "used to demand so much more from me than from any of her students. My friends used to ask, 'Why does she pick on you so much?'" On the one hand, Osipenko seemed to her ideally made for ballet. Soviet dance historian Vera Krassovskaya writes in her 1989 biography that Vaganova "could not remember ever seeing such beautiful legs and such a refined and graceful torso before, except perhaps in Olga Spessivtseva." But Osipenko's personality and her impulsive and emotional character manifested itself in her body's responsiveness. Her talent seemed "to impel her to imbue difficult movements with an even higher level of poetry," Krassovskaya writes, but simpler things, or combinations that she had already mastered could suddenly and unexpectedly flummox her.

Soviet ballet largely functioned according to the regimens of the *emploi* system of typecasting, whereby the dancers were slotted into categories and distinct repertories. This system functioned as well as any other; it certainly precluded the egregious miscasting that so often blights today's ballet stage. Vaganova believed in *emploi* but not as an absolute principle—she applied it liberally. But the extent to which Osipenko defied existing categorization as it was mapped out in Soviet ballet might have perplexed even Vaganova. Above and beyond category and the quantifiable utility of technique, Osipenko's body must have surely suggested its future propensity to prioritize the uniquely instrumental, kinetic possibilities of limbs moving through space without reference to a programmatic plot line, an inherited pretext.

Years after Vaganova died in 1951, Osipenko recalled reading about a conversation Vaganova had at the end of her life. "I worry about Osipenko.

She has an abstract kind of talent that I don't quite understand." Perhaps Osipenko's "abstract kind of talent" reminded Vaganova of the formalist experiments in art of the late Imperial and early Soviet years, now completely proscribed. "Formalist" was one of the most damning epithets of Stalinist cultural critique.

Between student and teacher, friction was perhaps inevitable due to the contrast in their own performing gifts. One of Vaganova's supreme accomplishments as a teacher was highlighting the individuality of her pupils so that she was able to groom a constellation of ballerinas with markedly different performing personalities. But even if she doesn't impose her own mannerisms, inevitably the teacher's approach to ballet is molded at least in part as a response to her own experience as a dancer. Talking about Vaganova's performing career, Osipenko mentioned her physical drawbacks—rather short arms and legs that weren't exceptionally flexible, a big head, a face that wasn't considered beautiful—and how they had forced Vaganova to develop an analytic perspective. "A pretty line is not the most important thing," Vaganova would say when discussing her Imperial colleagues Anna Pavlova and Tamara Karsavina. Yes, they had been major talents, but Vaganova implied that they had been too satisfied with their own beauty of face and figure to fulfill themselves as technicians.

Vaganova on some occasions went so far as to insist that "any fool" could shine in supported adagio; for her, it was in solo variations that a ballerina proved her mettle. Vaganova herself had spent most of her career as a celebrated soloist; she had been "Queen of the Variations." Only in 1911, after fourteen years as a member of the Mariinsky, had she danced her first ballerina lead. Her finest hours on stage were in solos while, as must have been apparent to her, most of Osipenko's greatest moments were destined to be in supported adagio.

It was in allegro that "the whole wisdom of classical dancing is revealed," Vaganova had stated in the textbook she wrote with Lyubov Blok. And this was the weakest point of Osipenko's technique. Yet Vaganova was not going to cede any ground, would not let Osipenko coast on beauty or facility.

"Alla was the most eminent student," a slightly younger contemporary at the school told me. "Everyone thought, 'It is ballerina.'" But Vaganova made sure the goal was set out of reach. Until Osipenko could dance *this*, Vaganova declared when she assigned her Kitri's act 3 *Don Quixote* variation at the highest speed, "I'll *never* believe that you're going to be a ballerina." In that case, Osipenko, thought, ballerina-dom was not for her, because that particular virtuoso variation was simply "impossible for me."

But Vaganova had certainly made major contributions as well to the character of Russian adagio. Once a week for center work, she assigned what she called "Italian adagio," which was lifted from the syllabus in which Vaganova herself had been trained, when Enrico Cecchetti worked at the school and theater. Osipenko didn't realize where the "Italian adagio" really came from until years later, when she began to teach in Hartford and watched other teachers give pure Cecchetti classes. These adagio steps were the same, but their character was quite different.

In her Hartford apartment, Osipenko demonstrated the difference between Cecchetti's and Vaganova's phrasing of the same steps. What in Cecchetti was an exercise in dynamic control, producing a smooth sequence of slow movements, became a blossoming in which an inner muscular vibration seemed to send movement scrolling past the limits of the body's actual extension. Producing its own cadences, the body could supersede the aural landmarks, often adding to its allure as a result. But going that far displeased Vaganova, who insisted on musical precision. "I was always late," Osipenko says. "I heard sound more prolonged than it was. Until I felt that my legs sang the music completely, I didn't move farther, but the music had already gone and I was late."

"Why don't you follow the music, Osipenko?' Vaganova would wail. "*Why?*" Vaganova scolded with a common Russian expression: "An elephant stepped on your ear!" Meaning "we were beat deaf."

Krassovskaya writes that Vaganova found it least interesting to work with students "whose bodies seemed to be ideally made for dance but who were unable or unwilling to overcome inertia or laziness. Vaganova considered them the most hopeless." While Vaganova certainly did not treat Osipenko as if she were a lost cause, she considered the student's friends, boyfriends, plays, movies, reading, long walks through the city irrelevant distractions: "If you love life too much, you're not going to make a career."

"Vaganova was afraid that I would be sidetracked by something or someone," Osipenko said. "You're very lazy," Vaganova chided her. "Maybe you will be a superstar, maybe nothing."

"With your character," she warned one time, "you'll wind up dancing in a music hall!" Sometimes she enjoyed rankling Osipenko capriciously. "How many days have you missed class?" Vaganova asked her when she'd been home sick. "Four days." "What?" "Four days!" "Don't yell at me! Get out of class!" Osipenko left in tears. Later that day she was taking an exam in music class. Vaganova appeared: "So, are you through crying? After the exam, come see me and we'll talk."

In the fall of 1949, Irina Kolpakova joined Vaganova's class and quickly became a favorite of hers. She demonstrated the single-minded focus that Vaganova accused Osipenko of lacking. "Look at her," Osipenko recalled Vaganova urging, "She uses her brain! What are you doing?!" As dancers and people, the two future ballerinas were entirely different. Perhaps there was never a question with Kolpakova that physical endowment could rival technique. Osipenko's "legs and feet were amazing," Kolpakova said at the Brooklyn Academy of Music symposium on Vaganova in 1998. "I never was blessed with anything like that. I had straight, nice legs; they looked nice, but they were never so expressive." But she had less beautiful yet stronger feet and batterie than Osipenko, and more stable pirouettes.

Not all was grueling work in Vaganova's classes; there was fun too. Vaganova's wit was often expressed at her students' expense, but they felt that what she said was designed to goad them into improvement. Sophia Brodskaya, "a perfect pianist," played for Vaganova's classes, and the two were close colleagues. When Vaganova prepared a second edition of her textbook she included musical excerpts from Brodskaya's accompaniment. The two were indeed such close and long colleagues that Brodskaya could on occasion go on autopilot. Osipenko remembered Brodskaya carrying a big bag with food and a romance novel into the studio. She'd put the book inside the score and eat throughout class. One day Sophia got quieter and quieter, then all of a sudden her fingers slammed into a chord. "What's going on?" Vaganova demanded. She said, "Oh, Agrippina Jacovlevna, excuse me. He left her." Vaganova laughed.

Osipenko chuckled too as she recalled a photography session with Vaganova and her class. Vaganova was grouchy because she had lost a gold watch. The photographer wanted to try a picture in profile next to one of the prettiest girls; Vaganova instead wanted to stand next to "*this* girl"—who had a flat nose like a Cossack's.

Vaganova remained in a bad mood for the next week, until one morning she walked in all smiles and whispered something to Brodskaya. The moment Vaganova left after class, the girls flew over to the piano. They learned that Vaganova had gone to the bathroom before class, pulled down her underwear, and the gold watch had spilled onto the floor.

If Vaganova knew she was going to be late to class, she'd send word to alert the girls to start on their own. They preferred to gossip and stretch, so they'd station a lookout at the windows. With Brodskaya's complicity, the minute Vaganova had been spotted, they'd rush to the barre and jump ahead to the place to which they should have progressed in that morning's lesson.

Mastering technique for Osipenko was always a matter of two steps ahead and one back. For a jubilee at the Philharmonic to honor Vaganova, Osipenko was to dance both the Waltz pas de deux and the Mazurka from *Chopiniana*. Vaganova promised her friends that they would be watching a wonderful new girl.

But things didn't go quite as Vaganova had hoped. Osipenko's landings were bumpy in the Mazurka. Then, toward the end of the Seventh Waltz duet, fatigue overcame her as she reached the traveling arabesques that the ballerina performs alone. Her legs almost gave way. She felt as though she had lost any connection to them. One choppy arabesque at a time, she reached the downstage wing.

After the performance, Vaganova was holding a red rose and talking to the Philharmonic's principal conductor Evgeni Mravinsky. "Go away," she said to Osipenko out of the side of her mouth. "I can't see you. I'll talk to you tomorrow." In fact they didn't talk outside of class for a long time.

Another time, Vaganova took her to a trans-USSR convocation of ballet schools that was held every spring in Moscow's Tchaikovsky Hall. She insisted that Osipenko stay in her dormitory room all day and rest before dancing the *Nutcracker* grand pas de deux. But Osipenko routinely craved ice cream so much that she would just as soon have a single scoop as a full-course meal. She stole out of the dormitory and was patronizing a street vendor when none other than Vaganova happened to walk by. Vaganova yelled, Osipenko sobbed, and pedestrians stopped to gawk. Osipenko was still sniffling at her dressing room table later that evening, when Vaganova walked in, tossed an apple—fresh fruit was something hard to procure at the time—in her lap and walked out without saying a word. "It's a good thing you danced well," Vaganova told her after the performance.

Here as in *Chopiniana*, Osipenko's cavalier was Anatoly Sepagov, then a student whose *emploi* was classical, although when he joined the Kirov he became instead an electrifying character dancer. She had also danced *Nutcracker* in the tiny school theater, and she danced it again with Sepagov on the Kirov stage. Then as now, it was a custom in the theater for students to dance *Nutcracker* at the theater during the first days of January.

After Vaganova died, Osipenko found that she had been one of Anna's sewing clients and had frequented their apartment for fittings. She and Anna were friendly and perhaps, Osipenko thought, had indulged their mutual fondness for cognac. But Osipenko never saw her at the apartment and nobody ever told her of the connection until after Vaganova's death.

The closest she came to seeing a private Vaganova was when she visited her apartment to rehearse. Vaganova was beginning to experience heart trouble and was resting in bed. Osipenko didn't wear pointe shoes, but even moving in soft ballet slippers wasn't easy on the bedroom's parquet floor. Yet Vaganova remained demanding, intent on perfection. But her manner was softer than in the studio. Osipenko was intrigued by the apartment with its prominently displayed photograph of Vaganova's common-law husband, the cherrywood furniture, and copious books.

In her own apartment, Osipenko at seventeen had decided that her elderly relatives were culturally retrograde. They read pre-Revolutionary novelists influenced by the French—and were fond of Alcott's *Little Women* and *Little Men*. At that time, Erich Maria Remarque was popular in Russia. Osipenko would insist that Maria and Anna sit around the big dining room table after dinner while she read for them as they sewed. The two old ladies sobbed as she read Remarque's *Three Comrades* and *Arc of Triumph*.

Nina never participated and seemed to hate hearing her daughter's recitations echo through the apartment. "Can't you find something better to do?" On the subject of Vladimir Mayakovsky, mother and daughter were drastically at odds. Osipenko loved his poetry; Nina hated it. Osipenko was determined, however, that her grandmother and great-aunt would listen to it. "You've got to listen," Osipenko insisted, "because you're behind the times."

During her second year in Vaganova's class, Osipenko started to gain weight. Nina's response was to put her on strict rations. More arguments ensued. To thwart her mother completely, Osipenko would insist that she didn't want to become a ballet dancer after all. Waking up hungry during the night, she'd sneak into the kitchen to treat herself. Nina was baffled about why her daughter didn't lose weight. Vaganova was, too. It was only several years into her career that Osipenko would transition into the sleek silhouette for which she was ultimately known.

Vaganova showed her students the exercises for the final exam no more than two weeks before they took it. "It was a real exam," Osipenko said. "Now it's a prepared performance," since, she claimed, teachers review the exam with their classes for weeks before. Privately uncompromising, Vaganova was intent on showing each of her pupils in the most flattering light. Vaganova placed Osipenko at the center of the studio for the adagio. But when it came time for thirty-two fouettés, she signaled to Osipenko to sit them out. "Yesterday she hurt her foot," Vaganova fibbed to the jury. That day Osipenko had awakened trembling; when it was all over, she slept straight through for twenty-two hours.

For the graduation performance to be held on the Kirov stage, Vaganova assigned Osipenko the White Swan adagio, and to partner her she recruited Vsevelod Oukhov, a principal dancer in the company. She impressed upon Osipenko that the Swan Queen is a very proud and powerful bird when she first appears to Prince Siegfried. It was not until later in the ballet that her capacity for love should become apparent. Nevertheless she was exasperated by Osipenko's reserve when she rehearsed with the principal dancer. "You see how handsome he is; you've got to flirt with him!" Vaganova insisted. "Why are you so timid?"

Over the years, Vaganova revised her class continuously, often responding to things she saw around her. She told her students to watch everything and not be censorious of the new or unfamiliar. To Osipenko she seemed progressive in matters of evolving style and aesthetics. Tugging at Osipenko's neckline during rehearsals for the graduation, she gave instructions to a costume attendant that it be lowered for the performance. "If this girl's bust comes out of her costume in the middle of the performance, you have to sweep it up and give to me!"

A panel of critics discussed the students' interpretations in their graduation performance. Vaganova and Osipenko listened to them critique her performance. They objected to moments when the graduate herself intruded upon the character of Odette, when her face brightened reflexively if her pirouettes worked. Vaganova said in turn, "If you give Carmen to a singer for the first time you're also going to tell her it's in her future, so how dare you criticize Osipenko?"

As soon as they were alone, however, Vaganova true to form insisted that Osipenko not attach any artistic credence to her defense of her pupil. Instead she was to take what they'd said to heart and go right back to work.

5

First Love

OSIPENKO WAS SIXTEEN when she met Vladimir Nahumov, the man she would describe to me as "my very first love and the love of my life." After her success in *Meditation*, the school had sent her and two other students to a big resort near the Finnish border. There she met Nahumov, who was twenty. He was from Leningrad but was studying in Moscow at the Institute of Cinematography. For three weeks students spent most of their time together. He flirted with all three girls, but among them Osipenko considered Angelina Karbarova the most beautiful. She assumed that he was really pursuing her. As their vacation came to an end, she hid in the bushes and cried, afraid that she would never see him again.

Sometime later in her apartment in Leningrad, the phone rang: "Hello, you probably don't remember me . . ." Nahumov had come to Leningrad to shoot his first film, *Taras Shevchenko*, which he was co-directing. He asked if she'd like to go with him to see a new movie about Peter the Great. "Babushka! Mama!" She was shaking with excitement. Permission was given warily: "Who is this?. . .Watch yourself! Come home right after the movie!" But their relationship developed slowly during his infrequent trips to Leningrad. Her entire family came to love him, for he was talented, intelligent, good-looking, and, she said, "a very good man."

In the summer of 1950, Osipenko was enrolled in an all-arts competition in Karlovy Vary, the spa town just outside Prague in Czechoslovakia. Vaganova prepared her in the White Swan adagio and the Bluebird pas de deux from *Sleeping Beauty*. Vaganova again accommodated Osipenko's style and her technical limitations. In Bluebird she had difficulty with the fast little tour de basque jumps, so Vaganova changed the step to a walk on pointe. She left from Moscow, the lone Leningrad member of a delegation sent from there to compete. Vaganova didn't go with her but instead went on vacation, swimming as was her wont in the Black Sea.

There had been an undercurrent of anti-Leningrad sentiment, and Osipenko had been admitted to the competition only after a tussle. When she received a gold medal for the *Swan Lake* adagio, Vaganova from her vacation cabled Osipenko's family in Leningrad: "The truth prevailed." ("She never gave me direct praise," Osipenko said.) Truth, however, was crushed to the ground for a while due to a big man from the Ministry of Culture in Moscow, Fyodor Kaloshin, who was also in Prague at that time. Unannounced, he arrived at her hotel room, closed the door and started caressing her, all the while telling her that she could be prima ballerina at the Bolshoi. She would go abroad whenever she wanted. Her response was a slap. With that his mood drastically shifted. "I will never forget this," he warned her. "As long as I am alive you will stay in Leningrad. You will never leave."

To this day, dance competition awards mean more in Russia than they do even in Europe or America, despite the fact that they are frequently blighted by the most blatant corruption. A school administrator invited her to his study and expressed his regret that she hadn't won anything in Prague. The astonished Osipenko corrected him. Apparently, Kaloshin had acted to prevent the school from being informed about her victory.

In tears, she told Nahumov what had happened. He decided that they should confront Kaloshin in his Moscow office. His secretary didn't want to let them enter without an appointment. Nahumov was insistent until Kaloshin agreed to see them. Had he done what Osipenko accused him of? "Yes, but I warned her that I would." With extraordinary audacity, Nahumov insisted that he pick up the phone and call the school and inform them. Amazingly, he did just that. But although performance opportunities abroad arose, she was never allowed to leave the USSR over the next six years.

THAT FALL, OSIPENKO entered the Kirov as a member of the corps de ballet. The opera house that was to be her professional base for the next twenty years was located on Theatre Square a few blocks off the Moika canal, lined with huge homes that made it one of the most privileged of Imperial neighborhoods. Ticket prices were subsidized by the state, and the theater was an immense source of pride to Leningraders from all walks of life. Visiting Leningrad in 1944, British reporter Iris Morley watched feverish repairs being made so that the theater could reopen in May after two years of darkness. The performers had been evacuated and the theater seriously damaged by German shelling. Scaffolding filled the beautiful sky-blue and gilt interior, originally dating to 1860. The administrator directing repairs told Morley, "It makes us feel when the theater is open that life has really begun again."

The ballet and opera companies, as well as the theater itself had all been named for Sergei Kirov, Party chief of Leningrad. His assassination in 1934, perhaps ordered by Stalin himself, was used by the dictator as pretext to begin the purges. Stalin deeply distrusted Leningrad, the czarist capital constructed by Peter the Great in a spirit of homage to Europe's monarchial baroque capital cities.

During the war Leningrad civic leaders had enjoyed relative autonomy, and city heads were widely popular for their role in saving the city from extinction. Stalin's response was savage and quick: as Osipenko entered the ballet company, the dictator was actively prosecuting the "Leningrad Affair," a dragnet against Communist chiefs in Leningrad.

Not surprisingly, Leningrad's Kirov always took second place to Moscow's Bolshoi where government patronage was concerned. The Bolshoi was allowed to raid the Kirov's roster whenever it wished. But it actively pursued a more rarified, less robust, performance style than the Bolshoi, in keeping with its continued identification with the city's aristocratic past.

All art forms were mandated to be created in a style conforming to didactic Socialist realism, installed as state doctrine in 1934. The inherent contradictions between the ambiguity of ballet movement and the programmatic mandates of socialist realism proved an ongoing challenge to the creation of successful new ballets.

Around half of the performances each season were dedicated to revised versions of full-length Imperial ballets. The balance were mostly *dramballets*, dating from the 1920s onward. They were plot-driven, thus satisfying the Soviet demand for explicit storytelling, often based on classic works of Russian literature, but by no means always easily characterized as Socialist Realism.

In the Kirov, Osipenko began to be given small solos right away, but she considered the time she spent in the corps valuable. The corps mandated the closest of contact with colleagues. Dancing in the ensemble of *La Bayadère*'s Kingdom of the Shades or *Sleeping Beauty*'s Vision scene, she needed to maintain a cantilena through her body that was transmitted to and worked in synergy with twenty or thirty other women. She had to be acutely aware of who was sharing the space around her.

She was the fifth or sixth corps member to descend into the Kingdom of Shades, and later in that entrance adagio, she bourréed in the front line when the snaking procession turned to face front. The Kirov customarily cast tall women in the front line of Shades, using shorter dancers in the rear, thus enhancing a perception of vanishing perspective. Osipenko stayed in the Shades corps long after she had moved out of all other ensemble assignments, even after she had danced both Gamzatti and Nikiya in *La Bayadère*. The administration cast soloists in the front line at important performances.

Shiripina coached her in her first coryphée roles: the big swans, one of Giselle's six friends in act 1 and Myrtha's lieutenant Moyna in act 2. "Her expression was really not nice," Osipenko said, and her tone of voice just as withering. Very seldom did Shiripina have praise to give.

Early on, Osipenko was assigned the adagio variation danced by one of the three solo Shades, a supreme test of line, control, and versatility. After the slow unfolding of the opening measures, the dancer negotiates a sudden tempo increase halfway through. Decades later, Elena Tchernichova would recall her childhood enthrallment with Osipenko's performance, as she writes in her autobiography. Osipenko in the opening grand scissone ouverte, "picked her leg up from a perfect fifth position, her working leg caressed her supporting leg, passing distinctly through every gradation while maintaining a flowing momentum until her leg was fully extended."

In a role like one of Giselle's friends, she was surrounded by senior, experienced coryphées who commanded their own measure of deference. "When a young girl joined this small team it was an honor," Osipenko said. She was careful to treat them with respect, and if the newcomer needed help, they supplied it.

Pyotr Gusev had directed the Kirov since 1945. He was a direct link to the immediately post-Revolution years of hope, privation, and experiment. He had graduated from the school in 1922 and had danced with Balanchine's Youth Ballet and with the Kirov for a decade before moving to Moscow to teach at the Bolshoi school and then direct the company, before returning to Leningrad.

"I loved him," Osipenko said. "I thought Gusev was wonderful." She considered him the most vigilant of all the ballet directors for whom she worked. Over a backstage loudspeaker he would comment following the performance, assessing a technique, a coiffure, anything that attracted his approval or censure. The dancers anticipated that his comments would be blunt but honest, and this was a further incentive for them to excel.

A pride of great ballerinas headed the company, but Natalia Dudinskaya was de facto prima ballerina assoluta (the title was not used after the Revolution). Vaganova's tutelage and protection, together with Dudinskaya's gifts as well as her relentless ambition and hard work, brought her to a position of dominance. Although she was now forty, she had a decade on stage ahead of her.

Dudinskaya defied *emploi*, dancing virtually every leading role, even though not everything she did was equally persuasive. She was stronger in allegro than adagio; andante was really the slowest tempo in which she was comfortable. This of course brought her close to Vaganova's own tempo and rhythms.

Dudinskaya "had all the energy in the world," Osipenko recalled. "She lifted up the whole performance." As a result, when Osipenko supported Dudinskaya's *Raymonda*, dancing her friend Henrietta, or dancing one of the grand pas couples in the final act wedding festivities, "we celebrated her" as much as the character of Raymonda herself. Although Dudinskaya's way of announcing to the audience "Here I am!" was far from Osipenko's aquiline reserve, the younger dancer liked her intelligence and aplomb, and was even prone to imitate her on occasion.

Alla Shelest, Tatiana Vecheslova, and Ninel Petrova occasionally danced the role during these years, but Dudinskaya's near-exclusive hold on Giselle aroused enmity. There were many who felt that the bravura technician was entirely unsuited to a character so innocent and a choreography so mysterious and impalpable. But despite the role's long performance history in St. Petersburg, "we didn't really know how Giselle was supposed to be." Osipenko assumed that, Dudinskaya being prima, she was doing it the way it was supposed to be. But visitors from the Paris Opera in the late 1950s, first Liane Daydé and then Yvette Chauviré, made her understand that Dudinskaya was not the role's ideal interpreter.

During that first 1950–51 season Osipenko was also given her first principal role, Maria in *The Fountain of Bakchisarai*. Choreographed in 1934 by Rotislav Zakharov, it was a seminal template for Soviet *dramballet*. It combined passages of traditional classical vocabulary, some of the exotica flavor of Fokine's mélanges of Eastern and Caucasian dance, as well as the enduring influence of Stanislavsky on Russian ballet, by which classical vocabulary was supposed to read as psychological revelation.

Maria is a Polish princess whose lover is killed by invading Tatars. Their chief, Girei, brings her back to his harem, awakening the fatal jealousy of spurned mistress Zarema. The saintly, submissive role was created by Ulanova, but it was atypical of most of what Osipenko herself would perform over the balance of her career. "I don't know why they cast me." Looking back she thought that perhaps the role was simply something that needed to be filled, for at that time not Maria but Zarema was the role that was coveted.

All the leads were young: Osipenko's classmate Viacheslav Kutznetsov was her young beau Vaslav, mowed down by the Tatars. Olga Moiseyeva, a Vaganova graduate from 1947, was making her debut as Zarema. "She wasn't very good," Osipenko said. "And I was terrible, unfortunately." Part of the reason was lack of conviction. "I was crazy, racing through life," Osipenko recalled, and rather than spend an entire three-act ballet supplicating, "I wanted to scream, 'Go away, Zarema!'" And perhaps her true feelings shone through. "You looked like a strong, healthy Soviet girl!" Gusev scolded her after the performance. "You could even have hit somebody." Nor was he happy about the performance as a whole. He didn't like the character makeup that Moiseyeva had applied: a big putty nose, a black wig, and body paint. "Why did you do this? It's terrible. I don't want to see it." Another young future Kirov star, Askold Makarov, was making his debut as Khan Girei. Gusev admonished him: "You looked like you were chewing lemon through-out the entire performance."

"The one person who defended me was Vaganova." Her verdict was that Osipenko was still a little young for a principal role, but all she needed was time—she was someone to watch. But to Osipenko's face, Vaganova said, "It was the first time I saw such a bad performance in a principal role. You were mindless. Think about the role instead of which movie you're going to next. Probably it will still be terrible."

Zarema stayed in Moiseyeva's repertory: "Olga started to work hard on it and she was good." But Osipenko performed Maria no more than three times, and, she said, "it didn't get better."

A role she performed more frequently during her first Kirov season was the Queen of the Ball, mistress of Peter the Great in Zakharov's 1949 *The Bronze Horseman*. Transferred to the Soviet ballet stage, Pushkin's poem was mined for its contrasting scenes of high life and proletariat desperation. Osipenko presided over a court assembly. There was a Polonaise and a pleasant party atmosphere. She danced a variation that wasn't difficult, culminating in a manège of soutenu turns. The only problem was that the hem of the costume was decorated with coins. If she turned to the right, they pulled her to the left.

One of the reasons that Osipenko danced the role frequently was that Alla Shelest, whose career suffered constant buffeting engineered by Dudinskaya as well as her own neuroses, found herself often cast in this supporting role. It affronted her, and she was not at all averse to canceling performances for a variety of reasons. Shelest was "always nervous," Kolpakova recalled, "and it immediately goes to the body." She recalled sitting in the audience watching Shelest dance Giselle with Kolpakova's husband, Vladilen Semyonov. During the intermission, a regisseur approached: "Irina, come on the stage! You have to dance the second act!" And whenever Shelest was scheduled for Queen of the Ball, Osipenko was advised to be prepared to step in.

Director Gusev was handsome: "All the girls loved him." He was a womanizer, but according to Osipenko, he was seriously involved with a young woman in the corps who later became his wife. Gossip around the theater placed him, however, in compromising relationships with some of the younger rising ballerinas: "There were rumors," Osipenko recalled, " 'Moiseyeva is his lover, Petrova is his lover; Osipenko isn't but she will be . . .' " Defamatory letters were released, which probably helped to trigger his dismissal in 1951. Unlike government officials who fell out of favor, ballet dancers were not shot—simply reassigned. Gusev worked many places in Russia before he died in 1987.

The defamation campaign might well have been the handiwork of Dudinskaya and her common-law husband, Kirov premier danseur Konstantin Sergeyev. "Sergeyev wanted to oust him," Osipenko said. In 1999 Dudinskaya described Gusev as "a very good man," which certainly did not mean that she and her husband would be any less anxious to dislodge him. Sergeyev had the right credentials. Traditionally there was a chief choreographer at the helm of the Kirov, and Sergeyev had already choreographed Prokofiev's *Cinderella* for the Kirov in 1945, and in 1950 revised *Swan Lake*.

But Osipenko was on Gusev's side. When Sergeyev eventually prevailed, Osipenko as well as many other young company dancers were distraught. She, Petrova, Moiseyeva, Makarov, Igor Belsky, and Yuri Grigorovich turned his last week at the theater into a marathon good-bye. "Osipenko, I am sorry I'm leaving because I could have made you a ballerina," Gusev told her. Seeing the way he had "worked morning till night with Moisyeva, Zupkovskaya, Voichnis," she was sure that indeed he could have.

Vaganova had insisted that rather than take the corps de ballet's company class, she return to her graduating class for her daily lesson, which Osipenko did throughout the 1950–51 season. But by the spring of 1951, Vaganova's heart condition was worsening rapidly. Her students were aware that she was failing. She attended the graduation performance attended by a doctor. A spotlight was trained on her box and she stood up and accepted the audience's applause, but backstage her students made sure to carry over to her the bouquet traditionally presented to teachers by their classes at graduation.

After the summer break, Vaganova did not report to work in the fall but was largely bedridden at home. One morning in the fall of 1951, Osipenko was taking the company class when she looked up at the balcony surmounting the studio and saw Vaganova standing there, looking very frail, a scarf wrapped around her shoulders. That morning Vaganova toured the building she had worked in for sixty years, greeting people but not stopping to talk. Her colleagues were convinced that she had come to say good-bye, even though Vaganova herself was not yet ready to concede defeat and even planned to resume work on November 9. On November 5, she felt well enough to walk in the Admiralty Garden near her apartment, but soon after returning home she suffered a fatal heart attack.

A memorial service was conducted in the Kirov's main rehearsal studio. Then Kolpakova, star pupil of Vaganova's final graduating class, together with Osipenko, joined a funeral procession to the cemetery carrying pillows on which were placed the many government medals Vaganova had acquired. That night Osipenko stood in the wings of the theater, tears streaming down her face as she prepared to dance the Queen of the Ball. She loved Vaganova despite her severity, for which she was certainly grateful—all the more so from the perspective of ensuing decades. Parallel to Vaganova's graduating class was one taught by Maria Romanova. "Romanova was softer, delicate," Osipenko said to me, "but it was very important to have that push that Vaganova gave us."

For Nina, Anna, and Maria, every time Osipenko stepped on stage was a gala occasion, not to be missed. Anna and Maria would leave as soon as the curtain fell and go home to cook dinner. Nina would wait for her at the stage door. When Alla rang the bell her elders opened it exclaiming "Oh, you are beauty!" regardless of how she had danced and how the performance had gone. Eventually she took to announcing her arrival with "Here's your beauty coming home!"

By now Osipenko had declared to her family that she was going to marry Vladimir Nahumov. As fond of him as her family was, her mother objected strenuously. Osipenko would have had to leave them, move to Moscow, lose her position in the Kirov, and start over again in the Bolshoi, should she find a way to be allowed to transfer.

Nahumov sometimes came to Leningrad for the day to see her. Once she was leaving her apartment to meet him for a walk. "You are not going anywhere," her mother announced. "I will not allow you to go." Osipenko replied that she loved him, she wanted to see him, and she was going. "No," Nina insisted, "you will not go!" Osipenko went down the stairs. Her mother followed. On the landing a window was open. Nina leaped onto the window sill and threatened to throw herself out. In blind shock, Osipenko pulled her mother down from the window. And it was trauma, not the sudden performance fatigue of a yet unformed balletic instrument, that now caused her own legs to give way.

6

Sidelined

KONSTANTIN SERGEYEV'S FIRST major project as Kirov artistic director was a new production of Petipa's *The Sleeping Beauty* in 1952. The ballet had been undergoing a steady process of revision there dating back at least to 1914, when Fyodor Lopukhov had staged a new production of the 1890 original. But Sergeyev's staging was the most radical to date, an amalgam of two contradictory forces: Soviet intolerance for anything recondite in art, combined with the primacy of formalism in the avant-garde of the pre- and immediately post-Revolutionary years. Sergeyev deleted the old dialogues performed in conventional pantomime, which were claimed to be incomprehensible to the mass public and outdated. At the same time he homogenized much of the dramatic specificity of the ballet, although most of the individual solo set pieces remained the same. The Lilac Fairy was taken out of the act 2 Vision Adagio, where the prince glimpses the sleeping princess. This became less a dramatic pas d'action in which Lilac's intercessions were key, and more a generic lyric adagio. Where characters had formerly expressed themselves in gesture, they now performed classical steps, thus adhering to the formalist doctrine that disciplines of art should be streamlined to their uniquely irreducible components. In fine art, formalism had been proscribed by the Soviets, and the doctrine of Socialist Realism substituted. But Sergeyev's *Beauty* was thus actually to some degree in tune with developments in contemporary Western ballet, a concession perhaps won—maybe without the apparatchiks' conscious awareness—by his production's officially mandated elimination of the old Imperial aesthetic.

Sergeyev's *Beauty* was performed exclusively at the Kirov until 1999. Ironically, when the company visited London in 1961, its version seemed to the British less authentic than what was performed by the Royal Ballet there. The Royal's production had originally been mounted in 1939 by

Nikolai Sergeyev, the ex-Mariinsky regisseur who had fled Russia after the Revolution taking with him the choreographic notes he'd compiled in St. Petersburg.

But in 1999, Sergei Vikharev used these same notes—*Beauty*'s notation dated to 1903, thirteen years after the Mariinsky premiere—to direct a visual and choreographic reconstruction at the Kirov. It was certainly not an exact resurrection of the 1903 text, since the notes were incomplete, but it revealed the exotic, intricate, uniquely hybridized theatrical world of the old Imperial ballet and of this particular masterpiece of Petipa more fully than what any other company was showing.

In April 1999, I went to St. Petersburg to see the world premiere of Vikharev's production. Two months later the Kirov brought it to New York. It won great acclaim from me and many other Western critics. But I avoided discussing the production with Osipenko on my regular visits to her, even before she herself had seen it. I knew about the antipathy of virtually all the Kirov toward the restoration—among the company's elders, but also among the young whom they taught. Within Osipenko's generation, a kind of teleology seemed to have taken hold. Just as the Soviets had told them that their history proceeded on a vector of ever-constant improvement, so too the Kirov dancers would consider that the 1952 Sergeyev version was the true *Sleeping Beauty*, the *Beauty* that Petipa himself would have made in 1890 if only he'd known how.

Another reason I avoided extolling the Vikharev restoration to her was that it had been the nineteen-year-old Osipenko whom Sergeyev had selected to create the Lilac Fairy in his production. Prior to that, she had danced Lilac in the Kirov production that dated from Lopukhov's 1914 revival, which retained considerably more pantomime than did the Sergeyev production. But from 1952 on it was Konstantin Sergeyev's production that she danced until leaving the Kirov in 1971. Lilac became one of her greatest roles. Certainly with her, the endless arabesques, part of what Vikharev described as the "fidgeting" substituted by Konstantin Sergeyev for the original mime dialogue, must have had an altogether different meaning than with other less physically imposing and expressive interpreters.

Sergeyev was immersed in the legacy of Stanislavsky adopted by the ballet after the Revolution. Osipenko recalled to me his own performances—in 1952 he was forty-two but still had another decade on stage. When Sergeyev as Albrecht circled the stage, pursuing the fugitive specter of Giselle, "he really touched, included the whole audience." In his work as choreographer the same principles applied. Over the long and painstaking rehearsal period, Sergeyev encouraged her to construct a matrix of subtextual relationships between the fairies and the King and Queen. Onstage it made for the vibrant connection that was needed to make up for gestural detail that had been deleted.

It was highly unusual that a dancer as junior as Osipenko would be assigned a lead role at the production premiere, given precedence over the high-ranking Shelest, who was relegated to the second performance. It would be unrealistic to discount the intrigues of Dudinskaya and Sergeyev at work. But Osipenko insisted that her selection was more than that. She said that at a meeting of Kirov artistic staff, music director Boris Haiken had recommended that she be first cast. Over the course of our interviews, Osipenko several times referenced the proceedings of meetings such as this. I asked her how she knew what had transpired. "Within five minutes" after a meeting adjourned, she assured me, virtually the entire theater would be familiar with all that had happened.

The Kirov observed the European custom of the *répétition générale*, dress rehearsals open to people in the art and social world, although for "social," one needed to substitute "political" when discussing the Soviet Union. The *Beauty* dress rehearsal in March 1952 was an exciting afternoon for Osipenko. Dudinskaya as Aurora danced beautifully. Osipenko's pirouettes were steady; she was proud at having met the technical requirements of a lead classical role. Osipenko received many compliments from colleagues: the consensus was that, four months after Vaganova's death, her faith in her student had been vindicated.

However, when Osipenko returned home, she discovered that her mother, concerned as usual about her daughter's weight, had nothing more prepared for her than two hot dogs served with cabbage. She was angry at the meager rationing and went out to buy an ice cream. She took a bus back home; when it pulled up to her stop, it wasn't close to the curb. She leapt onto the wet March pavement and slipped. At home her right foot started to swell. Ice wasn't kept in most Soviet households; instead her grandmother put cold compresses on her foot all night long.

She called in sick the next day, but Sergeyev called back, insisting that she dance the premiere. She tried pointing her foot as she talked to him: what he was asking was just not possible. Shelest danced in her place. Two weeks later, Osipenko's foot was still swollen, and she could walk only with difficulty. She went to the hospital, where the diagnosis was that she had torn a ligament connecting the tibia and the fibula bones. A specialist told her that that he was at a loss about how her injury could be treated. His prognosis was that she would never dance again.

Two young doctors, however, also visited her room soon after. "Alla, don't cry. We will try to help you; we will try to do something. You will be able to dance." They were interested in devising new techniques for treatment. A steady stream of visitors from the Kirov were also reassuring, pledging that the company would do everything to make her return possible. But first she would have to wait until the ligament healed.

Nahumov called her at the hospital. She needed to hear assurance from him, too, that she would be able to dance again. Instead he was jubilant. "It's wonderful. You won't dance, but you will be in my movies. You will be a great actress. We will have a boy and we'll be happy!" She was shocked. He seemed not to realize that she was devastated. "Never ever call me again," she told him. "Forget me. Everything is over." He kept calling, but she refused to speak to him. She remained in the hospital for a month. All told, eighteen months passed before she could fully resume her career at the Kirov. In Leningrad, she went out frequently with many friends, too frequently for her mother's satisfaction. Nina told Osipenko angrily that she was doing everything she could to delay her return to the ballet stage. But what she was really doing was staving off her fear of being alone—for walking by herself over the Antichekev Bridge on Nevsky Prospect she had begun entertaining thoughts of throwing herself into the Fontanka Canal.

Yet she felt tremendous support from the Kirov. Representatives of the dancers' union visited her frequently, bringing flowers, encouraging her, saying they were awaiting her return. She was given supernumerary roles on stage so that she could continue to earn her full salary rather than get a disability cut. She was even given a raise.

Finally, the pain in her foot numbed by anesthetic, she began physical therapy, working on machines. When in 1953 the Black Swan pas de deux was filmed with Dudinskaya and Sergeyev, she stood in for Dudinskaya during some camera rehearsals and walked on as an extra in the crowd.

That summer, she went on a month's vacation to Batumi, a resort on the Black Sea, where she would swim and have mud treatments. Traveling there by train necessitated a layover in Moscow. She didn't have money for a sleeper so she was forced to sit up all night on her trip to the capital. Nahumov had found out from Nina that she was stopping over in Moscow. He met her train and proposed that they get married immediately. His parents were waiting. He had bought plane tickets for a honeymoon. By the time she was expected to arrive in Batumi, they would instead be arriving at their honeymoon destination and could contact her family.

She was in turmoil. If he had already told her once that it was fine if she didn't dance, what would happen next? The injury had made her realize that ballet was the most important thing in her life. How could she live with someone who didn't realize that? And yet she knew that she was in love with him. "Before I'm certain I'll be able to dance, I cannot talk about it at all," she finally decided. The train was pulling out. She told him good-bye. "It was my first sacrifice," she recalled to me. "I sacrificed my love."

In Batumi she was joined by her former teacher Lidia Tyuntina. For two hours, from six in the morning until eight, she would perform basic exercises at a jury-rigged barre, held in place by Tyuntina's groggy young son. Then at eight she would swim. Tyuntina became as close as family during the months of her convalescence. In Leningrad, she also sometimes took private classes with Tyuntina and sometimes took a barre with Tyuntina's class at the school, or with the intermediate boys' class taught by Lidia Yementova. "Take a look at this boy," Yementova told her about student Nikita Dolugshin; "he's going to be great." Later he became one of Osipenko's favorite dancers and partners.

She had no fear of the water; in Batumi she'd sometimes take long swims at night by herself, guided home by the moon. A coach who worked on the beach told her that if ballet didn't work out he could turn her into a champion swimmer.

Osipenko and her friends routinely socialized with students at the Academy of Arts on the Neva. A Vaganova classmate had already married one of them, when Osipenko began to be courted by Georgi Paysist. He was an outstanding student in the fine arts division. His father was a distinguished doctor. He and his family lived in an apartment behind the Hermitage on what had been called "Millionaire's Row" before the Revolution. They also had a dacha. Paysist started courting her. After a while, he asked her family for her hand, pledging his unconditional support. If she needed any treatment for her leg, his father could help. And, he told them, he was going to buy a car.

"Too bad, too bad, Lalasha," her grandmother weighed in after he left. "You had Valody. Now you have this one and you want to marry him. He bought you with his car." (Cars were at that time uncommon in Leningrad.)

But she liked him very much and his support was encouraging. He was talented, smart, and his words carried authority: he was seven years older than she. She told him, yes. But she wasn't ready to marry. Sex was a taboo subject in her family. When men asked her to dinner, Maria would fume, "He invited you to a restaurant? Does he think you're a prostitute?"

Marriage meant signing a license at the wedding registry, housed in an old mansion on Nevsky Prospect. Two friends accompanied the couple, and then all went on to a party at a restaurant. She moved into his family's apartment, where it did not take her long to realize she'd made a mistake. "I realized that it wasn't Valody Nahumov at all. With Valody it was real love. Here it was something totally different." In a month she moved back home and faced the inevitable. "Too bad, too bad, Lalasha." Yet the disapproval of her mother, grandmother, and great-aunt was less than their excitement that she was once again living with them.

Osipenko and Paysist didn't divorce because he elected to be patient. They went to parties together; they visited each other's apartments. He assured her that one day she would fall in love with him.

AS A TEENAGER, Osipenko's later antagonism and disillusionment with the Soviet state would have seemed remote. Soon after the war ended, she'd gone with friends to visit the ex-Imperial estate at Peterhof, in the Leningrad suburbs, which had been devastated by the Germans. She saw how diligently it was being rebuilt, and she and her friends believed that their parents' taxes were being used for worthwhile endeavors.

When she entertained wounded soldiers during the war, they told her "We fought for our country and for Stalin." No distinction was made between the two. Despite the genocide he engineered, he remained to vast segments of the Soviet public "our leader and our teacher," so much so that in March 1953, Osipenko went to Moscow for Stalin's burial. A massive column of mourners moved slowly through the streets, trying to reach the Kremlin to view his casket. People watched from roofs and balconies. Police on horseback controlled the crowds, but nevertheless panic ensued and mourners were trampled. By the time she reached Mayakovsky Square she was so sickened by the spectacle that she decided to turn back. Her belief in authority had been altered irrevocably.

Given the original prognosis Osipenko had received after her injury, her return to performing was nearly miraculous—but it was not unqualified. Her jump was originally prodigious, and she was quickly, upon her return to the stage during the 1953–54 season, given the jumping role of Gamzatti in *La Bayadère*. But if she wasn't very careful about the way she landed she would be jolted by a sharp pain in her foot. She could never really jump again with the old freedom.

In the immediate post–World War II years, exposure to Western societies and culture made inevitable by the war was again stigmatized with a vengeance. However, in the final years of Stalin's life, the Soviets began to recognize the diplomatic value of cultural exchange. Stars of Soviet ballet, jewels in the crown of the nation's cultural life, began to be selectively exported for guest appearances in the West. Ulanova was sent to Florence in 1951, Shelest to London in 1953. Reciprocal exchanges with the West accelerated once Stalin was dead.

In May 1954, a gala of Bolshoi and Kirov stars was planned at the Opera in Paris, in exchange for a visit by Paris's Comédie Francaise, the venerable theatrical troupe. It was undoubtedly a wish to palliate the very real hostilities between the two countries that motivated such an exchange. For France and the USSR were indirect adversaries in Indochina, where the French were battling the Kremlin-supported Communists.

Nearly fifty dancers were scheduled to appear in Paris. Osipenko was eager to go, thinking that she could dance something that wasn't technically taxing—perhaps Chabukiani's Gluck adagio or Jacobson's *Meditation*. But Sergeyev advised her that perhaps she remained in too delicate a stage of recovery. She thought too that the long arm of her thwarted protector in the Ministry of Culture, Fyodor Kaloshin, had perhaps extended from Moscow. "We've had some calls," Sergeyev told her. "It's better for you to be in Leningrad and go next time."

She attended the dress rehearsal, where Ulanova, Dudinskaya, Shelest, and the Bolshoi's Raissa Struchkova danced. But for Osipenko the two most exciting performances were given by Ninel Petrova and Inna Zubkovskaya, two of the Kirov's leading young ballerinas. Petrova had joined in 1944. Zubovskaya had joined in 1941, after graduating from the Bolshoi school in Moscow. A relative who had a high-level post had been able to arrange for her to travel by fighter plane to Sverdlovsk, where the Bolshoi had been evacuated. But her plane was forced to touch down in Perm, and the Kirov soon claimed her for its own.

Petrova danced Lully's Gavotte extrapolated from Zakharov's French Revolutionary opus, *The Flames of Paris*. The entire company was familiar with it to the point of boredom. But when the curtain went up at the dress rehearsal, the spectators saw that a new, lighter-colored backdrop had been built, in grays and silvers. Wearing a blond wig, Petrova looked like Marie Antoinette. The audience of invited guests leaped to their feet and stopped the show with cheers.

The Gavotte was more customarily danced by Ninel Kurgapkina, who was far from Osipenko's favorite ballerina. Osipenko believed that Petrova gave the role higher style. Similarly, Zubkovskaya's performance in *Walpurgisnacht* rescued Leonid Lavrovsky's divertissement from a borderline of kitsch. The Kirov performed the bacchanal both as part of Gounod's complete *Faust* and extrapolated on its own. The ballerina and her scampering satyrs embody the coy prurience that probably could only be produced by a society so dogmatically puritanical. But Zubkovskaya at that dress rehearsal generated a genuine eroticism that Osipenko recalled with undiminished admiration more than forty years later. Lit by dim reds and oranges, the scene was mysterious and beautiful. Zubkovskaya, wearing a short red chiffon dress, her black hair pulled back tightly, "was something out of this world."

Scheduled for May 7, the Paris gala was first postponed for several days as it became clear that the French were going to lose the battle of Dien Bien Phu, which ended their influence in Indochina. It was then canceled outright when the French informed the Soviet delegation that their safety in Paris could not be guaranteed. Agitations by the French Communist Party had additionally raised tensions.

The dancers received offers from several other countries, but the Soviets sent them to East Berlin, where they danced with tremendous success. Originally scheduled for nine performances, they danced twenty in both East and West sectors of the city before returning home. The propaganda victory was thought in this instance to belong to the Soviets.

The elderly Osipenko was convinced that she might never have become the ballerina she did had she not been sidelined so long with her injury. After her graduation *Swan Lake* adagio, Vaganova had told her that her muscles were too lazy, too languid to the point of looking wilted. They weren't yet primed by the determination needed to command rather than simply execute the steps. But now, Osipenko felt, they began to respond differently. Certainly she had changed over the course of her nearly two years away from the stage. She was no longer happy-go-lucky. The months of enforced rest had turned her inward as she tried to examine her personality for the first time.

"What are you eating?" Gusev had asked her, frustrated as had been Vaganova by her unpredictable weight gains. "Spit it out! Spit it out!" Now she started to diet. She felt that there was no life for her without ballet. Having reached a point where she could again see a professional identity for herself, her marriage to Paysist now seemed irrevocably futile, and she insisted that they divorce.

As Gamzatti in *La Bayadère*, Osipenko shared the stage with Natalia Dudinskaya as an equal—at least in theory. Osipenko was making her debut as Gamzatti, the princess who orders the death of her love rival, temple dancer Nikiya. But Dudinskaya's name, presence, and technique was so puissant that although it is Gamzatti who is of noble caste, Dudinskaya's Nikiya "had the upper hand entirely." When Osipenko was required to issue an order for

Nikiya's execution, the line between balletic incarnation and Soviet performing legend vanished. "I thought, Oh my gosh, I can't do it to her."

Gamzatti was difficult for her not simply because so much of it was jumping. She was dancing choreography dating to Chabukiani and Ponomarev's 1941 revival, although she said that the variation had become more difficult since then. At an orchestra rehearsal she struggled with Gamzatti's rapid bourrées in her entrée before the betrothal adagio in act 2. Conductor Pavel Feldt stopped the orchestra. "Again you're behind," he reprimanded her. She responded, "But it is so difficult, and I just cannot keep up with your music. Please slow down just for me." He looked at her thoughtfully and said, as if talking to himself, as if genuinely perplexed, "Osipenko, you cannot do anything. Why on earth is everybody thinking that you will become great?"

Her legs still might give out unexpectedly and disastrously, just as they had at Vaganova's Philharmonic jubilee years earlier. It happened again when she made her debut in *Don Quixote* as act 1's Street Dancer. Here she was required to bourrée between eight matadors' daggers as she made her way downstage toward her intended destination, the dashing matador Espada, who was standing with a rival Flower Girl on his arm. Osipenko was supposed to tap him with her fan and fall coquettishly onto his cape. But this night she felt that her legs were once again failing her. To slide sinuously between the daggers didn't seem possible. Finally she was reduced to standing rooted in one position, doing no more than swishing her skirt side to side. She had already run out of music. "Just run, run!" nearby dancers whispered. She somehow reached Boris Bregvadze's Espada, swatted him, and fell, not onto his cape but down to the ground. "You didn't die, did you?" he asked. Indeed, Osipenko anticipated some form of annihilation from the authorities as soon as the first-act curtain fell. She heard conductor Feldt's voice offstage. "Where is Osipenko?" Now he was coming toward her. "Are you kidding? What did you do to us?"

"He was about to hit me," Osipenko remembered, "but he was afraid to break his baton."

7

Finding Herself

IT WAS IN 1954 that Osipenko danced her first *Swan Lake*, a ballet for which she would eventually become renowned. Replacing an injured colleague, she danced the two White acts, while Nina Timofeyeva danced the Black Swan Odile. The role was sometimes split up this way at the Kirov. In this case, the administration was concerned about resting the entire performance on either dancer: Osipenko had just returned from her injury, and Timofeyeva was technically strong but had graduated only in 1953.

Soon after the performance, Osipenko went to have her nails done at a beauty parlor that she patronized regularly. Nina Jelesnova, an actress at the once-Alexandrinsky, now-renamed Pushkin Theater, at the head of the Rossi Street complex that housed the ballet school, was sitting nearby. She had apparently seen the *Swan Lake* performance; she offered her help should the young ballerina desire coaching in the dramatic aspect. Jelesnova told her to call anytime she wanted to meet and work together. Osipenko was excited at the idea and told her family about it the minute she got home. "Mama, Grandma, Can you imagine what happened to me?. . ."

"What is her name?" they asked. "Forget it! Forget this phone number! We forbid you to go there. . . . Jelesnova is a lesbian and Studentsov"; her husband, also a star at the Pushkin, "is a pederast!" The two stars lived together on Fontanka Street but allegedly their apartment had separate entrances. Even now, when Osipenko was twenty-two, the disapproval of her family could carry weight. Artistic guidance would have to come from other sources.

For Kirov head Konstantin Sergeyev, with his wife Dudinskaya still dominating the stage, grooming young ballerinas was not his—or her—priority. At the same time, neither the director nor the first lady put roadblocks in the young Osipenko's progress, and for that she was grateful. "Dudinskaya loved me. I was falling down all the time so I wasn't a rival of hers. I was a little girl to her."

However, "they never thought or planned ahead," Osipenko claimed. If a dancer was indisposed, a substitute learned the role quickly and went on. She was able to learn fast and so it was easy for them to throw her on stage. "On the one hand Dudinskaya and Sergeyev let me dance, but on the other they never worked with me. They never tried to groom me as a future ballerina."

She knew she had been singled out since school by choreographers who wanted to create for her. But Osipenko herself did not feel that technically she was completely sound or capable. Even though she'd been able to continue in Vaganova's class during her first year in the Kirov, she "didn't really have time to teach me everything," Osipenko said. She believed that she had needed more work on coordination, on certain technical steps. In Vaganova's class she had been "a bit lazy, too," she admitted. Now she developed "a little bit of an inferiority complex," because the conductor Feldt was not alone in saying that Osipenko would prove problematic.

Nevertheless, in 1955, Osipenko conclusively re-established herself as a rising ballerina in the company when she assumed the lead in *Taras Bulba*, a balletic adaptation of Gogol's novella that was choreographed by Boris Fenster. Fenster was in his late thirties and had already been chief choreographer at the Maly theater in Leningrad for the past decade. Now he was starting to work for the Kirov, where he would become director three years later.

Originally Osipenko was scheduled for the supporting role of Oxana, a country girl, dancing in the second cast that would be headed by Shelest as the Polish governor's daughter. She is simply "Pannochka"—the Polish honorific for unmarried woman—for whom the young Cossack Andrei forsakes his allegiance. After a few rehearsals, Fenster told Osipenko that instead he wanted her to alternate with Dudinskaya as Pannochka. It was close to the opening night of the new ballet, and they worked after hours as he rechoreographed a new version of the role. The solos were less virtuosic than Dudinskaya's, but the pas de deux more intricate.

Boris Bregvadze danced the role of Andrei with both Osipenko and Dudinskaya. Dudinskaya in the role was "very aristocratic, with enormous charm," he recalled. "Alla was younger. Also aristocratic. But more like a young girl leading her own life." In her first scene in the ballet, Andrei sneaks into her bedroom window, and she playfully but imperiously dresses him in her clothes. With Osipenko, the escapade had greater appeal for the audience than with Dudinskaya, as both Osipenko and Bregvadze recalled. With them, the relationship between the two attracted young people was more conspiratorial, as social disparity between wealthy Polish girl and Cossack youth narrowed.

Osipenko was nervous in the first performances. Her friend Nina Smirnova told her, in the particularly blunt way that Russian ballet dancers have when speaking to each other about their work, that she'd been good but "you were much better in rehearsal. Dudinskaya was much better than you." Osipenko had a different performance temperament than Dudinskaya; Osipenko described both Dudinskaya and Olga Moiseyeva as two ballerinas who always danced on stage better than they rehearsed. Others danced up to the level of their rehearsals. Throughout her career, Osipenko herself would often find to her chagrin that technique that had worked in the studio faltered on stage. But her performances in *Taras Bulba* became more assured and she attracted significant attention. "The critics said that 'Osipenko is not your traditional ballerina,'" she recalled. "'There's something very different and special about her. We don't know exactly how, but she is different.'"

She saw the role as a reflection of herself, a portrait of her, her life, her attitude toward life. When the stage lights rose on her first scene in her bedroom, it was as if she had always lived there, so much so that she would have preferred "to live there on the stage all my life." The role became even more personal when she danced it with Viacheslav Kutznetsov. Whereas Bregvadze was already an established star, Kutznetsov was her classmate and friend. With him, she understood what the degree of collaboration was in a true partnership. Thirty years later, dance historian and critic Natalia Zozulina was writing a biography of Osipenko. She had never seen her in *Taras Bulba*, and the ballet had long since been dropped from the Kirov repertory. Zozulina asked Kutznetsov and Osipenko if they could illustrate the choreography for her. Osipenko warned her that she didn't remember it all after so many years. But she and Kutznetsov retained a pianist and once they started dancing together the choreography soon returned to their muscular memory: it was all there, in its entirety.

Belief in the role as well as her ability to perform it often determined how she fared technically. Osipenko was fascinated by the Lilac Fairy in *The Sleeping Beauty,* by the idea that every gesture and every step could be a bestowal of benevolence. Emanating from that raison d'être, the technical difficulties became easy. She enjoyed illuminating the contrasts and complexity of this ballet incarnation when her gentle benignity pivoted to potent determination to vanquish the evil fairy Carabosse. "I really enjoyed being able to be strong and order her out."

Sometimes her adversary was played by an actual female, Nina Federova. But sometimes its *en travesti* traditions were adhered to in the person of the Kirov's Mikhail Mikhailov or Alexander Chavrov. The two men left a strong impression on her. Mikhailov was tall, portly, older—big and powerful. Chavrov was smaller and reptilian, scurrying and slimy. "Their temperament was very masculine. I felt I played off them well and really reached the heights of acting and interpretation."

Her appearance at the conclusion of act 1 felt like a participation in a ritual. As she cast her spell over the court, her gestures were timed to signal the raising and lowering of the drops and curtains that prefigured nature's reclamation of the court in its hundred-year sleep. She believed herself empowered, invincible, dispelling chaos and strife. Finally, as the front curtain slowly descended she felt as though she was enclosed in her kingdom.

Nina loved *Sleeping Beauty*, so much so that after Osipenko's graduation, her mother had said to her, "I will die peacefully if you dance Aurora." That was unlikely to happen. Even when she was very young, she never looked like an ingénue. But when she danced the Lilac Fairy, her mother was to a degree mollified—she was "more or less satisfied."

8

Seeing the West

SOVIET CULTURAL EXCHANGES picked up pace alongside the program of de-Stalinization. In February 1956, Nikita Khrushchev, First Secretary of the Communist Party, denounced Stalin and the "cult of personality" at a closed session of the Twentieth Party Congress. That summer, Osipenko became the first of her generation of Kirov dancers to captivate European audiences. Moscow's Stanislavsky-Nemirovich Danchenko Ballet performed in Paris for a month's season at the Théâtre du Châtelet. The Stanislavsky company had decided to augment their ranks for their European debut. Osipenko and Kutznetsov were taken from the Kirov, although not as a performance team. Kutznetsov was then married to Tatiana Vecheslova, who had been a lover of Vladimir Bourmeister, artistic director of the Stanislavsky troupe. According to Osipenko, Vecheslova had asked Bourmeister to take Kutznetsov. But Osipenko didn't know who had recommended her or why she had been chosen. Bourmeister came backstage and extended his invitation after watching her dance Gamzatti. She was thrilled.

Overseas performances were always meticulously prepared. Osipenko spent a month and a half in Moscow rehearsing. "You had to fall in love with him," Osipenko said about Bourmeister. Then fifty-two, he was intelligent, cultured, and interesting looking. She considered him talented and innovative. She'd seen the ballet, *Tatiana*, that he'd created for the Kirov a decade earlier, which starred Vechelova as a Russian guerrilla. In 1953 at the Stanislavsky, he had made a new *Swan Lake*, which he was now taking to Paris. It preserved act 2, considered to be the work of Lev Ivanov in the 1895 Mariinsky premiere. However, Bourmeister created new choreography to music included in the unsuccessful Moscow premiere in 1877 but deleted when the Mariinsky introduced its production in 1895. Osipenko found Bourmeister's version altogether livelier and more accessible to contemporary audiences than the Kirov's *Swan Lake*. During the overture, a prelude made visible the backstory of Odette, who has been turned by von Rothbart into a swan by day. Rather than being confined to the Black Swan pas de deux, Odile was a vital presence from the rise of the second-act curtain, making fleeting appearances amid the character dancers before the pas de deux. Osipenko considered Bourmeister's Odile almost a sister guerrilla to his Tatiana.

In the West, these were the years of emerging counterculture: the Beats, Mods, and Rockers. And in Moscow, Osipenko noticed that some comparable rebel populations were emerging even in Russia. Whereas Soviet holidays had been the traditional times when young people threw parties, now they occurred more spontaneously. In Leningrad she went to parties called "meetings of physics and lyrics"—engineers with ballet dancers, actors, poets—and parents. But Moscow was less supervised. In Leningrad she danced the waltz or fox-trot; in Moscow she met rock-and-roll for the first time.

Bourmeister was dating a young woman who invited Osipenko and Kutznetsov to a party in her family's apartment in a building reserved for members of the government. Her parents weren't around to supervise; they had gone to their dacha. The guests sampled an abundance of delicious food that could not have been purchased in any ordinary Russian store during that period. Live musicians played and the guests started to dance. These sounds and the accompanying gyrations were something completely new to Osipenko. She asked the pianist if the combo could play something quieter. "Girl," the woman responded with sullen condescension, "what do you want—a waltz?"

On the flight to Paris, their plane encountered turbulence. Anxiously, Osipenko and Kutsnetsov made their way to the pilot's cabin, where they saw one pilot trying to control the bucking plane; the rest of the crew were crossing themselves. After they touched down safely, a Paris newspaper called them the "resurrected Russians."

The Parisians loved Bourmeister's *Swan Lake*, and in 1960, the production entered the repertory of the Paris Opera. During the five-week season, Osipenko also danced Chabukiani's Gluck adagio. The Châtelet stood in a red-light district, near the quays of the Seine. One prostitute had a contact in the theater and started watching from the wings night after night. "I lost so much money," she told them at the end of the run, "but I'm not sorry about it, because I saw so many wonderful performances."

"The aroma, the soul, the flavor" of the Parisian streets were endlessly intriguing. They seemed joyous, flavored with an openness palpably different from Leningrad. But KGB agents swarmed around the company, warning them never to venture out except in groups of at least five, chaperoned at all times by an agent. Casting an eye toward back doors and basement kitchens, however, Osipenko learned ways to shed her surveillance and explore the city the way she wanted.

While St. Petersburg pulled up the sidewalk early, Paris never slept. She ate onion soup at Les Halles at 5:00 A.M., watching the chic women who shopped early and stopped to snack. She saw Montmartre and Sacre Coeur. However, the KGB managed to thwart her chance to meet ex-Imperial prima ballerina Olga Preobrajenska, who had been a good friend of Vaganova's. Reportedly, Vaganova had also incorporated into her teaching elements of the classes that Preobrajenskaya taught at the school before fleeing to Paris after the Revolution.

In Paris, Preobrajenskaya's assistant, Elvira Roné, contacted Osipenko and arranged for her to meet the elderly ex-ballerina. Osipenko walked out of the hotel and saw Preobrajenskaya and Roné waiting in a cab, but before she could reach them a KGB agent buttonholed her and demanded to know where she was going. To a museum, she said, and steered clear of the cab. She later explained what had happened to Roné, who realized that it was probably best for them not to try to meet again.

A Moscow friend of Osipenko's was Ludmilla Maksakova, the teenaged daughter of a prominent opera singer. She later became a noted actress, and she was a ballet fan. Despite the danger involved, she enjoyed a friendship with Michel Renault, étoile at the Paris Opera Ballet. Through this friendship, Renault took Osipenko and Kutznetsov under his wing in Paris. Renault owned a car and he toured them through Fontainebleau. He took them to nightclubs in the Place Pigalle—among them a conventional striptease club as well as a nightclub where there were transvestite and cross-gendered entertainers. Their beauty startled the Russians. A program booklet showed small pictures of the men they'd been "before," opposite larger ones in their current feminine incarnations. Renault called over one of "the girls" and asked her to show them her breasts. She was dissuaded from showing them more.

Further enhancing their education, Renault invited them to a lesbian nightclub. When they arrived shortly before dawn, the floor shows were all finished, but on tables as well as under them were pairs in various stages of affectionate demonstration. Were they really all women, Kutznetsov asked Renault incredulously. Yes, he told him; they two were the only men present.

Despite the risk of imprisonment, there was of course an active homosexual population throughout the Soviet Union. Five years earlier, Osipenko had been in Yalta with several girlfriends. They decided to go to a restaurant where a woman invited her to dance and was irate when a young man tried to cut in. "This was my first acquaintance with this kind of love." Five years later, Osipenko still carried with her the full freight of Soviet Puritanism as well as relative inexperience. Paris's gender-bending spectacles disturbed and disoriented her.

On a free night, she and Kutznetsov bought tickets to see Edith Piaf at the Olympia. Then sometime later they were sitting in a café frequented by performers, when Piaf came in with friends, and Osipenko experienced at close range her huge eyes, her charisma. At a reception attended by Gina Lollobrigida, Osipenko and some of her colleagues drank champagne and fielded questions about how they liked Paris. She admired Lollobrigida's ensemble and felt her own clothes were dowdy by comparison.

Seeing Osipenko dance the excerpted White act on a mixed bill during the Paris run, *Dance and Dancers*' Clive Barnes praised her grace, her "lovely extensions and poetic feeling." Noted French dancers came backstage at the Châtelet. They invited her to cafés because they realized that the Russians weren't getting paid much at all. They took Osipenko and Kutznetsov out to dance the tango and fox-trot. For ex-Diaghilev star Serge Lifar, longtime director of the Paris Opera Ballet, the Kirov's descent from the Imperial Mariinsky, cradle of the Ballets Russes, made the company something sacred for him. He invited Osipenko out to dinner, which resulted in "unpleasant talks with security," she recalled. A KGB agent escorted her when Lifar made her that year's recipient of the Pavlova Prize that he had recently instituted. The ceremony was held at the Academy of Dance. In attendance were many stars of the European ballet, among them Claude Bessy, Nina Vyborouva, Alicia Markova, and Yvette Chauviré. But Osipenko's win fanned underlying Leningrad-Moscow rivalry, and after the presentation, her relationship with the Bourmeister troupe turned chilly.

At a reception after one performance, Leonide Massine told her that her dancing was illuminated by the soul of their common country. He invited her to spend a year dancing with a company he wanted to form in Monte Carlo. He promised that she would debut with Fokine's *Spectre de la Rose* and dance Massine's entire repertory. She was surprised when he started to show her *Spectre* in a Paris studio. It was a discovery for her because until then she had only read about that ballet in books. Except for *Chopiniana*, the Kirov dancers were unfamiliar with the old Fokine repertory that had been created for the Western tours of the Ballets Russes. Technically the Young Girl in *Spectre* was not very difficult: the role is mostly partnered. But it demanded an elusive quality, something internal.

Massine rehearsed her in it a couple of times together with Serge Golovine, the Paris Opera–trained star of the Marquis de Cuevas's troupe. She was meant to be an actual adolescent, whereas the spirit of the Rose was a phantom almost impossible for her mortal eyes to apprehend. He didn't have any human responses or understanding. "Massine made it like a reminiscence. He didn't give us the possibility to make contact in reality." The Rose and the Girl were to exist in two different styles of performance.

These rehearsals, however, went nowhere, for when Osipenko broached the subject of a leave with some of the authorities, her request was not only refused but mocked. "You, a member of the Komsomol, a Soviet, you're going to work in the West?" Did she want to find herself barred from ever leaving Russia again? She told Massine only that she would be too busy at the Kirov to work with him.

A rupture with the Soviet Union was something she couldn't entertain and didn't want to. A great irony of Osipenko's career is that while, much to her frustration, her travel options were eventually severely restricted by the Soviets, she never at any time during her career seriously entertained the idea of defection. As gratifying as was the Parisians' response to her, as intoxicating as was her first experience of European capitalism, when she returned to Russia her stay abroad assumed the quality of an alien, almost cinematic unreality.

For the Leningrad ballet community, Osipenko's honor resonated in ways that wouldn't have been possible only a few years earlier: this is the picture given by Valery Panov in his 1978 memoir *To Dance*. In 1956, Panov was a student on Rossi Street. He would join first the Maly, then the Kirov, where he was acclaimed in the heroic and character repertory. Later his star would plummet when he requested permission to emigrate, the Soviets' resistance sparking a cause célèbre in the early 1970s.

Panov notes that official response to Osipenko's victory marked a clear departure from the era that ended with Stalin's death three years earlier. Rather than being pressed to express an overwhelming emphasis on the gratitude she owed the leader and Soviet state for its largesse in fostering her talents, Osipenko seemed to be encouraged to own the award and her individual achievement. Panov was startled by this: "It was described almost as if she had something in common with Western stars, as if the state should be grateful to *her* for winning the competition!" Doors seemed to be opening; more things would be possible in the months ahead.

9

Creation

WAITING FOR OSIPENKO in Leningrad was the breakthrough creation of her career, the Mistress of the Copper Mountain in Yuri Grigorovich's *The Stone Flower*. Grigorovich was a twenty-nine-year-old Kirov dancer who had already created some choreography for the school. *The Stone Flower* was Prokofiev's final ballet score, completed shortly before his death in 1953. Written by Myra Mendelssohn, Prokofiev's second wife and frequent collaborator, the libretto was based on the fairy tales from the Ural mountains in Central Russia compiled by Pavel Bazhov in 1939. In February 1954, the Bolshoi had premiered a *Stone Flower* choreographed by Leonid Lavrovsky, but it had not been well received. Now Grigorovich would have his chance, an opportunity that wouldn't have been possible if Fyodor Lopukhov had not been made co-director of the Kirov in 1955, following a dancers' revolt against Sergeyev.

A 1905 graduate of the Rossi Street academy, Lopukhov had served the ballet company in various capacities, as dancer, choreographer, and artistic director. His restaging of *Sleeping Beauty* in 1914 initiated a pattern that accelerated after the Revolution, when he became director of the former Mariinsky and made more new productions of the classics so that they resonated with the burgeoning post-Revolutionary aesthetic. He also choreographed works that were his own entirely, sometimes to Stravinsky scores that Diaghilev had already used for his émigré Ballets Russes but had not yet been staged in Russia.

Lopukhov's choreographic vocabulary was inclusive and exploratory, riding the crest of artistic liberation following the Revolution. Young George Balanchine had danced in his ballets and been influenced by them. When New York City Ballet visited Russia in 1962, Lopukhov invited Balanchine to his Leningrad apartment, which was adjacent to the school on Rossi Street.

Lopukhov asked from where Balanchine's choreographic inspiration origi-nated. "From you," Balanchine replied. In 1971, Balanchine cabled eighty-fifth birthday wishes to Lopukhov, thanking him for "your help during my first feeble attempts to choreograph."

Lopukhov had fallen out of favor in the mid-1930s as the Soviets began insisting on a retrograde traditionalism in all the arts. His career had waxed since then, but it had also on occasion waned, including another, two-year stint as Kirov director in the mid-1940s. By the 1950s, Lopukhov had become as much a hero to the generation of Osipenko and Grigorovich as he had decades earlier to Balanchine and his colleagues. Osipenko too vis-ited his apartment on occasion. She appreciated his dry humor. "Osipenko's very skinny," he said once, "but on the bones meat is sweeter." Years later, Osipenko would dance the adagio from Lopukhov's 1927 *Ice Maiden* at an eightieth birthday tribute to him. He subsequently inscribed a picture to her partner and husband John Markovsky: "Don't let go of this woman; she has a beautiful ecarté."

Lopukhov was prone as well to absolutist pronouncements in the inim-itable manner of Russian ballet dancers. "Vaganova is nothing," he said to Osipenko. "She wasn't the Queen of Variations; she was just ugly." It is likely that Vaganova had played a role in his ouster as ballet director in 1930, which resulted in her obtaining his position.

At the Kirov, *Stone Flower* was originally going to be choreographed by Sergeyev, using Grigorovich as his assistant. Lopukhov, however, soon insisted that the younger choreographer take over the project. Sergeyev and Grigorovich quickly became adversarial poles around which the Kirov coalesced.

It was after seeing Osipenko in *Taras Bulba* that Grigorivich asked her to create the Mistress of the Copper Mountain in his *Stone Flower*. The Mistress is half woman, half lizard. She reveals to the stone-cutter Danila a malachite flower hidden in her mountain: the Platonic essence of all sculptural repre-sentation. She betrays her artistic mandate by falling in love with him but is able to relinquish him to his peasant sweetheart Katerina.

Lopukhov's appointment represented a power-sharing arrangement, in which his authority was not absolute. In *Swans of the Kremlin*, Christina Ezrahi describes the two-year process that slowly and laboriously brought *Stone Flower* to the stage, despite the opposition of Sergeyev and his sphere of influence.

Grigorovitch was forced to rehearse his cast privately, often in his own apartment. His choreography, in particular the duets the Mistress danced with Danila in acts 1 and 3, were conceived as homage and sequel to Lopukhov's choreography of the 1920s. Osipenko slithered over and around Danila, the entire surface of the two bodies interfacing in ways that had been taboo throughout the Stalin era. Grigorovich wanted of course to expand his own statement beyond his mentor's inspiration: Osipenko would clamber into a lift or slide out of one, and Grigorovich would analyze her trajectory, searching for new mechanics.

The theater's Komsomol organization, fifty-eight dancers strong, lobbied authorities for *Stone Flower* to be officially included in the theater schedule. After months of underground preparation, the cast demonstrated excerpts to Lopukhov, who then officially posted the ballet on the rehearsal agenda.

For Osipenko, Grigorovich's choreography was really a new style, different from anything she'd danced to date. There were fast turns, jumps, bourrées, and a consistently sharper outline to arabesques and attitudes. Sergeyev told Osipenko that if she danced Grigorovich's work she would no longer be equipped to dance the classics, which was nonsense. But certainly Grigorovich's kinetic signature influenced her style, which became starker, more graphically etched.

Grigorovich chose Tatiana Vecheslova as his assistant. She now worked closely with all four young dancers cast in the lead roles—Osipenko, Kolpakova as Katerina, Alexander Gribov as Danila, and Anatoly Gridin as the Bailiff who menaces Katerina.

Osipenko had watched Vecheslova on stage for years before the ballerina retired in 1953. While she was still performing, Vecheslova had also been Osipenko's acting teacher at the school. Since retiring, Vecheslova had directed the school for a time, but administrative positions were not the best venue for her. She was impulsive and outspoken. Midwifing a vanguard artistic enterprise was much more her style, enabling her to share with the dancers her immersion in cultural and literary communities. "She was not just a coach," Osipenko said. "She tried to make us cultured people." Vecheslova took them to museums, assigned them reading material, and insisted they formulate their own opinions. "She made us think. She made us find ourselves. She enriched our souls."

At Vecheslova's apartment, Osipenko became acquainted with the Moscow Art Theatre's Olga Androvskaya, and with Nikolai Akimov, the radical stage designer of the NEP epoch. Vecheslova was also a friend of Anna Akhmatova and liked to recite her and Marina Tsvetaeva's poetry as well as verse she herself had composed. Some of her love poetry was even published. In these years of youthful fulfillment and exhilaration, Osipenko

The Stone Flower with Alexander Gribov.
Photo courtesy Alla Osipenko.

also enjoyed composing poetry for a while. She returned to the pastime thirty years later, when her life had turned much more problematic.

The role of the Mistress sustained the protean character of the great ballerina roles of the classical canon. Over the course of the ballet's three acts, Osipenko made chameleon-like changes in costume and personality. From her initial appearances, she was identified with omnipotence, seen high above Danila, watching him stage left, then stage right. In their first encounter, he was to respond to her as if she were an alien creature. In act 2's village fair, the Mistress disguises herself as a peasant matron in order to vanquish the Bailiff menacing Katerina, dragging him down to some kind of inferno.

It was important to Osipenko that the audience not perceive the Mistress as bereft after Danila's desertion in act 3. Falling in love with him, she had wavered from her artistic obligations, risking Danila's equilibrium as well as her own sovereign detachment. But ultimately she had stayed true to her vision, realizing that he needed an earthly consort. In the final scene, she is shown overseeing his wedding to Katerina, a benign but remote observer. Osipenko wanted to ensure that the audience realized that while love hadn't worked out for the Mistress, she still had her gems, her career, as it were, remained. Her concern for them was and would be essential to her identity.

Grigorovich and Sergeyev's enmity belied the fact that Osipenko was in some way picking up where she had left off as Sergeyev's Lilac Fairy. Grigorovich instructed them in the history of the Soviet *dramballet* and its reliance on gesture and facial acting. Now he wanted his interpreters' bodies to be the exclusive conveyer of emotional information. The four *Stone Flower* leads read Bazhov's original stories together and copied out dialogue that they committed to memory and, so they hoped, to muscle memory as well, to give the choreography a dramatic clarity even though there was to be no pantomime.

At the first run-through onstage, the lead dancers felt that they had danced wonderfully. They were shocked when Grigorovich gathered them together and told them that it hadn't been what he wanted or expected. It wasn't their bodies but their faces that had transmitted the appropriate emotions. All was ruined: the opening night, he announced, was not going to take place. There was a long pause. Gribov picked up his towel. "Yura, we don't even know yet who will be more successful: you because of us, or we because of you. Good-bye."

Osipenko recalled that after their shock wore off, the four dancers took his words to heart and brought their performances into line with what he wanted, but she didn't think what they'd delivered in that rehearsal was worthy of his censure. They were committed to his aesthetic and had spent months immersed in it. But they were nervous, running through the entire ballet onstage for the first time, and so was he—even more than they. The premiere was scheduled to take place in April 1957, and it was certainly not going to be canceled. But a twitch began to be visible on Grigorovich's face. "Be quiet," Osipenko told him once; "You're making me nervous!"—for the ballet itself had already become a moment of sheer fulfillment for her. She wanted to engage with every aspect of the production; when the orchestra rehearsed the score, she came to listen. Prokofiev's score was different and in every way more complex than the music she customarily performed to.

For her it was glorious not to contend with a tutu—Osipenko was the first ballerina on the Kirov stage to wear only a unitard, outlining her ideal proportions and silhouette. Her appearance created a sensation: watching her move unencumbered, Russian balletgoers felt that the future had arrived.

A magical quiet prevailed in the audience of invited guests at the public dress rehearsal, an absorption that Osipenko was afraid of disrupting. On the opening night, Grigorovich as well as each of the four young stars of the ballet enjoyed a success that sealed their status in the Kirov. "Until then we were just promising boys and girls," Osipenko claimed. She went on to a party at the apartment where Grigorovich lived with Alla Shelest. "You remember, Yura," Gribov said, "you didn't want to allow us to dance the premiere?!" Grigorovich was conciliatory. Colleagues and students at the school carried Osipenko's flowers to her apartment. She woke up the next morning and her bedroom was carpeted with bouquets.

"I made the role for her," Grigorovich recalled in 2009 to his friend Helen Atlas. He coached other ballerinas in the role, "but she was the best." Nevertheless, Inna Zubkovskaya who was second-cast Mistress told Osipenko that she had erred by making the choreography too serpentine: "A lizard is not a snake." Zubkovskaya's Mistress was described by Osipenko as less sinuous, more predatory than hers. Zubkovskaya was a decade older and Osipenko wasn't going to argue with her. But they soon became friends, and this was only the first of many topics over which they would have amiable but blunt disagreements over the years. In 2000 I asked Osipenko about friends and colleagues with whom she might reminisce. It would be interesting to talk to Zubkovskaya, she told me, because "we always had different opinions about things." I actually had talked to Zubkovskaya in 1999 about her own career. But in 2001, Zubkovskaya died of a stroke at age seventy-eight.

The euphoria over *Stone Flower* continued for weeks. Late in May, Osipenko was at Grigorovich and Shelest's apartment after the debut of either Zubkovskaya or third-cast Kaleria Fedicheva as the Mistress. The choreographer suddenly decided to drive to the Finnish Harbor close to the city. Osipenko went along, as did Askold Makarov, Igor Belsky, and critic Ivan Karp. They swam at a boating club. Eventually, when the police started to evict them, they protested "We had a premiere; we're all celebrating! Let us do what we want!"

The Stone Flower has long been absent from the repertories of both the Kirov and the Bolshoi, where Maya Plisetskaya took on Osipenko's role when Grigorovich's production went into its repertory in 1959. Looking at the ballet today on video, much of it seems tame. The music contains passages of greatness, but it shares with all of Prokofiev's full-length ballet scores a degree of torpor that defeats Grigorovich at times. For Katerina alone and in her duets with Danila, Grigorovich created a valid neoclassical blend of ballet and folk, although in her solo passages his habit of visualizing every folk motif in the music becomes tiresome. Danila's solos are reliant on bravura tricks that become distinctive if the man ensures that the indigenous flavor is retained.

Despite Grigorovich's inveighing against the *dramballet*, it is virtually impossible to construct a narrative ballet without readily legible gesture. Pantomime is present in *Stone Flower*, but it is simplified, neither codified in the old Imperial manner nor realistic in the style of Soviet story ballets that preceded it. These vaguer and more generalized gestures have not aged well; they seem like a compromise.

Fernau Hall, who had reviewed *Stone Flower*'s London premiere during the Kirov's debut there in 1961, thought that much of the ballet was "very conventional in the usual Soviet neo-Petipan manner," referring undoubtedly to the long Jewels divertissement over which the Mistress presides in act 1. But Grigorovich here was using familiar antecedents, not making direct facsimiles; the choreographer's own voice is apparent. But the most artistically venturesome as well as spectacular passages in the ballet belonged to the Mistress. Hall mentions "some very effective exotic moments for the great Osipenko, exploiting her gift for strange soaring leg and arm movements and her flair for the mysterious and magical."

The highlight of her role was the act 3 duet between the Mistress and Danila, her final appeal to him to remain with her in her mountain. The throws, catches, and aerial lifts recall the surviving duet from Lopukhov's 1927 *Ice Maiden*, but the coiling, spinning character in this duet establishes a clear distinction as well.

The spell that the ballet had once cast is vivid in surviving footage of Osipenko rehearsing and dancing on stage opposite Griov, as well as her dancing the act 3 duet on a concert program with Igor Tchernichov. Also released on commercial DVD is the entirety of act 1, in which she was filmed in London in 1961, together with Soloviev and Sizova. Osipenko negotiates the animalistic assaults of the Mistress's appeals to Danila with a blend of abandon and serene physical composure, an integrity of line and position that makes these flights of daring sublime.

With the Kirov, Osipenko danced *The Stone Flower* in Yugoslavia in 1958. She found Yugoslavia under Tito rather different from other Communist bloc countries. It was closer to Europe. Pressure from Moscow wasn't felt as much as in the Soviet protectorates farther east, and Tito had begun asserting some independence from the Kremlin. In Yugoslavia, no one tried to stop her from accepting invitations to parties. "There are beautiful men there," Osipenko said when I asked for her impressions of Yugoslavia. There were, specifically, the dark-haired prototypes she was attracted to all her life.

In Belgrade the ballet's artistic director and the general director of the opera house asked her to remain in Yugoslavia. She was a ballerina of her own time; what was she doing interred in the nineteenth-century repertory of the Kirov? They offered her a good apartment and salary, but she didn't want to stay. The state of relations between Tito and the Soviet Union was too ticklish. Defection was impossible because now she was supporting her family. These were the happiest years she was ever to spend at the Kirov: "I had my *Stone Flower* and I didn't want to leave it!"

10

Her Way

WHILE I WAS interviewing Osipenko in Hartford, the Hartford Ballet faculty staffed a bachelor of fine arts dance program at the University of Hartford. In the fall of 1998, Osipenko was rehearsing the university students in excerpts from the Kingdom of the Shades scene in *La Bayadère*. She didn't think that they were technically equipped to do them, but took seriously her responsibility to make their performances "look somewhat good." She knew the ballet intimately; it had been part of her life for fifty years. In 1947, she had watched Vaganova rehearse Olga Moiseyeva for her graduation performance as Nikiya in the Shades scene. A couple of years later, Osipenko herself was dancing in the Shades corps soon after joining the Kirov. She never forgot the instruction given to her and her colleagues by Natalia Komkova: "Don't forget that you are Shades." Just as important as lining up strictly in correct formation was keeping in mind that each woman was one of a special species, hallucinatory figments of antihero Solor's opium-inflamed psyche.

During the 1990s, when Osipenko saw Rudolf Nureyev's *Bayadère* for the Paris Opera, she felt that the verdant setting and bright lighting vitiated the unique mystery of the cosmos she had stepped into at the Kirov. There the stage had been dark, the scenery minimal, the wings black. The Shades emerged from a netherworld.

From the corps, Osipenko had taken on the slow solo Shades variation, then the villainess Gamzatti, then the heroine Nikiya in the excerpted Shades scene, which was frequently performed as part of a mixed bill at the Kirov. Finally she danced Nikiya in the full-length ballet.

I couldn't get to Hartford to watch Osipenko's rehearsals that fall of 1998, but I asked her what she had told the dancers. She was "working them very delicately." She wanted to make sure that they weren't smiling excessively, a pitfall that was by this time becoming a growing tendency in major ballet companies as well as regional ones. But she also did not encourage any other kind of overt self-expression.

From watching Vaganova coach Moiseyeva in 1947, Osipenko remembered her insistence that the dancer's face be impassive. "Now it's done always wildly," Osipenko complained, "with too much expression. She's a Shade. It's not like an elephant."

She impressed upon the Hartford students the need to listen to the Minkus score and let it instruct them about what to do. The different and contrasting technical demands of the three solo Shade variations were strictly delineated. The quick and staccato steps of the first variation were different from the big broad cabriole jumps in the second. Osipenko considered the third variation, the one she had danced, the most deceptively difficult. Certainly she had found it a challenge, a taxing test of adagio technique, of strength and control, demanding buttery smooth descents from pointe. Nikiya's variation, she pointed out to the dancers, combines elements from the dances of all three solo Shades, as befits her status as regent in their transcendent kingdom.

Dancing Nikiya in the Shades had been one of her favorite classical assignments, giving her the chance to proudly display her classical physique and style. "In the Shades I was a little more sure of myself. My form gave me confidence." The Shades scarf adagio contains pitfalls for many ballerinas but she found it surprisingly easy. The scarf itself has undone many performances, entangling the ballerina as she turns while enclosing herself in the bolt of chiffon. But in Osipenko's case, not only did it not get in her way but instead she felt that it aided her equilibrium. She compared it to a tiny piece of elastic used by her mother's cousin's daughter (granddaughter of Osipenko's great-uncle, a revolutionary). At nine months old, the infant had used it to pilot herself. One time she let go, but kept on walking, powered with the confidence that it had instilled.

Osipenko's Nikiya existed in the Shades scene as a cold voice of Solor's remorse at abandoning her for the rajah's daughter, Gamzatti. No love for him remained. She was a recriminatory reminder of his betrayal, a different specter entirely than the ghost of Giselle who is reconciled with Albrecht in act 2. Nikiya was a queen, unrelenting, unforgiving. While Solor supports Nikiya in pirouettes and arabesques, Osipenko noted the absence of the body-to-body contact that we see when the same vocabulary is performed in the White Swan adagio in *Swan Lake*. Several times, Nikiya raises her arm in a sickle-shaped port de bras, meant to indicate to Solor, Osipenko said to me, that "God saw everything."

Osipenko recalled critical notices that considered her interpretation as intriguing and unusual. And yet the coldness of her statement did not affect the quality of her articulation. Nikiya's limbs had to whisper in her Shades entrance. But she meant them to suggest a sigh, a swoon of pain.

When it came time to take on Nikiya in the full-length production, however Osipenko felt that her performance was "awful. . . . I don't even like to think about it." Osipenko never felt comfortable in the first two, plot-driven acts that precede the Shades. "If I couldn't identify with a character—on some level—then it was very hard for me. So Nikiya got bitten by a snake"—that being the method of assassination preferred by her rival Gamzatti. "Somehow I just couldn't relate."

She compared herself unfavorably to Alla Shelest, a chameleon who could delineate a character and inhabit a milieu wholly foreign to the person she was herself. (Maya Plisetskaya similarly said, "Shelest for me is number one because she was an actress.") "She really could get into the character and say, 'I am Nikiya.' She could really become that." Shelest scaled the temple dancer's plight to the peaks of tragedy. Like most of the company, Osipenko recognized Shelest as an extraordinary artist. No one else in the company worked quite the way she did, experimenting by herself for hours in the studio, studying her reflection to see how things worked. Shelest "thought about her parts very seriously." To prepare for the role of Nikiya, Shelest studied Indian dance; she read the history. Osipenko, on the other hand, sought to distill the role to its defining, symbolic attributes. By her own description, her approach was closer to *Abstrakne Mushlini*, or Abstract Thinking. Such thinking may have been much discussed in pre- and post-Revolutionary aesthetics, but was anathema after the implementation of Socialist Realism as national artistic doctrine in 1934. "When you don't think of the role per se but the role in the abstract," and that role is a creation of balletic melodrama like Nikiya, the results could certainly be novel. Yet Osipenko didn't perform the role enough times to develop an interpretation she considered satisfactory.

It was Shelest's perfection in another touchstone role that wound up preventing Osipenko from assuming it. In 1958, another toss of the directorial dice at the Kirov brought choreographer Boris Fenster to the helm. Fenster had created ballets for the Kirov and the Maly. At sixty-seven, Lopukhov was now retired as director, although he continued to teach at the Rimsky-Korsakov Conservatory. Fenster was recalled by Osipenko and others as a benevolent and relatively progressive voice. His directorship, however, was prematurely curtailed two years later when he died of a heart attack.

Fenster had asked Osipenko to dance Myrtha in *Giselle*, a role for which her height and authority were well suited. Certainly the role intrigued her. She saw Myrtha as a solitary avatar of female sovereignty, somewhat like the Mistress of the Copper Mountain. But unlike the Mistress, Myrtha's power was born of the frustrated energy of love thwarted. A mortal woman might easily take a disappointment in love and channel it into renewed determination to make her next relationship succeed. Instead, Myrtha takes the same disappointment and uses it to wreak revenge on all men in her supernatural dominion. Osipenko rehearsed Myrtha, but as much as she liked the role, finally she could not bring herself to try it onstage. A picture of Shelest's unique performance in this role remained in front of her eyes all the time she rehearsed. "I've never seen a Myrtha like that," Osipenko said of Shelest. "Her bourrées floated. She had an enormous elevation, a very beautiful upper body." Osipenko decided she could not improve on Shelest's interpretation and she did not want to try. She also thought that Fenster, who was rehearsing her, had doubts about whether she had the stamina to do it well.

Leonid Jacobson's *Spartacus*, which premiered at the Kirov in 1956, was an entirely different creation than Yuri Grigorovich's far better known version created for the Bolshoi in 1968. Both were performed to the same Khachaturian din, however. Whereas Bolshoi athleticism dominated Grigorovich's tale of the Roman gladiatorial slave's insurrection, Jacobson's by contrast was a conscious exercise in aestheticism, a sculptural recreation of Attic art. All the ensemble roles were highly individualized: "Nobody was like anyone else," said Osipenko, who danced the role of a maenad at the 1956 premiere in Leningrad.

In Jacobson's ballet, the role of Spartacus's wife Phrygia had been created by Zubkovskaya and later danced by Petrova. On one occasion, both ballerinas were indisposed and Osipenko was given a few days to learn the part. Both Zubkovskaya and Petrova were dark-haired and thus convincingly Roman. "I want to stay a blonde," Osipenko told Simon Virsaladze, who had designed the sets and costumes. "Nobody can argue with you," he said. "You will do it your way." She did, despite the fact that verisimilitude was important in the Kirov aesthetic at that time, and a blonde like Soloviev would duly don a black wig to impersonate the Indian warrior Solor. The conductor said, "It was very interesting: it looks like he found you in the northern reaches of the Empire."

As Phrygia in *Spartacus*, Osipenko again extrapolated the theme of feminine strength that she wanted her interpretation of the Mistress to convey. During her final monologue she was to weep and lament, but then rise from the ground after peering into Spartacus's inert eyes. Stronger and taller than at any previous moment in the ballet, she now made clear that his crucifiction had given her the strength to continue the fight for freedom.

At one performance she put so much emotion into her lamentation that her nose hit the floor and blood spurted. Jacobson told her not to let anything like that happen again. She needed to resemble a mourning monument—to embody quintessence. The exhortatory morale was both uplifting and achieved more subtly, less didactically, Osipenko believed, than the Socialist Realism optimism of an equivalent finale in the earlier Soviet ballets.

Jacobson wanted her also to dance Aegina, mistress and conspirator of Spartacus's Roman enemy Crassus. But once more Osipenko demurred on the grounds of Shelest's perfection in the role. Shelest had created the part. She was "the genuine Aegina," Osipenko said. "She was not just Crassus's lover but a political activist, his supporter, advisor. She attracted him with her intellect."

OSIPENKO'S EARLY MARRIAGE and subsequent divorce had been disillusioning; for a while she didn't want to get involved with anyone. This changed when she became interested in Anatoly Nisnevich, a young dancer who had graduated from the school and joined the company in 1956. He was blond and medium in height, the notable exception to her lifelong infatuation with tall, dark men. Nisnevich was in fact a complete and angelic contrast to her first husband's appearance. But he was what the Russians call "a blond devil," intelligent, with a harsh wit. Nevertheless, Osipenko said, Nisnevich "played a role in my life as a savior."

"Are you crazy?" Zubkovskaya said to her. "Do you realize you're marrying a man five years younger?" (Later, however, Zubkovskaya herself married Kutznetsov, who was six years younger than she.) "Every time Zubkovskaya saw me she asked, 'Tell me, what do you do with him?' Finally I said, 'Inna, I don't know; every morning I wake up, look around and think, Did I get married or did I give birth?'"

At 63 Nevsky Prospect, Osipenko had been sharing a large bedroom with her mother. Now after her marriage Nisnevich moved into her room, while Nina moved in with her own mother, Maria, into what had originally been the dining room. Great-aunt Anna lived in the third room. "My mother and my grandmother were too smart," Osipenko said wryly about their decision a decade earlier to surrender half of the apartment. "They couldn't even imagine that I would grow up someday. Afterward they could have kicked themselves." She asked the government to help her find a larger place. In return she surrendered these three rooms to the theater, who offered them to the Kirov dancer Robert Gerbek. Osipenko and her family moved to what was once called the Black River district, near the "church in the stable," where Alexander Pushkin's memorial service had been held in 1837—it was now a KGB headquarters. It was convenient for her, closer to the opera house than 63 Nevsky. Their apartment was large by the standards of the time, 200 meters in all.

Nisnevich had graduated from Feya Balabina's class. Balabina had been a virtuoso ballerina able to polish off steps in which only men usually excelled. It was perhaps for that reason she was assigned a senior men's class, a highly unusual example at the school of instruction by the opposite sex. Also in that class were future principal dancers Sergei Vikulov and Gennady Selutsky. "They were a troika," Osipenko recalled, each perpetually engaged in a friendly and sometimes less-than-friendly attempt to prove his superiority. Also in Balabina's class was Igor Tchernichov, who was equally talented and equally prominent. But Tchernichov stood apart from their rivalry because he was not cast in the danseur noble niche but always in dramatic or neoclassical roles.

Nisnevich's career in the Kirov was on the rise, but he was still an inexperienced and frequently tentative partner, whose ego did not allow him to admit any liabilities. "I'm better than Vikulov!" Nisnevich insisted to his wife. "I'm better than Selutsky. Why don't you want to dance with me?"

Osipenko had been invited to dance in Cluj-Napoca, Romania, by the ballet company's artistic director Gabriella Taub-Darvasch. Taub-Darvasch had studied in Vaganova's teacher's training course. Osipenko wanted to ask Vladilen Semyonov to partner her. Nisnevich "didn't like that at all. He thought he was the best Siegfried." She considered him a very good Romeo but not right for Siegfried. But she didn't see any way out of taking him. During these years she also danced frequently with Nisnevich at the Kirov. But his partnering did not enhance her performances in *Swan Lake*, nor in a series of Jacobson duets that she danced with him.

11

New Roles

RAREST AND MOST coveted by Kirov dancers were roles created especially to fit the dancer's talents, since new works were hardly created in profusion. Osipenko was the fortunate recipient of additional creations in the years following *The Stone Flower.*. For an official gala at the Kirov in 1958, Jacobson decided to make a pas de deux for Askold Makarov and Osipenko concerning Prometheus. Makarov wore briefs and chains, his pale Slavic skin darkened with makeup to suggest a more convincing Greek hero. As the eagle tormenting him, Osipenko was again costumed to show off her ideal balletic proportions and silhouette, in a black leotard and tights. She thought the duet was wonderful. It was successful with the audience except for the government officials who were there in force. They didn't like the way her black leotard became spotted with red blots from Makarov's body makeup. They thought it looked sloppy. Osipenko tried it wearing a gray jersey instead, but again her costume absorbed smudges.

Given that the government assumed responsibility for all costs, new ballets could gestate at a leisurely pace. That same year, Jacobson took a couple of months to create a ten-minute Rodin triptych, three duets inspired by the sculpture's compositions, performed to orchestrations of Debussy's *Suite Bergamasque.* Osipenko and Vsevelod Oukhov were "The Kiss," flanked by Petrova and Nisnevich as "Eternal Spring" (which resided in one of its original incarnations in Leningrad's Hermitage) and Shelest and Tchernichov as "Eternal Idol."

Originally, Jacobson wanted the dancers to wear flesh-colored tights to convey an impression of the nudity of Rodin's figures. This was nixed by the authorities, however, and the dancers wore filmy tunics over their tights. Yet intrusion from the government continued. Jacobson was told that what he put onstage was equivalent to sexual acts. "These are just like jokes, it's not something serious," he said in defense of his work. "You can be punished for such jokes," he was reminded.

But if intimacy forged in marble was now to be interpreted by human sinew, it remained at one remove from sensual actuality. "I never looked at him, as if the relationship was unreal," Osipenko said about "The Kiss." A painter told her that her remote eyes and averted gaze reminded him of Garbo. "The Kiss" was a pleasure for her to dance. Oukhov was considerably older than she and "an excellent partner, very sensitive." It was technically easy. None of the women in the Rodin trilogy wore pointe shoes. Jacobson used a lot of turned-in steps. He was so opposed to traditional balletic articulation here that he forbade them to point their feet, even when their legs unfolded in a supported extension. That required a different kind of effort.

The trilogy was filmed for the 1960 compilation of Jacobson's *Choreographic Miniatures* that also includes Osipenko dancing *Meditation* with Nisnevich. "The Kiss" seems like an adult sequel to the earlier ballet he'd made for the teenaged Osipenko. By the standards then applied by Soviet cultural authorities, it would have seemed provocative. Today it registers as Osipenko recalled it: more rarified than realistic. But it was certainly something different and undoubtedly memorable to its audience. On film, both Osipenko and Oukhov seem assertive and adult, existing somewhere on the cusp between idealized flesh-and-blood and nobly rendered iconography.

Watching "Eternal Idol," Osipenko didn't like at all the way Shelest's feet looked—unpointed according to Jacobson's directive, and not very arched innately. "I know your favorite ballerina was Shelest," Zubkovskaya was similarly fond of telling the Kirov's Igor Belsky, who later directed the company, "but her feet were [European] size 46!"—in other words enormous. Shelest's silhouette, proportions, and muscle tone were each closer to the balletic ideal than those of some ballerinas whose careers overlapped hers, but she was nowhere near as shapely as Zubkovskaya or Osipenko herself.

Osipenko praised Shelest with evident sincerity as one of the greatest artists, two of whose portrayals were so stirring that they had deterred her from repeating these roles herself. And personally, "I have a wonderful relationship with Shelest to this day," she told me in February 1998, months before Shelest died. But Osipenko also on occasion could denigrate Shelest's physical instrument.

Hearing her made me reflect on the perpetual competitiveness between dancers, seemingly a constant no matter how much admiration also exists. In an art form dictated by aspiration toward an impossible ideal, the smallest deviation from that ideal is noticed and provides grist for rivalry. Scrutiny extends to self-appraisal. Critical as well as collegial consensus acclaimed Osipenko's own proportions as being as close to perfection as those of any ballerina in history but, as she said, "no dancer is satisfied" with her or his own appearance. Her own conviction that her legs were proportionately too short for her height led her to abbreviate her tutus. The administration sent her a reprimand: Kirov costumes were made in one style and had to be maintained the way they were. "This is terrible. Don't do it again." She ignored their injunction.

As Virsaladze had said, she would do it her way. Her breaches of Kirov protocol were not exactly whims but expressions of her need for artistic self-determination. Her iconoclasm was to some extent shared by others in the company and accommodated by the administration, as well as by the somewhat more relaxed political climate of the Khrushchev thaw. And the Kirov at this moment was directed by the comparatively young and progressive Fenster. Furthermore, Osipenko at that moment had clout. She was riding the crest professionally and as yet was hardly on the political radar at all. Her real struggles with authority were yet to come. As she fell afoul of the Communist establishment, theater authorities would be less tolerant.

During the late 1950s, Osipenko also worked with another avatar of modernity, Kasyan Goleizovsky. Balanchine would cite him as a formative influence. Goleizovsky championed all the rambunctious, heterodox, formalist elements that had been curtailed by the more staid cultural mandate of the '30s. Since then, he had been relegated to the fringes of Soviet culture. But Lopukhov invited him to the Kirov to create a pas de deux for Osipenko and Igor Tchernichov. Igor's wife Elena watched some of the rehearsals and in her 2013 memoirs recalled the duet as "very beautiful, very intricate." It interpreted the shifting colors of a Scriabin score but was so lacking in narrative content that Osipenko herself felt a little baffled by it—in short, it was everything that was then aesthetically suspect. Goleizovsky seemed in a rush to finish choreographing the pas de deux. Before he could, however, his contract was terminated.

In 1959, Osipenko was given a challenging role in Igor Belsky's new ballet, *The Coast of Hope.* During the 1960s and '70s Belsky would direct first the Maly and then the Kirov. There was a streak of the provocateur in him. In his production of the Russian chestnut *The Little Hump-Backed Horse*, created for the Maly in 1963, he turned the courtiers around a fairy-tale czar into a veiled satire of apparatchiks surrounding Khrushchev.

In *The Coast of Hope* he adroitly wove together a common Soviet trope, the juxtaposition of the nurturing Soviet homeland and an evil foreign shore, with a message of spiritual transcendence that was at odds with Soviet empiricism. In his first major work, Belsky worked with distinguished collaborators. Young Andrei Petrov was already successful as a film composer. The scenario was by Yuri Slonimsky, ballet critic, historian, and one of the USSR's most distinguished men of letters. Trained as a dancer, he had been a member of Balanchine's Youth Ballet. The ballet's scenery by Valery Dorrer was certainly avant-garde for that time and place: it was exceptionally spare and distilled.

The Coast of Hope, 1959, Act 1.
Photo by Nina Alovert.

Belsky created the lead woman's role in *Coast of Hope* jointly on Kolpakova and Osipenko. They impersonated a fisherman's girlfriend, dancing with him in the ballet's first scene a long adagio where they dreamed of being able to fly. Then the fisherman was sent far away on a long expedition. The village maiden danced a solo of longing and waiting. Eventually, all the fishermen returned. Four lines of four men each were now reduced by one: the girl's lover. His absence provoked from her a mourning dance monologue—"like Sarah Bernhardt," Osipenko said. It turned out that he was imprisoned by a wicked populace on the far shore. To save him from their clutches, his girl somehow transformed into a bird. Belsky "wanted to show that a person's soul could fly." She took to the skies, found him in his cell, and imparted to him the means to vanquish his captors.

As the bird of deliverance, Kolpakova and Osipenko wore a unitard à la *Stone Flower*. The cast of Belsky's ballet believed that this work was as much in the vanguard as Grigorovich's. They often rehearsed in what was called Petipa's studio at the school, where he had once rehearsed. A balcony surmounted the studio's perimeter, which was now called the Vaganova studio as well because of the bust of the pedagogue that had been installed. One day the dancers came in and saw that the bust was turned around. "We all said that Vaganova just couldn't stand it, so she turned her face away"—away from the breakaway into neoclassicism that her students believed they were making.

Different parts of the ballet played to the strengths of each of the two young ballerinas. Osipenko's opinion was that she excelled in the first half, while Kolpakova was better when the bereft village girl transformed into a bird of deliverance. But she didn't think that either she or Kolpakova had done justice to both halves of the role and as a result it never received a total interpretation. "Belsky really didn't think about that contradiction, about Kolpakova's limitations and my limitations. That was his mistake. The ballet didn't look full, didn't look completed." Perhaps the problem was that the two halves of the role simply didn't fit together. "Not only I but a lot of people thought it was not right for the strong girl to turn into a lightweight bird," one more fragile than an avian doppelganger of the village heroine would logically have been. In the interests of internal logic, Osipenko's girl should have turned into an eagle. "I stretched it tragically, Kolpakova stretched it Romantically." It was one of the very few roles they shared.

Soviet ballet historian and critic Natalia Roslavleva writes in *Era of the Russian Ballet* that "Osipenko's Beloved was stronger, with a marked will

The Coast of Hope, 1959, Act 2, with Alexander Gribov.
Photo by Nina Alovert.

of her own, graceful and perfect in line. Kolpakova coloured the character with her own special radiance and warmth, and therefore was able to arouse greater compassion in the spectators' hearts."

The Coast of Hope was given its premiere in April 1959 and stayed in the Kirov repertory no more than two seasons. It was not Belsky's dalliance with transubstantiation that doomed it, at least officially. Instead, in the dance he made for the inhabitants of the distant shore where the fisherman was imprisoned, Belsky had been audacious enough to appropriate some of the gyrations of Western idol Elvis Presley, making use of jazz influences in the score. Rock-and-roll was judged something not fit for the eyes of the Soviet population, even when used to illustrate an alien population's infamy.

A Russian ballet beachhead had already been established in Egypt: Leonid Lavrovsky was directing a school he'd established in Cairo, staffed by Russian teachers and pianists. Now the Kirov went to Egypt for two months at the end of 1959, staying on through the new year. It was a delightful anomaly for them to be in warm weather at that time. Conditions were very good. The cook was a black man whom they called, Russian style, "Daddy Washa." His food was delicious. "Everything was memorable," Osipenko recounted. In a marketplace she was given a hookah to smoke, the tobacco "so strong it was like opium." Visiting the pyramids, Nureyev and Kurgapina climbed to the top, but Osipenko reached only midway before turning back in trepidation. Everyone found unforgettable the sudden manifestations of a green desert oasis at sundown.

In the Cairo museum, the bust of Nefertiti stood alone in a large room with a wide window through which the sun illuminated it differently at different times of the day. "By the hour we looked at her." Shelest looked longer than anyone else. Osipenko thought that the Kirov ballerina slightly resembled the queen of antiquity.

They returned to St. Petersburg later in January 1960. It wasn't possible to buy fresh fruit in the winter in Leningrad, only canned or dried. Osipenko brought sweaters and blouses for her relatives, but it was the fresh strawberries and tomatoes she'd managed to bring back that most impressed them.

She always was worried because her grandmother and great-aunt were old, and returning from a long tour she was always overjoyed to see them. One time she said, "It's so good to come back and see you're both still alive!" They laughed about it. Once, returning to Leningrad via Moscow, she called her mother and asked her to bring the two old ladies with her to the train station, not far from their apartment. Nina said, "Babushka can't come because she's a little bit sick." Osipenko was concerned. "If she's a little bit sick let her come to the train station." Her train pulled into Leningrad the next morning. Nina and Anna were accompanied by someone bandaged, assisted by two aides: it turned out to be Maria, who had fallen in a store and suffered multiple fractures.

By her own admission, at times Osipenko exploited their devotion. Once, she bought a very beautiful dress and high-heeled shoes to wear to a party. The shoes were so stiff she couldn't walk in them, so she asked Anna to walk all day in them to break them in. It was painful for the elderly woman, but she did it.

Good shoes were all but impossible to find in Leningrad. Whenever she was abroad she purchased more; Italian were the best, but any bought abroad were better than what was produced domestically. "You can't imagine what we had and what we didn't have," she said. Where any kind of consumer luxury was concerned, "it was almost nothing." She told the story of Simone Signoret and Yves Montand purchasing women's underwear in Moscow and putting it on exhibit in Paris, where the lingerie was denounced as shockingly ugly. "At that point they became enemies of the Soviet Union," Osipenko recalled tartly.

Now the Kirov troupe was touring more frequently, and individual dancers were also sent to perform in the West. Osipenko and Vladilen Semyonov went to Holland to dance at a gala featuring all sorts of dancers from around the Soviet Union. In Amsterdam, Osipenko and her colleagues watched the prostitutes ply their trade in their allotted district. It was fascinating for them because this type of frank admission of life was so unlike anything permitted in the Soviet Union. In their windows, the prostitutes played cards and drank coffee. One very popular woman worked out of her basement apartment. Alternately they would see her sitting inside, her curtains wide open; then they would not see her because her curtains were pulled tight shut.

On the plane they had met a Soviet jiu-jitsu team arriving for a competition in Amsterdam—seven or eight tall, healthy boys from different Soviet regions. They wanted to visit the prostitutes but they didn't have money. "They said, 'OK, we are healthy, we are beautiful; they will take us without money.'" Two of them went into one woman's house. The rest, along with Osipenko and some of her colleagues, waited for them outside. Ten minutes later the two young men came running out, followed by a prostitute yelling at them never again to darken her doorstep without an entrance fee.

In 1960, the Kirov made its first visit to Japan. Watching from the wings one night during *The Stone Flower*, Osipenko saw Kolpakova stumble on stage. When it was time for her entrance, the same thing happened to her. They didn't realize it but a small earthquake was occurring each time. That night she was awakened by a larger convulsion. She looked out of her window and saw tall buildings swaying. Then she understood.

An admirer from the Grand Kabuki invited her to attend his performance. Multi-segmented Kabuki performances could last an entire day. The audience arrived with food and with pillows to recline on. Osipenko was uncomfortable and she couldn't stay more than several hours, but the Kabuki fascinated her. A ballet dancer could learn a lot from its plastique, and the actors' gestures, poses, and movements.

Vakhtang Chabukiani had choreographed a full-length *Othello* in 1957 for the state ballet in Tblisi, where he remained as artistic director. In March 1960, the Kirov took the ballet into its repertory. Chabukiani was invited to stage it as well as dance the lead, as he had in Georgia. When he came to Leningrad, he auditioned Kolpakova, Petrova, and Osipenko for Desdemona. He lifted each ballerina in turn, then he turned to Osipenko. "You will dance with me." She warned him that her stage persona was now too sophisticated, that Kolpakova and Petrova were more suited to the role. But Chabukiani's criterion was above all his own comfort as a fifty-year-old partner.

Osipenko didn't think the ballet was first-rate, but it was exciting to dance a premiere opposite Chabukiani, a measure of whose old magic remained. She was riveted by an Ethiopian dance he performed while she watched on stage. But he was not the ideal partner. His hands were small. Supporting a

With Kabuki star during Kirov tour to Japan, 1960.
Photo courtesy Alla Osipenko.

ballerina, no matter how ideally her weight was distributed, was not his priority. "Hold yourself up!" he admonished her.

For Osipenko it was very interesting in 1961 to rehearse the lead in Sergeyev's *The Path of Thunder* with Mikhail Mikhailov. He had coached her as far back as her debut as the Queen of the Ball in *The Bronze Horseman*. Mikhailov had graduated with Balanchine and participated in his early choreographic efforts. In his fifties, he remained on stage in acting roles such as Girei, Peter the Great, and the opium-smoking captain in *The Red Poppy*. He was also dancing the acting role of a father in *Path of Thunder*, which was based on South African writer Peter Abrahams's 1948 novel about interracial romance under apartheid. (The liberation of subject black populations was a cause championed by the Soviets.) Mikhailov insisted that the dancers create a fully realized character, that they arrive at rehearsal with a cogent mental approach toward what they were going to work on.

Osipenko was also rehearsed by Dudinskaya, who had created the role opposite Sergeyev at the premiere in January 1958. Both Sergeyev and Dudinskaya were still fulfilling a full docket of performances, and Osipenko never felt that their attention was directed at grooming potential replacements. "Dudinskaya may have loved me at one point," she said, "but there was never a time when she took me for a month and worked with me and let me dance as her student," she said. "She worked with me on *Path of Thunder* just because she had to."

Dudinskaya "insisted that you do what she wanted. I was trying so hard to please her." Without realizing it she fell into the habit of imitating Dudinskaya's own mannerisms. By the time Sergeyev visited their rehearsals, there were parts in her interpretation where she was giving her own performance and parts that looked imitative. And here Sergeyev did display the correct directorial perspective. "Natalia Mikhailovna," he said, using the formal patronymic as he invariably did when talking to her in public, "give Alla the freedom to do it her own way. Don't insist on making her do exactly what you did." By the time Osipenko made her debut in the role, critics acclaimed her for standing not only on her toes but on her own two feet artistically.

The Path of Thunder endured in the repertory. It was popular with the public, she believed, because it had a modern edge; it was "a love story, but not sentimental. There was a lot of acting: I came to the village where he lived looking for a chance to meet him." Both lovers were killed in the end. "The choreography was all right," she said, but "the duets were good. Sergeyev could do easy, light pas de deux. I was pretty strong in them." Her partner Boris Bregvadze concurred. "It was not very rich choreography," he said. "There were only some adagios where she could open her heart. When she fell in love she opened her soul; she danced wonderfully, too."

Such was Osipenko's luster during these years that she was appointed a delegate to the Komsomol's Central Committee, which consisted of several thousand outstanding young exemplars from all professions and republics of the Soviet Union. She served for two years. Once a month they convened for one day in Moscow, and annually a one-week convention was held. They stayed in the best hotels. They were treated to baronial cuisine and bountiful champagne and cognac. Their per diem of 45 rubles was equal to many workers' monthly salary. At the Committee meetings, minutes would be read, as she described: "Right now we decided this person will be replaced by this one. All in favor raise your hands! All against?" But "we didn't know the position, the name, who was being replaced by whom," Osipenko recalled. All hands rose nevertheless.

In the evening there was top-flight entertainment—the Bolshoi might dance—and no shortage of debauchery. One morning she and her roommates opened a cupboard and found a Committee secretary there, a hungover refugee from the previous night's festivities. Along the way his pants had gotten mislaid. "Alla, during the night I lost my pants somewhere," he explained. "I don't remember where. I beg you, just walk around and try to find them. I'm meeting my wife and I need them."

PART TWO

12

Nureyev Defects

THE BOLSHOI HAD made its London debut in 1956, its New York debut in 1959. Now in 1961 it was the Kirov's turn to see and be seen on the global stage. Osipenko described Georgi Korkin, general director of the Kirov opera house, as a highly disciplined "iron manager." He was sometimes cruel, but on other occasions displayed a sense of fair play and appropriateness. Korkin faced down Dudinskaya and Sergeyev in their insistence on dancing in the Kirov's Paris and London debuts planned for that spring. She was forty-nine; he was fifty-one, and the European presenters did not want them onstage. In her memoir, Elena Tchernichova writes that since "Dudinskaya's prestige had to be maintained," her archrival Shelest, who was six years younger, was also scratched from the tour. Word was sent out throughout the company that it was the company's young stars who would be featured in Europe. This most definitely included Osipenko, although all tour arrangements were unpredictable.

Alexander Gribov, who created Danila in *The Stone Flower* opposite her in 1957, was yanked off the roster shortly before the company left Leningrad. Osipenko believed that his putative crime may have been his marriage to a Romanian. Gribov, who had been one of the Kirov's most prominent young dancers, was so angry that he started to come late or not at all to rehearsals, and his career declined.

Among the young men who would be featured in Europe were Rudolf Nureyev and Yuri Soloviev, each of whom had graduated from Rossi Street and joined the Kirov in 1958. Over the course of his career, each would have a profound influence on the shape, style, and technical accomplishment of

Dress rehearsal, *La Bayadère* "Shades," Paris 1961 with Rudolf Nureyev.
Photo courtesy Jerome Robbins Dance Division, The New York Public
Library for the Performing Arts, Astor, Lenox, and Tilden Foundations.

male dancing. And the Kirov's Paris season would have an irrevocable impact on each of their lives and careers, as it would on Osipenko's.

In 1958, then-Kirov director Boris Fenster had ignored company precedent and let Nureyev bypass the corps de ballet, giving him a soloist contract immediately. Soloviev's career had moved at a slower and more prudent pace. He was much more technically accomplished than Nureyev, but also much less flamboyant and assured in personality projection. In Paris, Osipenko would be dancing with both Nureyev and Soloviev for the first time. She was not entirely sold on this new generation. For her they lacked distinction of manner. As Albrecht in *Giselle*, "Sergeyev was a real noble person," whereas Soloviev and Nureyev were "like boys from a village. The critics liked it. They explained it as something new. But in my opinion it was nothing new, it just wasn't as good." But Nureyev would prove to be the dominant dancer of the Paris engagement. He created a sensation on stage, and he created a sensation defecting at Le Bourget airport as the company was on its way to London.

The Kirov's monthlong Paris season opened at the Opera on May 16 with *Sleeping Beauty*. At the open dress rehearsal, the *répétition générale*, the day before, Osipenko danced Lilac to Xenia Ter-Stepanova's Aurora and Nureyev's Desiré. This was a *répétition générale*, traditionally in Paris an important social and artistic event to which friends, patrons, and intelligentsia were invited.

After dancing her Prologue variation, Osipenko walked offstage and was chatting with colleagues when suddenly she heard a voice calling for her to reappear onstage. One person was applauding, and protocol dictated that she accept the applause even if it was only a rehearsal. In the second act, Nureyev danced Desiré's Hunting scene variation, and now the invited audience "went bananas," Osipenko recalled. The next day she saw a newspaper article about the dress rehearsal with photos of her and Nureyev.

Nureyev was furious when he found out that he was not going to dance, as originally scheduled, the opening performance as well as the *répétition*. This type of scheduling preference never concerned Osipenko very much, since she knew her work attracted attention regardless of when she danced. But Nureyev was convinced that Sergeyev was deliberately suppressing him because he remained a rival danseur as well as director. With Osipenko, the young Nureyev wasn't very sure of himself. There was something of a distance between them. With her, he always used the formal "Vy," while she talked to him in the familiar "Ty." But it was comfortable to be with him, which made her overlook his shortcomings—that he was somewhat short for her and not the most experienced or adept partner. Her response to a partner depended to a large degree on personal feelings. If she didn't like him, she could become agitated and demanding. If there was a bond of affection it was easy for her to work out any difficulties.

Nureyev's technique, anything but secure when he joined the Kirov in 1958, was now challenged by the platform stage of the Palais des Sports, the arena where the Kirov continued its Paris run after the Opera. *New York Times* dance critic Anna Kisselgoff, then a graduate student, was visiting Paris in the summer of 1961. Watching the Kirov at the Palais, Kisselgoff saw Nureyev slip on its platform stage and leave the stage immediately. *Swan Lake*, including music, came to an abrupt halt. Disarray ensued onstage until Nureyev reappeared and the performance resumed. Future Kirov ballerina Gabriela Komleva was dancing in the corps at that performance. Decades later, Kisselgoff ran into Komleva and asked what her reaction onstage had been. She said it was terror about how to restart the performance, as well as what the fallout from Nureyev's transgression might be.

Similarly, Osipenko recalled Nureyev falling at the end of his Shades variation. Once again he left the stage, then returned, signaled to the conductor, and danced the entire variation again from the beginning. The Kirov management called him on the carpet. Nureyev danced his next Shades with Osipenko in a white fury. During the coda, he whisked Osipenko across the stage so buoyantly that the audience burst into applause as never before. It was for her the most memorable moment of their brief partnership.

When *The Stone Flower* was shown on May 23, Soloviev took Gribov's role. Tatiana Legat, whom Soloviev had married the previous December, recalled that "Osipenko was a senior master, but she wasn't a typically standard type of dancer. She was complex . . . interesting." Soloviev was "so young, and he was beside himself with excitement that he was going to dance with her." Her performances with him went well. She always liked him personally and his excitement could only have been flattering. She also felt from him something emotionally so genuine that it touched her. When Soloviev's Danila bid farewell to Osipenko's Mistress of the Copper Mountain, his response seemed to her suffused with his apparent guilt about usurping Gribov. This heightened the final scene's emotional intensity.

On her first visit to Paris in 1956, Osipenko had been aware that her clothes were drab compared to those of Western performers. Now, at the Christian Dior ready-to-wear boutique she bought a cream-colored evening suit: chemise dress with a matching jacket. She loved it so much that she couldn't bear to part with it even twenty-five years later, when it was frayed. Instead, she had it remade into a lampshade. In Paris, she wore her new ensemble to a performance and party given by impresario Marquis George de Cuevas at the Théâtre des Champs Élysées. "This is the way a Russian ballerina should dress!" Nureyev announced to her when they met there.

Kirov dancers on tour certainly bought as many goods as they could afford. But the company was kept on very strict rations. Most dancers didn't have enough money to go out to eat. They bought their own food in markets and ate in their rooms. On tour in Italy five years later, the dancers were told that juice, water, and beer were free at their pensione. Osipenko recalled one ballerina ordering a beer, then asking to have the bottle opened. The waiter returned with the open beer, but told her that a mistake had been made, and only juice and water were free. She sent the beer back.

Osipenko was entirely satisfied with her reception in Paris, by both the critics and her French colleagues, some of whom she'd met in 1956. Violette

Verdy, by then a star of the New York City Ballet, was visiting Paris at the time. She described her initial experience of Osipenko's dancing. "She had a body that allowed her to show you her imagination, her incredible sense of neo-classicism—using the classical technique in a completely personal way to create shapes and emotions that one didn't expect."

"She was so stunning," Jean-Pierre Bonnefoux, then a rising star in the Paris Opera Ballet recalled fifty years later. "There was a sense that she was a personality like nobody else: otherworldly and sexy and grand. That was a mystery in her: you didn't really know what she was thinking, what world she was coming from." He parked himself outside her dressing room and presented her with flowers. "I fell in love with her."

During the season, Nureyev repeatedly flouted regulations. Alla Sizova had graduated with Nureyev in 1958 and was frequently paired with him on stage. In Paris, Nureyev "was warned not to meet the French artists," Sizova recalled. "None of us would do that, but he had enough courage to do whatever he wanted." His explanation to the authorities was that fraternizing with the Parisians would enhance his achievements on the Soviet stage.

His infractions were being minutely reported and Osipenko herself had also apparently aroused suspicion. She began to find herself singled out for surveillance. Night after night, one KGB agent invited Osipenko out on the town, to the types of places that the dancers were forbidden to frequent, even had they the money to afford them: the Lido, the Folies Bergère, clubs on the Place Pigalle. The agent was "an idiot," Osipenko said, lacking in conversational wiles, but these were invitations one was not easily able to refuse.

One night she had on a new pair of shoes that pinched her feet, and pleaded that as an excuse not to go out with him. But he forced her hand by insisting that her lack of interest in visiting their planned destination could mean only one thing—that she had been there already. But she had not been. She agreed to go out with him once more, but walked home barefoot, her shoes in her hand. The next night Osipenko asked him if they could visit a boîte with television "because I'm sick of talking to you." She invited Zubkovskaya to join them. Finally, she reached her threshold of boredom and refused to continue going out with him at all. Zubkovskaya warned her to be careful, that her career would end if she continued to behave like this. But things were only going to get much riskier.

During her first visit to Paris in 1956, Osipenko had become friends with Vera Bakadora, whose mother was Russian and her father French. A couple of years later she moved to Moscow to study at GITIS, the graduate theatrical institute. She married and stayed in Russia for thirty years; however, her mother lived in Paris and Vera often returned to France. She was in Paris for the Kirov season. Her uncle worked in television and he took her and Osipenko to the film set of *Les Amours célèbres* to watch Brigitte Bardot and Alain Delon.

Bakadora told Osipenko that another backstage visitor, Attilio Labis, premier danseur at the Opera, had become infatuated with her. He wanted to take Osipenko on a Sunday, her day off, to visit Sur-la-Seine, a village by the river on the outskirts of Paris. "Are you kidding?" was her initial response. Such an invitation was out of the question. But Bakadora told her that Labis was importunate. Still, Osipenko wouldn't risk going alone. Her roommate Natalia Makarova had other plans, but Kolpakova agreed to accompany her.

Labis arrived at the hotel to pick her up. There the two ballerinas sat waiting. He had no choice; he took both of them, but his anger was apparent. The village was enchantingly beautiful. He showed Osipenko a small pensione, and indicated a suite "that was going to be ours."

Subsequently she obtained permission to attend a performance by Maurice Bejart's company. During intermission an elderly French couple came up to her and gave her a bouquet. A KGB agent pounced, demanding to know who the flowers were from. "Give them to me!" "Why do I have to?" She took her seat, but despite the fact that a KGB agent was sitting directly behind her, once the lights were out she slipped out of the theater. She met Labis as planned and he took her to a small restaurant. It was empty. Only a gypsy orchestra played. He had rented it especially for them. They danced as the candles burned low.

In Paris she reunited with Serge Lifar, with whom she hadn't communicated since her 1956 debut in Paris. He invited her to a vernissage, a private preview at an art gallery. She couldn't resist attending, although she didn't dare ask anyone from the Kirov to escort her. Labis couldn't go because he was rehearsing, but after hearing from Bakadora how Osipenko had rashly allowed herself to be photographed at the opening, he bought the film and destroyed it.

Another suitor was a good-looking young journalist who had interviewed her for *Le Figaro*. She turned down his invitations. When he found out that she was seeing Labis, he rushed to her hotel and said, "Don't you realize that Labis is a total idiot?" Not that she cared. Labis was "very manly, very handsome. Probably he evoked something in me as a woman." Labis's fiancée, also a dancer in the Opera, found out that he was visiting Osipenko and came to the hotel where she began buttonholing all and sundry about the possible presence of her husband-to-be.

Labis offered to make an exchange: he would go to Russia to dance and the Opera would host Nureyev. Despite the restrictions to which the Soviets were subjected, anything seemed possible at that exhilarating moment of cultural and personal rapport. That was all about to change, however.

In Paris, Nureyev had been boarding with Soloviev. One night, they were heard arguing, and the next day Soloviev appeared with a black eye. The KGB questioned him. He disclosed that he and Nureyev had been in the habit of massaging each other after performances; on the night before, Nureyev had made a pass at him. The die was cast for Nureyev's defection. Although virtually everything about his behavior in Russia as well as in Paris was suspect, the KGB now had evidence of a statutory transgression punishable by seven years' imprisonment.

On June 15, closing night of the season, Osipenko and Nureyev danced *Swan Lake* together. The entire Kirov was keyed up. Nureyev pointed out to Sergeyev the resounding success their performance had just enjoyed. The director's response was, "It's just because it was a Saturday." Afterward, Nureyev and Osipenko were invited out by some admirers. Osipenko dutifully requested permission and was told by the KBG that permission was granted, but Nureyev would be her responsibility.

During the month they'd spent in Paris, Osipenko's mother had called her frequently for news. Now Nureyev wanted to make sure that his teacher, Alexander Pushkin, was kept informed of his triumph. "When your mother calls just tell her the performance was superb," Nureyev advised. "It's probably too much," she said. "No; just tell her it was superb. Period. Let your mother call Pushkin and tell him."

"Go straight back to your hotel," she reminded him as they said good night. "Where else am I going to go?" Nureyev laughed. "I have to pack." In Paris he had spent all his free money on new Lycra costumes and arranged for them to be sent ahead to London. He was very excited about dancing Grigorovich's new *Legend of Love* when he returned to Russia.

The next day, June 16, was Osipenko's twenty-ninth birthday. She had saved a bottle of Starka vodka for the occasion. When she came back from dinner it was already 1:00 A.M. "It's your birthday and you're not even here, so I just decided to start without you," Makarova told her. They stayed up all night, consuming chocolate an admirer had handed her along with the vodka.

Korkin had been summoned to the Russian embassy in Paris, ordered to instruct Nureyev that rather than flying to London, he needed to return to Moscow immediately. But Korkin balked: Nureyev was so volatile and unpredictable there was no telling what his response would be. Korkin was a member of the Communist Party, he was reminded, and he was ordered to do as he was told.

But the next day, as Nureyev was standing behind Osipenko waiting to board the plane, it was a KGB agent who collared him. "Nureyev, you're not going to London. You're going to Moscow."

"Why?"

"Oh, just because. We decided." Ostensibly, however, he was returning to perform at a government gala there.

Through the airplane windows the Kirov saw Nureyev signaling to them, two fingers pressed against two fingers: the universal symbol for "jail." He tore his hair, beat his fists, ran toward the boarding staircase as it was being wheeled away from the plane. "Let's do something," Osipenko told Korkin as they watched. "Maybe I should go back with him straight to Moscow." "I can do nothing," Korkin told her. "I did everything that I could do, that I had to do. There's nothing you can do."

13

Repercussions in London

INSIDE THE AIR terminal, Nureyev, with the help of French friends who'd come to see him off, requested political asylum. The Kirov dancers flew to London in stunned silence, convinced that whatever exactly had just happened on the airstrip, Nureyev's defection was about to call forth terrible repercussions. British impresario Victor Hochhauser, who was presenting the company, had planned a birthday party for Osipenko in a restaurant on the Strand. Her colleagues were also invited. Hochhauser asked the birthday girl to cut a splendid cake, as Kolpakova, Zubkovskaya, and Moiseyeva stood alongside her. They "looked as though they were going to kill someone," Osipenko recalled. The impression she gave me was that they had not been overjoyed about occupying supporting positions in her limelight. But in 2007, a documentary on Nureyev's Russian career included a few seconds of newsreel recording this very same cake-cutting. The ballerinas wore glassy, dutiful, mask-like smiles that made me wonder more about how cognizant they were of the implications of Nureyev's act. What could it mean for him, for them, for the Kirov, for the Soviet Union itself?

As it turned out, everyone connected to the Kirov—from the dancers who subsequently denounced him, to those, like Osipenko, who refused to—was affected by his defection. But at that moment the ballerinas may not have yet known that Nureyev had indeed requested asylum in France. As Osipenko walked from the restaurant to the Strand Palace Hotel across the street, she found reporters standing outside. "Miss Osipenko, do you know that Nureyev has asked to remain in Paris?" She went in and ran into Simon Virsaladze, who said, "Alla, I just heard on the radio that Rudik has requested political asylum."

An Englishman named Parker who worked at the British Embassy in Moscow was a big fan of hers, and he was also then in London. He held his own birthday party for her the next day in the restaurant of the hotel, inviting Dudinskaya and Sergeyev as well, since he knew that for Soviets there was greater safety in numbers when fielding invitations from foreigners. They celebrated over many platters of food, and Parker presented her with some gifts.

But for Osipenko that was to be the end of celebrations in London. The simple fact that she had danced with Nureyev the night before his defection was enough to make her suspect. Her eagerness to continue to work in Europe in 1956 undoubtedly also implicated her. Her relationship with Labis, which of course must have been detected, undoubtedly sealed her status. She wouldn't be rooming again with Makarova; Osipenko was told that she would be a pernicious influence on the younger ballerina. Instead she was put in a room by herself one door away from a KGB agent.

The next day at the hotel a diplomat from the Russian embassy gave the company a briefing. "The Kirov Ballet is a wonderful company," he told them, "but Nureyev's defection in Paris has put a big stain on the troupe. You have to be very cautious not to go to any parties. Don't walk by yourself, only with someone else.

"There are a lot of provocateurs here. Not all of your dancers understand the seriousness of the situation. For example, yesterday one of your dancers, instead of staying home during this crisis, went out to a restaurant to celebrate her birthday. I want this to be the last time. If this happens again she will back in Russia in 24 hours."

Osipenko sat with goose bumps. "Also," the official continued, "they gave her gifts and she accepted them." At this very moment, Kirov dancer Galina Kekicheva, with whom Osipenko had created Chabukiani's *Musical Moment* years earlier, stood up. "And this ballerina had the right to celebrate her birthday and to accept gifts," Kekicheva insisted, and sat right down again. It was an assertion quite out of character for Kekicheva, who was customarily quiet. Later, Osipenko asked her what had come over her; even Kekicheva herself wasn't quite sure.

Osipenko danced *The Stone Flower* with Soloviev, Sizova, and Gridin when the Covent Garden season opened June 19. Together with a KGB agent, several young men in the company picked her up at the Strand Palace to walk to the theater a few blocks away. Before they got to the stage door, the agent asked her not to identify herself to any local fans.

On that night, Osipenko danced "magnificently," A. H. Franks would report in *Dance and Dancers*. After the performance, leaving the stage door in street clothes, without makeup, she was asked if she was indeed Osipenko. "I said, 'No, she's back there.'" In her hotel room, she heard a key turn in her lock and realized that she was in solitary confinement, as she would be every night for the monthlong season. Several young men in the company came to her room with a bottle of vodka, however, and they all played the card game "Stupid."

On tour in Lisbon, Labis had sent her an emerald ring tucked inside a bouquet. He called her in London: "Did my present fit?" She was confused about exactly what he meant as she had not found the ring, but staring at his bouquet she replied that it fit very well. She hung up and asked Vera Bakadora, who had come to London, what he could have meant. Bakadora knew about the ring and they took apart the bouquet but couldn't find it. Osipenko went to a KGB agent and asked what had happened. "It's not appropriate for a Russian ballerina to receive such gifts," she was told.

Nureyev's defection naturally provided additional opportunities for Soloviev, who was now to make his debut in *Swan Lake* partnering Osipenko. She was allowed to walk through London with him after rehearsal. Soloviev shared his anxieties, telling her repeatedly that "*Swan Lake* isn't for me. . . . I'm too short for you." In the classical prince roles, Soloviev's prototypically Russian face and round thighs stirred controversy for the remainder of his career. Osipenko, too, felt that he wasn't ideally suited to *Swan Lake*. But she impressed upon him, "We have no way out. We have to dance. You have to be prepared for this. It doesn't matter if you're shorter. Nijinsky was shorter and he was a wonderful ballet dancer. You will dance wonderfully. Don't worry."

The nightly performances that the Kirov gave on tour made their routine nothing like the leisurely pace of Leningrad. Osipenko danced *Swan Lake* with Soloviev first on July 12, 1961, and then again the very next night. "Everything was fine," she said about their *Swan Lake*s. "I'm sure it was a very correct performance" rather than an extraordinary one. But in *Ballet Today*, Fernau Hall described it as a triumph for each individually. "The whole season came into focus with Osipenko's magnificent performance of Odette/Odile. . . . Both in the 'swan' acts and in Act III her unique and miraculous line (with long, supple arms and legs curving upwards towards an ecstatic infinity) was seen to advantage in great choreography."

While Hall described the twenty-year-old Soloviev's partnering as "occasionally inept," once again, Osipenko's personal affection for a partner made her tolerant. "It was very easy to talk to Yura and explain things," Osipenko said. "So everything was fine." In any case he apparently did dance as brilliantly as Osipenko had promised him he would. Hall wrote, "One forgave Soloviev for everything as soon as he launched himself into Siegfried's variation, in which he brought pure male classical dancing to a higher point

With Yuri Soloviev in London, 1961.
Photo courtesy Alla Osipenko.

than anything seen in London for at least three decades, and probably since Nijinsky."

Together with Osipenko, I once watched Galina Mshanskaya's 1996 Russian documentary on Soloviev, *I Am Tired of Living in My Native Land.* The performance footage included seemed to astound her as much as if she were seeing him dance for the very first time.

Soloviev's London performances won the adulation of the city's balleto-manes, which continued unabated through the Kirov's return visits in 1966 and 1970. While Nureyev's defection undoubtedly accelerated the oppor-tunities given Soloviev, it also was a fateful turning point for him. In 2005, Soloviev's paternal uncle Alexander recalled that beginning with Nureyev's defection, his nephew became "more cryptic, especially on that topic, about what had happened then between them. How Nureyev had left. They were living together in the same hotel room, after all. He did not like to discuss this topic."

Guilt-by-association continued to reign in Soviet society. Soloviev's paternal grandfather had been sent to a camp in the Ural mountains for a three-year "check-up" after he returned from a German POW camp follow-ing World War II. Back in Leningrad, Soloviev was summoned to KGB head-quarters, "the Big House."

' "It was more than once that they 'invited' him there," Alexander said. "And obviously he was affected by—going over there. That played its role, I believe." Alexander believed that the trauma of Nureyev's defection had some measure of responsibility for the fact that in January 1977, Soloviev was found dead from a gunshot wound, apparently self-inflicted, at his dacha outside Leningrad.

14

Left Behind

ALTHOUGH HER LIBERTY was generally restricted, in and around London, Osipenko was able to accompany her colleagues on a number of tourist excursions. Once they went to Stratford-on-Avon to see *A Midsummer Night's Dream*. The play was long and naturally performed in English. It was hot outside, and news cameramen recorded some of the dancers dozing. Another day she spent browsing through London's stores with Zubkovskaya and bought a sweater for Nisnevich, who hadn't been taken to London or Paris.

She was nonplussed when a KGB agent approached her with a special warning. "Alla, tomorrow there is a free day. A lot of people are going to call you and invite you to visit Windsor Castle with them. So don't even think of going. Tell them you're tired." Sure enough the next day her hotel phone rang and a man asked in broken Russian would she like to go with him to see Windsor Castle. She was tempted. . . . What would happen if she said yes, she asked herself. But what if it was the KGB calling, disguised as a native Englishman speaking pidgin Russian? How else in the world could the KGB have known? He had to be a plant, she decided. No, she was sorry; she replied, she was just too tired.

Toward the end of the season, the Russian ambassador to Britain called another company meeting. "I want to congratulate the Kirov ballet for their very great performing." He asked his secretary to fetch a bouquet, then took it and brought it over to Osipenko. "I want to present you with these flowers in honor of your wonderful artistry, and to express my apologies for my earlier complaints. You are entitled to our respect."

At the closing night gala, Osipenko danced Jacobson's *Meditation* duet, partnered by Igor Tchernichov. The Kirov returned to Russia, and Osipenko went off with Nisnevich to spend time in the country. In August, he was summoned by telegram to rehearse for their upcoming debut in America.

They were scheduled to open at the Metropolitan Opera on September 11 for a three-week season that would be followed by a two-month cross-country tour. Osipenko, however, was not called. Nisnevich was suspicious: "You probably had a very good time in Paris, that's why they crossed you out. Do you realize what it's going to cost you now?" he reprimanded, not without some apparent satisfaction. Being left home after her success in Europe meant that a black mark had been entered against her.

The personal liberties Osipenko had taken were alarming enough, but Nureyev's defection had of course panicked the Kirov and Kremlin authorities. Cultural exchange could not mitigate rising geopolitical tensions: the Berlin wall had been erected that same summer.

Once again all tour arrangements were unstable, and vicious competition and scheming surrounded the selection of tour dancers. Zubkovskaya told Osipenko that a friend of hers found that he was not going to be taken along to New York but that Zubkovskaya's husband Kutznetsov was. He wrote an anonymous letter to the KGB, asserting that Kutznetsov was someone whom "you couldn't be sure would come back or not." Kutznetsov was scratched from the tour.

Osipenko too would stay in Leningrad, where the season would open at the same time the company began its New York appearance. "You will dance everything," she was assured, and she did dance frequently while so many of the company's ballerinas were in the United States, although this hardly assuaged her disappointment. She danced *Raymonda,* an infrequent role of hers, as well as adding a new role, the principal ballerina in Fokine's *Chopiniana,* partnered by Nikita Dolgushin. She enjoyed dancing with him on this and a number of other occasions over the next twenty years. He had graduated with Nureyev and Soloviev in 1958. His technique wasn't as rocky as the young Nureyev's, but it was in no way as spectacular as Soloviev's. Nevertheless, he had a Romantic presence, the long slim, rarified lines that Osipenko admired. She prided herself on them—she looked for them in her partners.

She had danced *Chopiniana's* Mazurka for Vaganova's jubilee fifteen years earlier, but now she danced the Prelude as her solo. By this time the Romantic ballet to which Fokine had made his 1908 homage seemed alien to her. "I didn't like Romantic ballet because I didn't have the style. I couldn't do it."

And yet Fokine's Prelude is one of my favorite pieces in ballet, and I wanted to probe its enchantment with her. In the Prelude, the ballerina is listening for, communicating with, unseen, mysterious spirits that only a sylph can discern. What is the ballerina talking about in the Prelude? "I completely have no idea," Osipenko stonewalled. I challenged her. Why, then, had it been one of Shelest's greatest roles? "She was smarter than I!"

"It's a different sense of fantasy," Osipenko said, and once more expressed the thought that Shelest's was richer. Shelest "could think about the partner without dancing with a partner; it was no problem to look at a window like a partner. Shelest could partner herself. For me, no." And Osipenko did indeed have some opinions about the Prelude, actually preferring the performances of Ninel Petrova and Marina Pomerantzova. For her, Shelest brought some needless complication and even some tragedy to it. "Shelest was too full out. She was trying to make something out of it. Petrova and Pomerantzova were really listening to the music, going with the music and were inside of it, and it was beautiful," Osipenko admitted.

In New York, the Kirov opened with *Swan Lake* starring Zubkovskaya partnered by Semyonov. "I was horribly nervous," Zubkovskaya recalled to me in 1999. "Since Diaghilev, there had been no Russian ballet in New York, so it was a big responsibility." I was amused: although Zubkovskaya had trained at the Bolshoi school before joining the Kirov in Perm in 1941, she had obviously completely sided with the Leningrad team in its perpetual rivalry with the Moscow troupe. The Bolshoi's debut season in 1959 she apparently considered an irrelevance.

The Kirov certainly could put on a great season without Osipenko, and yet her absence registered with those in a position to know. One of them was Shields Remine, who was associated with *Ballet Review* almost from its inception in 1966 until he died forty years later. In 1961 he had repeatedly been on the standing room line for the Kirov's season. He recalled that the big gripe among him and his fellow devotees was why, after her success in Europe, was Alla Osipenko not there?

Reviewing the season for London's monthly *Dancing Times*, Lillian Moore announced that "New York did not see Alla Osipenko, Xenia Ter-Stepanova, or Oleg Sokolov at all." Ter-Stepanova and Sokolov had also been prominent in the Europe seasons. Naturally, not every principal dancer was taken to New York; Boris Bregvadze, passed over for Paris and London, did get to New York, and the same was true for Osipenko's husband Nisnevich. But Osipenko, after her successes abroad, did have every right to consider that she had been shortchanged.

The dancers were staggered by the wealth of New York, more visible than even in Paris. "New York was a total shock," Zubkovskaya recalled. "The shop windows!" Zubkovskaya was a survivor with the drive to acquire such luxury as she could and the pragmatism not to dwell on disparities. Not all were so fortunate, however. The tour marked pianist Sonia Rostick's first trip out-side Russia and sadly it was her last. Before leaving Leningrad, Sonia was "a smart and happy and cheerful woman," Osipenko said. In Russia she'd been extremely frugal; in New York she bought herself a coat. When she came back to Leningrad she was "different, quiet, didn't talk to anybody," recalled Osipenko. She sat with the pianist during a rehearsal when Sonia turned to her said, "Alla, Alla, look: how terrible. I'm absolutely naked!" She eventually went into a psychiatric hospital and died there twenty-five years later. Like most in the Kirov, Osipenko seemed to believe that the shock of New York, its abundance and profligacy, had simply been too much for her.

15

Swept Off Her Feet

ONE MORNING ABOUT a month after the Kirov had left for America, Osipenko boarded a bus to the Rossi Street academy, now named for Vaganova, where the company took class and rehearsed. She sat down and opened a detective story when the doors opened and actor Gennady Voropayev got on. "He looked like Sean Connery," she recalled, "except Sean Connery was nothing compared to him. You could lose your consciousness looking at him." He gave her his trademark glance—"All women fell apart from this look"—and took the empty seat next to her. "I thought, What a shame. Such a handsome man is sitting next to me and what will he think about me reading such a stupid book?" She shut it quickly, hoping he hadn't seen. She got off at her stop and looked back.

"What's wrong with you?" someone asked her when she arrived at the Vaganova. "You look so nervous."

"On the bus I met such a man!"

Two days later, Nisnevich called her from America. She pleaded with him to return to Russia immediately: "Something is going on with me and I need you here." "Don't you understand that I cannot do it right now?" he said. "Nobody will allow me." What was it, had something happened? No, she told him, nothing had happened.

The next day, Viacheslav Kutznetsov called her. "Why are we sitting home like two old people?" he asked. He too had been left behind while Zubkovskaya was in America with the company. He invited her to the season-opening gala to be held the next night at the central V.T.O. ("Society of all-Russian Theaters") on Nevsky Prospect, customarily attended by stars of the ballet, opera, and drama. Grandmother Maria frowned. "Why are you going out so late? You're a married woman, going out alone?"

"No, he invited me: I'm going with Slava. I'm just going to a party. What's wrong with it? Once in a lifetime I can do it."

At the banquet she glanced at the door and she saw the very same man who'd been on the bus. Their glances met. She was wearing her Dior evening suit, which was "exactly what it needed to be." There was a pause. She stared at him and he smiled devilishly, then rushed toward their table: "Slava, please introduce me to your friend." Kutznetsov refused angrily. Voropayev was a well-known wolf. One of his former lovers called him "The Red Banner," after the prize given to Soviet worthies. But at the time Osipenko knew none of this.

Later on the dance floor he cut in on her partner, and they danced together until 3:00 A.M. When the ball ended they walked to her far-off apartment. He recited Pushkin, sang romanzas, and, once again, "I lost my head." He said good-bye to her downstairs. Maria and Anna were having breakfast when she let herself into the apartment. "Yes," Maria pronounced knowingly. "Too bad, too bad, Lalasha."

"I fell in love with Voropayev, because he was very much like Attilio: tall, handsome, passionate," Osipenko recalled. "I was carried away. I felt something that I didn't with Nisnevich. All of a sudden I realized that Nisnevich wasn't the right person for me." They had a mutual agreement that if something happened to estrange them they would inform each other honestly. "You wanted the truth from me and I'm writing you the truth," she said in a letter. "I fell in love and I can't do anything about it. I have to leave you." She gave the letter to a KGB agent who was joining the Kirov in America, but it never reached him until the plane trip home to Russia. By this time Osipenko knew that she was pregnant. She didn't go to the airport but she asked some people to meet the plane, "If he doesn't know, just let him know now." But she was sure that he had received the letter. "You made a fool out of me," Nisnevich told her when he arrived home. The KGB in charge of the tour was married to a classmate of hers, and later she approached him: "Alexey Sergeyevich, I sent him the letter—why didn't it reach him?" "Don't you understand?" he said. "We were on tour with a lot of responsibilities," and having of course read the letter themselves, they didn't know how Nisnevich would react. And only a few months after Nureyev's defection they were not taking any chances.

Nisnevich asked for her car as part of their settlement. She gave it to him, but balked when he said that he wanted her garage space as well. Very few people had one. Hers was private, next to her apartment building, and it was heated, so the car would start without a problem even in the Leningrad winters. "But probably I will buy another car." She did, and did not surrender the garage.

It was tradition in Russia for children to remain living with their family into adulthood, and this was exacerbated by the housing shortage in Leningrad. Osipenko had particularly close and binding ties to her mother, her grandmother, and great-aunt. But she summoned up her courage and told Nina, Maria, and Anna that she would now love to try living on her own, "to be responsible for my life." Voropayev and a roommate shared a two-bedroom apartment. She wanted to live there with him. Watching her move out her things, Maria and Anna were reduced to tears. "Lalasha, what are you doing? Think about it."

Two weeks later she came home to visit. Her mother was sitting with her head in her hands. "They won't eat or drink," she told Osipenko. "They miss you so much." She found Maria and Anna lying in their beds. "We cannot live without you," they told her. "We don't have a lot of time to live and we miss you so much. You're everything that we have." She told Voropayev she had no choice but to move back home. Eventually, once her divorce from Nisnevich was decreed and she married Voropayev, he moved in with her and her family.

It was after that that she was invited to the borough Komsomol center. "You married one man. You have a child from another man. Your moral degradation is obvious. It's not good at all. You're supposed to be a role model. A Komsomol member cannot behave like this." As she listened she thought of the dissipation she'd seen at the Committee shivarees in Moscow, and the way that peccadilloes there were always hushed up.

"Because you're such a model for your profession, we've already decided we want you to become a Party member," she was told, but her behavior had put them into a quandary. "I was going to write a reference for you. Do you understand what kind of position you've put me in? I was going to recommend you for the Party and now I don't know what to do."

"Wait a minute," Osipenko stopped him, "did I ask you to write this reference? Did I tell you that I wanted to become a Party member? Thank you very much for wanting to recommend me," she continued, "but I wasn't ever going to become a Party member. Do you have any more questions?" "No," replied the incredulous official, "no more questions."

She had curbed a lecture she found offensive, but her victory was of course Pyrrhic. "When I left that meeting I realized that my career was just down the drain."

But it was constitutionally impossible for her to be prudent, and the more she ran afoul of the system the more irreverent she became. When the Kirov's

Party secretary approached her and told her that her dues were in arrears, she replied, "I'm already almost thirty"—Komosomol officially ended for a member after turning twenty-seven—"and anyway I'm a monarchist!" Her voice was facetious but it was the kind of joke that would trigger official apprehension.

Defying powers in the theater was, of course, less dangerous than insulting the Party, although in short order theater and Party would begin to merge more decidedly than ever before. Opposition to Sergeyev's direction was growing within the Kirov. Osipenko said that "Sergeyev boasted that he gave good roles to 'Komsomols,'" the young generation of dancers, but the support and preparation they needed was not always there. Dudinskaya in her final years onstage customarily rehearsed for an entire week before every full-length performance, whereas her young rivals might get two or three days, and sometimes fewer than that. Osipenko resented being given bad press reviews for performances of *Raymonda* and Nikiya in *La Bayadère* where she'd had so little rehearsal time that she wasn't sure she was always doing the correct choreography.

Nevertheless, Dudinskaya was perfectly civil to her until Osipenko joined a number of leading dancers who signed a letter criticizing Sergeyev's direction in 1962. Osipenko recalled two letters: the first signed by senior dancers like Askold Makarov and Nikolai Zubkovsky, the second by younger dancers, Osipenko included. She was tasked with delivering that letter to the Moscow press when she went there as a delegate to the Komsomol Central Committee meeting.

Many bigwigs presided, the biggest, among them premier Nikita Khrushchev himself. A young man sitting next to her asked her who she was. "I'm a dancer from Leningrad." He said, "We are almost in the same profession. You dance and I write. I'm a journalist. You work with your feet and I work with my hands." She responded, "We dancers work with our brains also."

"Who is this man?" she asked a friend. "You don't know?" It was Khrushchev's son-in-law, Alexei Adzhubei, who was editor-in-chief of *Izvestia*, one of Moscow's major newspapers. Osipenko ran into him again at the meeting. "What did you mean when you said *you* work with your brains?" Adzhubei asked.

"I am sorry that I offended you," she said. "I understand that you have to have brains also; I didn't mean anything by it." And by the way, she had a letter to deliver to his newspaper. When published it triggered the beginning of open hostilities between Dudinskaya and Sergeyev and the younger generation.

A letter signed by Kolpakova, Kurgapkina, Moiseyeva, Osipenko, Petrova, Shelest, and Sizova was eventually published in the West. Among other grievances enumerated: "It has often been said in print as well as within our theater that it is incumbent upon us to cherish and keep alive the great works of Russian choreography such as *Swan Lake, Sleeping Beauty, Raymonda.* But it has also been noted that Sergeyev was making changes in these ballets for no apparent reason. Yet Sergeyev remains as convinced as ever that his position gives him the right to handle the national treasure of choreography as he wishes." Reading this in 1999, I marveled at the irony that it was many of these same dancers who were now prepared to defend Sergeyev's production against the perceived challenges posed by Sergei Vikharev's reconstruction of the 1903 *Sleeping Beauty.*

Not long after the letters were published, Dudinskaya's claque greeted one of Kolpakova's Kirov performances with a near-riot of derision. After Kolpakova's opening night Aurora in Paris, Dudinskaya had said to all and sundry, "They said they wanted a young cast? Did you see how her"—grabbing her own triceps—"arms wobbled?" And now Kolpakova had added her name to the same letter Osipenko had signed.

In April 1962, Osipenko took yet another risky and undoubtedly damaging step, testifying in Nureyev's defense at a hearing organized by his sister, Rosa. Nureyev had been tried and convicted of treason in absentia and sentenced to seven years' imprisonment, commuted from fifteen. Rosa petitioned her brother's Kirov colleagues to speak in his defense in an attempt to clear his name. Osipenko admired his strength, his rebel spirit, and she felt that his disgrace was an outrage.

Earlier she had been questioned by phone by some operative. Was Nureyev homosexual? Had he had a relationship with his teacher, Alexander Pushkin? "I don't know. I can't say anything because he was my partner and only my partner. About his intimate life, I know nothing." But she blurted out with typical rashness that in Paris she herself had been seeing Attilio Labis and wasn't paying the slightest attention to Nureyev's involvements.

On April 5, she provided testimony in Nureyev's defense. There was of course no Bible on which to swear, but each witness swore that he or she would speak truthfully. A judge presided. Witnesses were called. There was no public. A stenographer recorded the proceedings.

She was on the witness stand for several hours, as the government attorney attempted to prove again that Nureyev's defection was a preplanned act of treason. On the contrary, Osipenko insisted, it was the actions of the KGB that had made him decide; she had seen Nureyev seize his new life blindly, frenziedly, without premeditation.

She didn't see anyone else there from the Kirov that day but recalled her impression that Alla Sizova, as well as a number of stage hands and makeup and wardrobe personnel did appear to support him.

But it was announced in no certain terms within the company that Nureyev was a traitor. Dancers who had been close to Nureyev vociferously denounced him at a number of company meetings. "Now every time that there's a gala in honor of Nureyev, they're always there," she told me in 1998, five years after his death. "I heard with my own ears what they said against him."

Given the hypernationalism of the Soviet Union, there were many who genuinely believed he had betrayed the motherland. But undoubtedly as well, cooperation reaped career dividends. Among the dancers, "it was very clear who supported Nureyev and who didn't," Osipenko claimed. "The ones who didn't got promoted," whereas to the Soviet regime, her testimony in his defense made her "just as bad as he."

16

The Gates Close ...

LENINGRAD CONTINUED TO welcome ballet from abroad. When New York City Ballet visited in October 1962, Osipenko found Balanchine's work, *Apollo,* in particular, different from anything she had ever seen. Watching what was to a Russian very cool, abstract choreography, she was overcome with emotion. She understood how much ballet could express without narrative and, by extension, how much her own style of expression—skirting as it did the more demonstrative Russian tradition—could aspire to.

Also in Leningrad that year was none other than Attilio Labis, dancing with the Opera's Claude Bessy as guests at the Kirov. Bessy and Labis were touring the studios of the Rossi Street school with Osipenko together with Voropayev, as well as Soloviev, and others from the Kirov. Labis asked Osipenko to step into the corridor. "I despise you because you lied to me!" He took out a medallion containing a lock of her hair and threw it to the ground. "You told me you were married, but you've already divorced and married again!"

"What happened out there?" Voropayev asked her later.

"He threw my hair in the garbage can."

"It sounds like you."

Voropayev and his colleagues were in the habit of staging private performances late at night for an audience of their peers; this is a theatrical tradition in Russia, referred to as *Kapustniki*—"Cabbages." They took Labis to one of those, and then to an artist's studio. When Bessy and Labis returned to Paris, they told an interviewer, "Why do they say there is no nightlife in Russia? Alla Osipenko took us to a nightclub." But when Labis visited Russia again in 1969, she avoided him altogether because she didn't want a repeat denunciation.

Osipenko had come to believe that her body looked best as thin as possible, and that required diligence on her part. "The only people I envy are those who can eat and remain thin," she said to me once. She weighed 54 kilograms when she graduated from Rossi Street; by the time she finished dancing thirty years later, her weight was a full 10 kilograms less. Zubkovskaya chided her: "You're always on a diet; you don't eat this, you don't eat that; why are you like that?"

"*Now* are you eating?" she asked when she learned that Osipenko was pregnant. Osipenko assured her that she was taking vitamins and following all the advice given by her doctor. In May 1962 she stopped dancing to await her delivery. Her last performance was Desdemona opposite Kutznetsov's Othello—he joked that he was holding not one, but two. In September 1962, she gave birth to her son Ivan. The infant instantly became yet another issue of contention between Osipenko and her mother. Nina took charge of his care; she fed him, dressed him, bathed him. "Mom, it's my baby," Osipenko protested. "Let me be with him. Let me do something."

Resisting parental authority was for her always more complicated than defying Party or theater officials. She believed that her mother was taking over with the best intentions, a high sense of responsibility. On the other hand, Nina insisted that Osipenko put her career above everything else and thus provide her mother vicarious satisfaction. "She wanted me to be a great ballerina or die," Osipenko said. "She didn't even give me the possibility to be a good mother. She just pushed me to ballet."

What about taking in a movie, Osipenko suggested to Nina, or a visit to friends? "You know I hate movies!" Nina replied angrily. "You know I don't want anything else." Her mother preferred staying at home by herself. "It looked like something had died in her. It was very sad."

Ivan's birth coincided with or occasioned a closer relationship with her father, who had returned to Leningrad. During World War II he had been released from prison so that he could be sent to the front, but he never discussed prison, except once when he inquired whether she and Nina were still on good terms with certain old friends of the family. It turned out that they were. He told her that they had given evidence against him for the State to introduce during his trial.

Three months after giving birth, Osipenko returned to the Kirov stage, dancing *The Stone Flower* opposite Soloviev. But it wasn't long before she realized that the inevitable day of reckoning had arrived. Nisnevich's warning a

Osipenko with Ivan onstage at the Kirov.
Photo courtesy Alla Osipenko.

year earlier was now borne out. She had not only the Dudinskaya-Sergeyev axis opposed to her in the theater, but, more onerously, the state apparatus itself.

Moreover, during the past year there had been a ferocious pushback by cultural and political reactionaries against the gains made by the liberal arts intelligentsia. Only a decade earlier, even contact with foreigners in the USSR could easily be criminalized, and now, foreign success could be subject to revised paradigms. Acclaim in the West certainly conferred cachet on a Kirov performer within his home troupe. And yet, it's possible that, particularly given the personal liberties she'd taken in Paris, Osipenko's success in the West could now be held against her. This was grist for the contemporary persecution of poet Evgeni Yevtushenko, who had dared to publish his autobiography first in France. Khrushchev himself issued wildly contradictory statements about cultural policy over these months; it was his perceived laxity in tamping down the rebels that in part determined his ouster in December 1964. His "thaw" was over, and what became the years of stagnation under General Secretary Leonid Brezhnev began.

Osipenko now looked in vain for her name on the posters on the theater facade that announced upcoming performances. Theater regulation required principal dancers to appear on stage three times a month. Now Osipenko was to learn to her disappointment that three monthly appearances in her three-minute "Kiss" duet in Jacobson's *Rodin* could be counted as sufficient discharge of her obligations as well as the Kirov's.

At the same time, the Party's presence in the Kirov was rapidly becoming stronger, as Nureyev's defection prompted a crackdown and an influx of dancers joined. Many dancers had previously considered the Party not only barbaric but nouveau riche. Elena Lukom had graduated in 1909 and remained a leading ballerina into the early Soviet epoch. She was now a coach in the theater. One time she asked Osipenko about the younger wife of Lukom's old flame, ex-principal dancer Boris Chavrov: "How can he marry a woman who was in the Komsomol?"

All manner of rationalization could ensue, one of the most seductive being the idea that the Party could be transformed by the participation of outstanding artists of ostensible integrity. Osipenko asked a fellow ballerina why she was suddenly joining. To be specific, she asked, "Are you crazy?" because "we were friends and it looked like she would never do it."

"In the Party, there have to be good people," the ballerina replied. "In this case we will go different ways," Osipenko replied jocularly, but she was shocked. It was the beginning of the end of their friendship.

Nureyev's defection also brought about the dismissal of Georgi Korkin, who was replaced by Pyotr Rachinsky as general director of the opera house. Rachinsky's credentials were definitely not on the artistic side. He had been a fireman, and played in an amateur orchestra. Inevitably, it took him no time at all to become an adversary of Osipenko. Communist allegiance would become ever more important in the Kirov and hers was definitely lacking. Nor was she able to flatter his authority any more than she could anyone else's. He also began a long affair with Kirov ballerina Kaleria Fedicheva, with whom Osipenko shared a good deal of repertory. Fedicheva's interests were now going to be paramount in the Kirov.

"There are so many like you," Rachinsky told Osipenko. He began appearing in the wings just as she was about to dance her Prologue variation in *Sleeping Beauty*, which contains a series of double pirouettes that weren't easy for her. The variation finished, he'd be gone just as abruptly. "It made me very nervous," as of course it was intended to do. Although Lilac was one of her favorite roles, it became "torturous" to go to the theater and perform it.

In 1963 the Kirov was filming *Beauty* on the LenFilm soundstage. The intention was to concoct a uniquely cinematic experience, via Cocteau-like sets, with major cuts in the ballet as well as some reordering of sequences.

The role of wicked fairy Carabosse, traditionally danced by a man *en travesti*, was originally to be danced by solo performer Makmud Esambayev, a star of Soviet popular entertainment. However, Dudinskaya decided that she wanted to perform it instead, and so new choreography on pointe was created for her. The result was incongruous, since the crucial aspect of Carabosse is that she was not one of the idealized ballet firmament but instead was a creature of baseness. Still, most of the important sections of the ballet survived and, led by Sizova and Soloviev as Aurora and Prince Desiré, the film gives us a testament to the strength of the company at that time. Not surprisingly, Osipenko was not chosen to dance the Lilac Fairy; more surprisingly, neither was Zubkovskaya, whose performance ranked alongside hers as the finest in the company. Instead it was danced by Irina Bajenova, whose performance in the film is pleasantly competent, but lacks the older women's authority.

The Kirov was planning to return to America in the fall of 1964 for another New York season to be again followed by an extensive cross-country tour. In retrospect, Osipenko's inclusion that spring in a small group of Kirov dancers sent on a two-week tour to Greece looks like a mollification, for she would again be denied the chance to perform in the United States. And it was a standard Soviet example of plausible deniability: theoretically Osipenko was allowed to travel abroad, simply not, at that point, to any major balletic capital.

Artistically her trip to Greece ranked as *haltura*, something done with the tacit acceptance of far less than optimal result. The performance venues were informal; at one stop they danced on an outdoor stage in the town square. Cultural and scenic dividends were greater. Sailing the Aegean, she saw an island temple that stood starkly isolated. "It was so impressive, so beautiful, there aren't enough words to express it." She went with Makarova, who was going to be included on the tour to the United States, to a party in a taverna that turned raucous. As Osipenko got into the swing of things, her fellow revelers showed their enthusiasm by lifting her up onto a table. "Don't get a bad reputation," Makarova reprimanded her. "In those days Natasha always tried to play that she was proper and prim," Osipenko recalled wryly and fondly.

As much as she wanted to see the world, she wanted to dance on the great international stages. A Kirov dancer called her and said he'd heard that her relationship with Rachinsky was fraught. He advised her to ask Rachinsky's forgiveness, which she was not about to do. Perhaps it was not coincidental that in New York his wife danced Osipenko's own role of the Lilac Fairy.

Osipenko was sent with another small band of Kirov dancers to Syria and Iraq during the company's American visit. As she had been in Greece, Osipenko was partnered by Boris Bregvadze. Bregvadze had been one of the Kirov's greatest stars, and a heartthrob whose appearance had been known to arouse squeals from women in the audience. Now almost forty, his career had been in decline in recent years. He had been so put off by Nureyev's success in roles in which his fiery temperament had made him preeminent—Solor in *La Bayadère*, Basilio in *Don Quixote*—that he'd shied away from performing them. Although Bregvadze danced in the Kirov's 1961 New York debut, the company didn't present *Don Quixote* on tour during these years. They didn't discuss it, but Osipenko felt that a gradual demoralization took place. (However Bregvadze proved enduring, which is why I was able to interview him about Osipenko in 2005, when he had just turned eighty.)

In the Middle East, the Kirov dancers traveled as part of a mixed bill consisting of Georgian musicians and Armenian singers, among others. Osipenko performed an adagio by Chabukiani to music from Gluck's *Orfeo et Eurydice*, and the White Swan pas de deux, standard excerpts for this type of concert program. Again it was the experience of culture and place that was "an inspiration for me," she said. Observing the ancient cognates of Western civilization she started to fantasize that she had lived in now-ruined edifices in a past life, just as the Russian writer Alexander Kuprin had described his imagined behavior in prior existences. Not unsurprisingly, it was as a figure of importance that she imagined herself. "Sometimes you think maybe you were a king in another time. . . ."

She returned from Syria, and the company returned from its visit to America. She made a point of regaling her colleagues with stories about her trip: "I saw so many beautiful things. . . . America is nothing, but I was in Syria; that is something wonderful!"

"They just kept silent," Osipenko said as she recalled the situation thirty-five years later, "because there was no sense in arguing." Osipenko was wise to her own caprice; in terms of professional visibility, she assured me "I understood that you couldn't compare Syria with America."

Sergeyev's approach to her now became a matter of fulfilling the dictates of those in the Party hierarchy as well as nursing payback for Osipenko's participation in the letters that had sought to thwart his leadership. He lectured her on her technical shortcomings. "You can't do thirty-two fouettés. Even two pirouettes are a problem for you." She asked for the opportunity to dance Giselle. "You are not Giselle," was the response from on high. She asked for Juliet. "You are not Juliet. It is not your *emploi*." Strictly speaking, that was true enough. "And yet Sergeyev let Kurgapkina dance *Swan Lake* and *Giselle*!" This still bothered Osipenko. Kurgapkina had been a personal favorite of Vaganova's and she cast her carefully in pas de deux in student recitals. "Kurgapkina had a good head and did all these things beautifully." The perpetual soubrette, Kurgapkina was, however, hardly ideal for grand ballerina roles.

Virginal heroines had never been Osipenko's forte even in her first years in the company, as proved by her Maria in *The Fountain of Bhakchiserai*. And yet Juliet and Giselle are far less passive than Maria; what attracted Osipenko was their passion and courage in the defense of love.

"I was crying," Osipenko recalled, "thinking that I was useless, that I couldn't dance anything. I tried to find a reason why I had the right to dance." Ultimately she realized that although she could not do thirty-two fouettés, her body exemplified every canon of balletic fitness. She reviewed her career and saw that virtually every choreographer active at the time had wanted to create for her.

It was apparent to her as well that if she wanted to remain in shape she was going to have to make some new adjustments. During the 1980s, when Russian dance historian Natalia Zozulina wrote a biography of Osipenko, she was allowed to research in the Kirov archives. "Alla Evgenyevna, you didn't dance at all!" It was recorded that she had danced *Swan Lake* once in three months, that she hadn't danced *Stone Flower* for an entire year. Actually, Osipenko said to me, "I danced a lot," much more than she was officially scheduled for. "I replaced any who needed replacement. I never said 'No,'" although she certainly was entitled to, given the very short notice on which many of these substitutions were made.

In 1965 she made her belated debut in what would be one of her greatest roles, Queen Mekhmene-Banu in Grigorovich's *Legend of Love*. It was based on a play by Nâzim Hikmet, the Turkish Communist writer who spent his final years in the USSR. Grigorovich had choreographed the ballet on her and Nureyev before the tour to Europe in 1961. Dudinskaya, who saw the young Grigorovich as a potential rival to Sergeyev as Kirov leader, chose that moment to ask Nureyev to partner her in her last performances of *Laurencia*. Nureyev skipped several of Grigorovich's rehearsals and Grigorovich scratched Nureyev from the premiere—thus Nureyev's pleasurable anticipation in Paris of belatedly dancing the role when he returned as planned to Leningrad. When Osipenko pulled a calf muscle shortly before they left for Paris, Grigorovich told her not to come to rehearse with him but instead make sure she recovered in time to dance on the tour. He continued choreographing a somewhat different version of the role for Moiseyeva, who alternated with Zubkovskaya in the initial performances.

After a brief spell as an assistant artistic director at the Kirov, Grigorovich had moved to Moscow to become director of the Bolshoi in 1964. Now Osipenko sensed that his dramatic intent at points in this ballet had been diluted since he'd originally created the role of mythical Queen Mekhmene-Banu for her.

Mekhmene-Banu sacrifices her beauty to save the life of her sister Shyrin, then finds herself hopelessly infatuated with her sister's lover Ferkhad. Osipenko re-learned the ballet with Vecheslova, who was rehearsing this ballet as she had Grigorovich's *Stone Flower*. She was told that in her final exit she should pose like an eagle before running off stage. Recalling what Grigorovich had originally choreographed, Osipenko realized that she was not supposed to be posing at all. Rather, she was peering lower and lower into a pond, her reflection parting the waters until what she saw was so horrifying that she fled.

In 2009, Grigorovich confirmed that the role was made for her. He was looking for an "Oriental, lithe expressiveness," and was gratified by the way it manifested "through that particular plasticity she so well commanded."

In *Legend of Love*, Osipenko was "unbelievable," Roudolf Kharatian recalled. During the mid-1960s he was a senior student in Pushkin's class, having already graduated in Armenia. Osipenko's Mekhmene-Banu was lofty, noble, sublime: "Everything was up and up and up, moving up and up. She was a magician."

Legend of Love conformed to Socialist Realism precepts when the hero Ferkhad resolves his romantic turmoil by dedicating his life to the opening of a new waterway to bring succor to the famished population. But more than Grigorovich's *Stone Flower*, his *Legend of Love* was also everything that would have been impossible in the recent past. There was an attempt to suggest psychological conflict. There were trios in each act in which the principals seem to step out of the plot line, all dancing simultaneously but each in isolation, each immersed within his or her own psychological field. There was a dream scene where Mekhmene-Banu's frustration finds subliminal release. There were solos, configured as monologues, passages of steps meant to suggest emotion but easily defined simply as steps, and thus lacking what traditional Soviet aesthetics defined as "content."

In the climax of act 2, Mekhmene-Banu is required to dance twenty-two fouetté turns. Up to that point, they had been beyond Osipenko's technical capacity; she had never performed them on stage. As did many Kirov ballerinas,

The Legend of Love with Boris Bregvadze, 1965.
Photo courtesy Alla Osipenko.

she eschewed them in the Black Swan pas de deux. In her first two performances of *Legend of Love,* she performed relevés in attitude instead, while in
the studio Vecheslova drilled her in the challenging turns. Vecheslova insisted
that she aim for a count of thirty-two turns in the studio, to ensure that she'd be
ready on stage to ace the required twenty-two, no matter what the performance
vagaries or nerves that were in play. At her third *Legend of Love,* Osipenko was
ready to launch her fouettés. The audience, which was at that time a highly
knowledgeable public familiar with each dancer's attributes, was shocked and
delighted. "At last, Alla, you crossed the Rubicon!" a fan wrote her.

The original quartet of Grigorovich's earlier *Stone Flower* was reunited
when Kolpakova danced Shyrin, Gribov danced Ferkhad, and Gridin
was the evil Vizier. "It was a very interesting performance, one of those

once-in-a-lifetime things," Osipenko said. "The critics said that here we have the cast that was so close in *Stone Flower* and they brought a new life to *Legend of Love.*"

On other occasions, Emma Menchyonok rather than Kolpakova danced Shyrin opposite Osipenko. A 1953 graduate of Rossi Street, Menchyonok came to typify the Grigorovich doctrine of less as more. "It wasn't really important the way her acting was," Osipenko said. Menchyonok was "spiritual and mysterious," with an unusually beautiful style, movement, and physique. Of all the dancers surrounding Osipenko on the Kirov roster, Menchyonok remains one of the most fondly remembered by colleagues. Mikhail Baryshnikov partnered her in *Giselle* and *Chopiniana*; in 2010 he described Menchyonok as "very beautiful and very cool. Very internal. There was a kind of wonder about her. She was really interesting."

Menchyonok "wasn't ambitious," Osipenko said. "She didn't get any awards or titles. She didn't join the Party. She was offended by the theater and by the Soviet powers." Elena Tchernichova recalled that Menchyonok left the theater quickly after a performance. After the ballerina retired in 1977, she had very little to do with the school or the company, although her husband Boris Bregvadze taught there for decades until his death in 2012. Offstage as well, Menchyonok was an internalized presence. "I spoke out more defiantly," Osipenko said, "but Menchyonok was a silent person. She kept everything inside."

17

... And Open Slightly

BY LATE 1965, Osipenko's position in the Kirov was equivocal enough that she was not taken with the company when it spent four weeks in Paris, despite her success in this city in 1956 and 1961. Some weeks before the Kirov left for Paris, she was sitting in a V.T.O, the performing-artists-only clubhouse, with Olga Moiseyeva and an individual she recalled as "a friend of Rachinsky's." An upcoming Kirov performance would commemorate the anniversary of the introduction of running water in St. Petersburg.

Originally, *Don Quixote* was programmed: a comic ballet that seemed logical for a festive occasion. But then Rachinsky had substituted *The Bronze Horseman,* which ends tragically in a flood that destroys the world of the hero. "Maybe because in *Bronze Horseman* there's a lot of water," Moiseyeva joked. They all laughed.

The next morning a secretary pulled her out of class: "Alla, the director calls you for a meeting." "I'm going to the director's," Osipenko told her colleagues gaily. "Either they're going to fire me, or I'm going to Paris!"

Rachinsky was sitting with a Party chief of importance. "Osipenko, what were you saying at the table last night?" Rachinsky asked.

"I didn't say anything."

"So, tell me, you can say that *Don Quixote* is better to celebrate 100 years of running water than *The Bronze Horseman*?"

"Yes, it's better."

"So this is what you think?"

"Yes."

"Do you realize that last night you discredited my name, because you said that I could change this to that anytime?"

"I didn't say anything like that. I was just repeating what your friends were saying."

"What do you think, that you're not part of the collective?"

"Yes."

"My people and your people are different people?"

"Yes, they're different people."

"Osipenko, do you understand what you just said?"

"No," she said, practicing her own stonewall with a decidedly subversive tinge: "No, I don't understand what I was saying." She turned around and was going to walk out. He stopped her. "For now you work in my theater and if you work in my theater you're going to work the way I want you to work, not the way you want to work."

Now he had succeeded in striking her flashpoint. "I work in the government's theater, the Mariinsky Theater," Osipenko retorted, using its pre-Revolutionary designation, "not in your theater!" She turned and walked out.

"Oi," Osipenko sighed as she told me this story. Needless to say, she was not given a reprieve and taken to Paris; indeed she never danced in that city again. And Rachinsky's hostility only grew.

Osipenko and Makarova often commented to each other about their work. The younger ballerina told Osipenko that her performance in *Legend of Love* was too reserved. Osipenko replied that the scenery was minimal and that dictated the key of her performance. "Everybody loved Natasha's melting, vulnerable Odette," Osipenko recalled, "but I didn't feel that the swan could be very sexual. I told her, '*Swan Lake* is a story about your loneliness, not that you want a relationship with somebody.'" But Makarova and she understood the role differently.

Aurora was an infrequent role for Makarova, given Kolpakova's and Sizova's world-famous interpretations. "It's not coming out," Makarova complained about her rehearsals. "I don't understand what I'm doing in the Rose Adagio. It's just not working." Osipenko came to see her performance. Four cavaliers in this adagio didn't seem sufficient for this particular Aurora. "You're actually waiting for number five," Osipenko told her. "Maybe the fifth one will come some time, somewhere . . ."

In 1966 they were alternately dancing the Pearl of the World harvested by the fisherman Kino in the ballet that Konstantin Boyarsky made from Steinbeck's *The Pearl*. Steinbeck was at that moment acceptable to the Soviet authorities because he opposed America's aggression in Vietnam. Makarova told Osipenko that she had asked a critic which of the two he preferred in the role. "When you come out on stage," he told Makarova, "I want to jump out of my seat and come up and touch you all over. But when Osipenko does it, I can't move; it's like a vision has suddenly appeared. Which do *you* think is better, Natasha?"

The two ballerinas were again roommates in the summer of 1966, when Osipenko was finally allowed to return to Europe for the first time since the Kirov's fateful debut tour five years earlier. The tour opened in Verona at the gigantic Arena, where the Kirov not only danced *Sleeping Beauty,* but in addition performed Sergeyev's *Aida* choreography; they were filmed in performance, led by Leyla Gencer, Carlo Bergonzi, Fiorenza Cossotto, Anselmo Colzani, and Bonaldo Giaiotti, conducted by Franco Capuana.

Kolpakova went to Italy but she was injured and not dancing. Together with Sergeyev, Dudinskaya, and Rachinsky, she took her seat to watch one

The Kirov on tour in Italy, 1966.
Photo courtesy Igor Soloviev.
Sitting (l–r): Makanova, Kolpakova, Kurgapkina, Fedicheva, Osipenko, Dudinskaya.
Standing (l–r): Soloviev, Rachinsky, Sergeyev, Vikulov.

of the Kirov's *Beauty*s in Verona. No sooner had Kolpakova remarked to Rachinsky that Nureyev was reported to be in the audience than the group of Kirov-ites heard a loud throat-clearing behind them. They turned and were shocked to see Nureyev sitting only a few rows to their rear. No one dared turn around during the performance that followed. Over the years, Nureyev made persistent attempts to renew contact with ex-Kirov colleagues he could assume would be sympathetic as well as trustworthy. "I wasn't supposed to meet him," Alla Sizova recalled about another occasion. "But I had enough courage to pull myself together and meet him. But I did it quietly."

Osipenko danced the Lilac Fairy at that performance. A knot of spectators remained applauding after most of the audience had filed out. Nureyev was among them. He took off his dark glasses. His eyes met Osipenko's onstage. "You look fantastic" he signaled to her in balletic pantomime.

The Kirov went on by train to Venice, where the company boarded launches to take them to the center of the city. Rachinsky and the KGB stepped into the last boat to leave, but the crew said there wasn't room for Makarova and Osipenko. "What hotel is it?" they called to Rachinsky as he pulled away. "We don't know where to go!" "OK, don't worry, someone will be back for you!"

No one came back, but they took the next available boat and got off at the Piazza San Marco, which they did know was close enough to their hotel. It was midafternoon. They didn't see any other Soviets around. Osipenko had a detective story with her, which she read aloud to Makarova. They sat until it was dark, by which time they were almost in tears. What to do? Continue to stay put, they decided; somebody would eventually find them. Suddenly Viacheslav Kutznetsov appeared.

"Girls, where are you?"

"Where are *you*?" He had gone to their hotel nearby looking for them and found that they hadn't yet registered.

Osipenko recalled a KGB operative named Valentin whom the dancers jokingly nicknamed "our director." He frequently attended rehearsals. "He was merry, a good fellow, a mensch," Osipenko recalled. "May I, as a Soviet director, drink a glass of wine?" he would say and then toss it off in one swallow, as if it were a finger of vodka. "If you drink like that," they told him, "we will all know you're not a director."

At rehearsal the next day Osipenko asked Valentine how he could have been so negligent: they might have defected. "Alla," he whispered, "we wanted to drink and we just forgot about you. It was nothing personal."

The KGB gave the dancers extra money so that they could avail themselves of some tourist activities that were pricey, but "we were always kind of on a leash." Once, however, she and Makarova were out walking alone and found themselves lost. They asked two young men for directions. "Russian ballerina!" the two braves divined. "Piccolo! Piccolo!" the two women implored. They started walking alongside them. When they got to the hotel they discovered that their guides were anticipating something more than *Molto grazie*. "But you wanted to be with us a little . . ." The dancers dashed into the hotel.

Once Osipenko found herself sharing a gondola with only one other passenger, the Italian impresario who was managing their tour. He said that Nureyev wished to meet with her. He wanted her to remain in Europe, to defect, and to dance with him. She explained that neither a meeting nor a defection was possible, now that she had not only family but a child in Russia.

The Fenice theater and the Piccolo Hotel were so close that when Makarova in her dressing room realized she'd forgotten her pointe shoes, Osipenko was able to hand her some through the window of the hotel. In their room Makarova and she shared one bed, a tour arrangement to which they weren't accustomed. They spent the night alternately bumping into each other and apologizing.

On one occasion the two sat in the hotel lounge drinking wine. Kurgapkina appeared wearing a brooch she had bought in Italy on the advice of Yorgi, one of the assistant directors. Yorgi was intelligent and his taste was good. But Kurgapkina customarily looked and dressed like the proverbial *dunya*, a Russian village girl. She had pinned her brooch onto a *seraphan*, a type of loose Russian rustic dress. "Nelka, why do you need this?" they teased her about the brooch: "A priest doesn't need a harmonica," using a venerable Russian expression. Kurgapkina was not amused. "You know, girls," she retorted, "if you knew what lesbians were you would become one," and left in high dudgeon.

But Kurgapkina accompanied them when they went to a party given by the wife of a prominent artist. She had approached Osipenko in the wings of the theater and extended an invitation. They lived in a palazzo that once been occupied by Gabriele d'Annunzio.

Osipenko, Kurgapkina, and Makarova boarded a crowded vaporetto. The three ballerinas chattered in Russian. Sitting across from them was a heavy man wearing a white suit. "Look at that man," Kurgapkina whispered, "he's sitting with his fly open!" They all had a good laugh. Where were they supposed to go once they got off? Kurgapkina asked. They'd been told to ask where d'Annunzio's villa was.

"Dear ladies," a voice behind them remarked in Russian, "can it be that you are looking for my villa?" Osipenko stood rooted to the ground as she realized that this was the very same man whose fly had occasioned hilarity.

She managed a "Hi," but "we were so ashamed we were ready to go back." The man, however, hurried them along to his home. The three ballerinas sat together at one table, and their host realized how uncomfortable they felt. "These young ladies just saved me on the ship," he stood up and announced. "I didn't notice that my fly was open, but they let me know about it." The ballerinas laughed and relaxed and ended up staying for hours.

The Italian tour concluded in Milan. The Kirov gave a gala performance, in which Osipenko danced the second act of *Swan Lake*. Unlike her previous visit to Europe in 1961, Osipenko had not committed any outrageous infractions on this tour. But when the company went on to London in September for a season at the Royal Opera House she was not included, a cruel and injudicious decision that Osipenko tried to appeal. "I was there already," she petitioned the authorities. "They remember me." She was told that her customary repertory was not going to be performed in London. This was nonsensical, since in London the company again danced *Sleeping Beauty* and *Swan Lake*, in both of which she had been acclaimed in 1961.

"It made me very nervous," she recalled. Like most Russian performers, she remained vulnerable to this kind of insidious undermining. Intellectually she could realize what was at work, but on an emotional level "I thought that it was because they thought I wasn't good in these roles. It was demoralizing." Instead, Fedicheva danced Lilac Fairy while Odette/Odile was shared by Fedicheva, Makarova, and Moiseyeva during the Kirov's four-week season at Covent Garden.

By now she believed that colleagues were colluding in her exclusion. Another ballerina said to her before a tour, "Alla, I'm so surprised, why aren't they taking you on the tour with us?" "I should ask you that," Osipenko replied. "Why are *you* asking *me*?"

In Paris in 1956, Osipenko had attended a farewell party for Maurice Chevalier, who was leaving for an extended trip. He told an amusing story comparing Russian, French, and American diplomats. "Da, da, da," was the Russian diplomat's response to everything the petitioner requested, but when it came time to sign the relevant document, he wrote "Nyet, nyet, nyet."

While dialogue with many authorities was "simply impossible," she asked one KGB agent with whom she was on more pleasant terms why the authorities would not let her go abroad. But he too, gave her the standard snow job. "Alla, we love you. You are charming. You're such a good dancer. You go to Syria, you go to New Zealand. We're good to you. ... You go where you want to go. We do everything for you. If you don't go somewhere it's not our problem; you have to talk to your director about it, not us." Sergeyev in turn responded to her inquiries by referring her back to the political authorities. Osipenko felt as if "I wasn't involved in the life of the theater. I was just coming and going." She began to think about how she would mark time until she would reach her twentieth year with the company and be able to collect what would be a sizable pension.

But 1966 also brought one of her career's highlights: *Syrinx*, a solo choreographed for her by Georgi Alexidze, a twenty-five-year-old Georgian choreographer who had made some pieces for Vaganova student recitals. Now he was planning a program of new ballets at the Philharmonic. Also participating were Kolpakova, Makarova, and others from the Kirov. Alexidze asked them if they were willing to work for free. Not only were they willing, they even defrayed some costs from their own pockets, so hungry were they for something new to dance, something made for them specifically. The Philharmonic allowed them to rehearse there after performances, whenever its stage was free.

Prior to Osipenko's *Syrinx* on the Philharmonic program, husband-and-wife Budarin and Klefshinskaya would dance a duet by Alexidze showing Pan's pursuit of the nymph. Osipenko's solo was meant to evoke Syrinx's transformation into a reed, a refuge achieved by the intercessions of water nymphs. Osipenko would share the stage with flutist Lev Perepelkin, performing Debussy's eponymous flute solo, named for the pipes of Pan.

Young as he was, Alexidze nevertheless knew exactly what he wanted from his dancers. Osipenko's legs were going to do what they did famously: describe long slow lines paid out in space in slow ecartés and développés. She danced *Syrinx* in pointe shoes from which she'd removed the hard box that allows the ballerina to rise on the tips of her toes; Alexidze's choreography required her to rise no higher than high demipointe, thus allowing her to hold her extensions longer than was possible in an unsupported pointe solo.

In her telling, however, her arms were challenged by his instruction to let them move freely as flora. Initially she told him that she felt that she couldn't do his piece because she was afraid her arms wouldn't be expressive enough. But he reassured her: "You only have to do one thing: try. We will see if it is good or bad."

Why she felt inadequate here I was somewhat at a loss to understand. Watching her performances on film I see the clear classical foundation of the recognizable Vaganova port de bras. "Everyone said to me, 'Your arms are not good,'" she claimed, however. Perhaps this was the result of stylistic iconoclasm: certainly there is visible in her port de bras, even in the classical repertory, a certain neoclassical freedom that was particular to her. And perhaps her interpretative decisions were unorthodox. In *Swan Lake* she didn't want her arms to be as fluid as Makarova's or Moiseyeva's. She had observed that swans moved differently from most birds, and too much rippling or flapping violated their nature. She liked to establish a pose and then let her arms linger in a magisterial stillness. Critics, she said, complained that her legs were singing, but her arms only speaking.

In any event, she worked hard to release her arms from the geometry of classicism, or the stark angularity of Grigorovich's modern choreography, so that they could embody the vagrant drifts of Alexidze's imagining. His intent was explicit in his instructions to her: her arms and hands were reeds blowing in the wind; they were rain parting the clouds. But the movements themselves were enigmatic; they could be read formally just as eloquently, as they could illustratively. In fact, it's not clear how much the audience would have been able to decipher each of Alexidze's specific intentions, and that fitted the particular paradox of her kinetic imprint. What they undoubtedly saw, in this performance that Smakov in *The Great Russian Dancers* calls "magnificent," was a pliant torso and scrolling arms constructing a plastique of responsiveness particular to the vegetation into which the nymph Syrinx dissolved.

In *Syrinx* she seemed to find a dance dimension outside time, as much beyond metric division as was Debussy's watershed composition, written originally without bar divisions or breath marks. Her phrasing of Alexidze's prolonged stillnesses owed something to what she had seen of Kabuki. She described flutist Perepelkin as "a genuine flute player—a genius." Earlier he had played for her performances of Chabukiani's Gluck adagio, performed to *Orfeo*'s Dance of the Blessed Spirits. In *Syrinx,* the flutist's pauses became musically significant. "They weren't pauses, but rather prolongations of sound," which she could use as fermatas enabling her to sustain extended lines into space.

And Osipenko in *Syrinx* found a timelessness, perhaps unique in all her career, establishing a link between points archaic and contemporary. In the film of the dance made several years after its premiere, we see that here she did not entirely present herself as a ballet dancer. There are times when she moves with an earthier attack that speaks of everything in the composite image we have of "pagan." As always she exemplifies the Russian gift for finding movement in immobility. When she raises her leg in écarté, the movement pulse continues after her leg is fully extended. In the pauses taken by the flutist, her body's vibrato permeates the silence.

Ballerina and musician each heard in Debussy's composition the bittersweet gift of solitude. Osipenko and Voropayev were separating; neither sobriety nor monogamy proved to be his strongest suit. "I was going through turmoil," Osipenko recalled. Syrinx, an acolyte of chaste Artemis, was granted refuge at the price of selfhood. As she danced Alexidze's solo, Syrinx's metamorphosis awakened a transporting experience in Osipenko: "I was not a woman anymore; from within I felt a different kind of life."

18

Staying in the Game

INNA ZUBKOVSKAYA WAS a pragmatist. Whereas most Kirov ballerinas didn't do much on the day of a performance, for Zubkovskaya it was a free day when she could do her housework. Osipenko asked her how she could possibly focus on mundane things in the hours before a performance. "You think the whole day about the performance at night," Zubkovskaya replied. "I don't need to. Nobody else is going to wash the windows if I don't."

But from the morning of the performance Osipenko didn't want to talk to anyone at all. There were ballerinas who liked to sleep in, take a late class, have tea, and then rest until the performance. She preferred to take an earlier class and then sit in the Alexandrinsky Garden and think about what she was going to do that night. And yet no amount of preparation blunted the inevitable vagaries and nerves. "There's a Russian saying, 'There's never enough air before death,'" she said to me. "You go onstage the way you already are."

On a performance day her mother knew not even to bother asking her questions. In general, where professional matters were concerned she kept her own counsel, independent of her family. She did not want to talk to her mother about the vicissitudes of her career. Nina wanted her to be a ballerina of the Kirov but stayed out of the how and the wherefore. If she did question her daughter's decisions, Nina was told to mind her own business. Nina worried about her daughter and her career, but she tried not to discuss these with her.

Nor did Anna and Maria give her professional advice, apart from the customary rebuke that they had been issuing to her since she was a girl: "Lalasha, your tongue is your enemy. Sometimes you have to just keep your mouth shut."

Zubkovskaya asked Osipenko once in the Kirov cloakroom why she was so continuously up in arms. "Everybody is in your situation. Nobody does what they want to do in the theater. You are famous. You are a very good dancer. Be quiet."

"Maybe I do it because I want to create a little bit more in my art." Perhaps Zubkovkskaya was satisfied dancing once a month and concentrating on her husband and daughter, but for Osipenko, ballet was the most important thing in her life, "especially after I had almost lost it" when sidelined by injury in 1952.

Nevertheless, Osipenko remained in pursuit of a perfect romantic alliance. Following her divorce from Voropayev, a rare sensible romantic move on her part was her affair with Georgi Ufeet, who was dean of a department at the Leningrad Theatrical Institute as well as the right hand of director Georgi Tovstonogov. Ufeet's previous romance had been with cinematic bombshell Tatiana Doronina. Ufeet came from a traditional Jewish family. "Please eat," his mother would tell her, "don't go out hungry." Among all of her husbands and lovers, Ufeet was "the most educated, well-bred, intelligent," Osipenko recalled. "He was just wonderful."

After Vaganova died in 1951, Dudinskaya took over her company class and graduating class at the school. Although Osipenko studied with her for more than a decade, she said Dudinskaya "danced in class," complaining "she really didn't pay much attention to us." Using the prima ballerina's execution as a benchmark could be a matter of "Do as I say, not as I do." Dudinskaya used expedients that did not always correctly conform to academic precept.

On the other hand, Osipenko was grateful for what tutelage she did receive. Like Osipenko, Dudinskaya's legs were hyper-extended, although by the end of her career they appeared to have become straighter. Hyper-extension means that the knee sways back in the socket, creating a very decorative curve to the supporting leg in arabesque. Rather unusual at the time, it is sought after in ballet today despite the fact that it can create equilibrium issues, by shifting weight back toward the ballerina's heels. Dudinskaya once said to her en passant, "I always kept my knees slightly bent." Osipenko tried working that way and it helped, particularly in adagio, especially in second position.

Eventually, however, an exodus from Dudinskaya's class ensued. "She didn't really teach, so we left." Marina Shamshova was a retired Kirov dancer who now taught at the Maly, and she also began teaching Osipenko privately. Shamshova encouraged her to improve the presentation of her already renowned legs. "Your legs are very expensive, but you must price them even higher by the way you present them."

For a time later in the 1960s, Osipenko took a company class taught by ex-Kirov ballerina Lubov Voichnis. Voichnis gave her class at the theater, while Dudinskaya's was held at the school, where she also taught the graduating class earlier in the morning. Some of the Kirov's leading ballerinas had requested that Voichnis be invited to teach.

Unfortunately, the experience turned out to be just as fraught as so much of Voichnis's life. "Voichnis is a victim of fate," Osipenko told me. Born in 1924, her father was executed in the purges of the late 1930s. She was adopted by the Pevsners, whose daughter Irina was also studying on Rossi Street. The two girls became close friends. Osipenko still remembered Voichnis's graduation performance, while the school was stationed in Perm in 1942. She danced the *Corsaire* pas de deux. Her jump was remarkable, and "there was a magic about her." As a young woman, Voichnis was romanced by the much older choreographer Leonid Jacobson. But then, ironically, he married Irina Pevsner, and Voichnis started to separate from her adopted family. She rose to the top level of the Kirov roster, but two knee injuries resulted in two different operations and a long recuperation. "She was very smart," Osipenko said, and attributed the fact that Voichnis began to drink to her realization that she could never again attain the level at which she had danced before. Her husband left her. At forty she retired and went to teach in Cairo at Leonid Lavrovsky's school. She was in Egypt for several years, "all by herself, like I am," Osipenko told me in Hartford. By the time she returned to the Soviet Union and began teaching at the Kirov, it was too late. Sometimes she came to class under the influence of alcohol. Not surprisingly, in her condition the class that she gave was unremarkable. Eventually she was dismissed. She died of cirrhosis in 1971 at age forty-seven.

In 1966, Osipenko herself began teaching at Vaganova at the request of the administrative director, Valentin Shelkov. It was a tradition for Kirov dancers to begin to teach while they were still on stage. While she was only thirty-four, Osipenko understood that teaching was a way out, a way forward into "the second part of my life." She taught what was called the "experimental" class, girls admitted at age twelve and taught for six rather than the traditional nine years. During the 1950s, this was how both Makarova and Emma Menchyonok had reached the Kirov. Osipenko taught all six years, shepherding this class to its graduation in 1972. Six days a week, she taught from 9:00 A.M. until 11:00 A.M., before taking her own class at 11:45.

Osipenko's renown and her rank in the theater meant that in the post-Khrushchev Soviet Union she could be harassed but not extinguished. New opportunities came her way despite her problems with the Party and

Kirov brass. A film of excerpts from the Bolshoi's repertory was being made in which Maya Plisetskaya was cast to dance *The Dying Swan*. But apparently Plisetskaya had objected to something and quarreled with Leonid Lavrovsky, who was directing the movie. He worried that Plisetskaya's pulling out would doom the entire project. He and Osipenko had never met, but he called her and asked if she could travel to Moscow immediately as the substitute. They would have only one day to film the solo. But she told him that she had never danced the Dying Swan, and other Kirov ballerinas did it regularly. Nevertheless, he wanted her and she decided to go. From the train she went straight to the film studio. He showed her the steps, which, simple as they were, had been easily subject to many variants since Fokine had originally choreographed the dance for Pavlova in 1907. Lavrovsky's version was "not the style of Russian ballet," Osipenko said, being more neurasthenic than the norm: "He understood my possibilities." Nevertheless, "I never risked dancing it this way again because if I did people would say I was crazy."

Lopukhov's adagio from his 1927 *The Ice Maiden* stayed much longer in Osipenko's concert repertory. Partnered by Igor Tchernichov, she initially danced it at a gala in honor of Lopukhov's eightieth birthday in 1966. She was the first ballerina to dance this since it had been created by Olga Mungalova, for *The Ice Maiden* had been permanently stricken from the repertory in the 1930s, when its strange and novel partnering devices provoked accusations of Western influence and formalism. She filmed it with John Markovsky in 1974, recording some astounding partnering feats, among them Osipenko standing on Markovsky's shoulder in a fully-extended arabesque. She found it terrifying, even with partners as reliable as Tchernichov and Markovsky, but it is accomplished with deceptive ease in this recording. There is also the famous Lopuhov ring, in which she stands in profile to the audience, extending an attitude so high that her foot meets her head. It is a complete refutation of the explicit verticals and horizontals of traditional ballet architecture, an iconic image that Grigorovich used in *Stone Flower* in 1957 and Balanchine quoted in *Agon* the same year.

Alla Shelest had retired soon after Dudinskaya did and very probably at the implicit order of Sergeyev, for it was reportedly only after the theater announced that she was retiring that Shelest herself discovered that fact. But she returned for this gala to dance a pas de deux.

Osipenko was very nervous that night and remembers little about it. Tchernichov was a superlative partner, but the dance had too many risky and unorthodox maneuvers for her comfort. Furthermore, Mungalova's performance had been a landmark in Russian ballet. Osipenko was sensitive to the usual sidelines grousing: why was it being revived with anyone else? But she was a fitting interpreter because Lopukhov's choreography had directly influenced what Grigorovich had made for her in *Stone Flower*. Gusev, who had danced it opposite Mungalova, taught the duet to Osipenko and Tchernichov.

Osipenko began looking at guest performances around Russia as a way to enhance her sometimes sparse performance docket at the Kirov. She had contracts in different cities: in Odessa, where she danced as many as a dozen *Swan Lake*s annually. She also visited regularly Chelyabinsk in the Urals; Slamata, the capital of Kazakstan; and Sverdlovsk, which was a major theatrical capital also in the Urals.

These invitations were often arranged by schoolmates who had been posted to these cities. She suspected that her performances outside Leningrad were more interesting because she felt freer to experiment. Once she danced act 3 of *Swan Lake* swathed in black: tutu, tights, shoes. Sergeyev, who objected to any change in tradition unless he himself made it, learned about it and asked her if she had lost her mind.

In Odessa, Natalia Bar, a soloist in the state ballet company, studied Osipenko's performances, noting the quality and variety of her arabesques. Looking back, Bar realized how much they stood in contrast to today's often distorted articulation, where legs are often indiscriminately and monotonously hiked. Osipenko's leg could be high, but didn't need to be high at all; she "could paint any picture with a forty-five-degree arabesque," Bar recalled. "The way she stood so high on the hip"—supporting leg and torso creating an integrated line continuing through "endless arms and endless neck"—meant that "the breadth of the pose would be much more expressive" than the militantly hiked legs often promoted in Europe and Russian ballet in recent years.

Osipenko's "brush was very impressionistic," Bar said. Her body created lines that allowed a prolonged impression on the retina and imagination of the spectator. By contrast, kicking a leg straight up to the sky left the spectator "nothing you can take home with you," instead imposing a finite picture not suggestive to heightened interpretation or speculation. Osipenko's extension was never pushed to its limit and so never registered as finite. Thus did she generate "poetry of movement" and sustain a lingering afterimage.

Once in Minsk, capital of Belarus, Osipenko was rehearsing *Swan Lake*; the conductor was a woman, and rather eccentric. In Odile's act 3 unmasking, von Rothbart pushed Osipenko a little too hard and she tripped. "Pick me up; pick me up," she told him. "Alla, it's something unusual and wonderful," the conductor told Osipenko afterward. "I never saw such a thing in *Swan Lake*. Everybody must do it like this." She had imagined that Rothbart was deliberately throwing Osipenko toward the Prince to revel in his humiliation.

Both Osipenko's enormous arch and the weakness of Soviet pointe shoes meant that her shoes sometimes broke. In Chelyabinsk she was again dancing *Swan Lake*, partnered by Semyonov, when her pointe shoe collapsed. "Vladik, something happened with my shoe!" He lowered her down slowly in fondu arabesque and she remained standing in a pose. There was nothing else she could do. The corps de ballet saw it and again thought it was something new that she had introduced into the ballet. They told her it was wonderful.

After Shelest retired, she directed the ballet company in Kubyeshev. Osipenko was flattered when Shelest called and said she'd checked with the theater: Osipekno was free for ten days. "Come here, dance *Swan Lake* and I will rehearse with you." Shelest had her own system that focused the muscular equilibrium in intersecting diagonals. "This shoulder is pushing this hip, and if I lift this hip . . . your ear has to be in line with this bone here, otherwise . . ."

At the performance, "I came out on stage and I was like crazy. I tried to think about everything: Where do I push this? I'd forgotten already." She couldn't tell how she had danced. Nevertheless, Shelest was pleased, hosting a supper for her after the performance. "Alla, you made such strides in ten days; you never danced as well as you did here with me!"

She also danced as guest artist at the Maly, Leningrad's second center of opera and ballet, across town from the Kirov. Indeed, there were times during the mid-1960s when she was dancing *Swan Lake* at the Maly and in Odessa more than she was appearing at the Kirov. Kirov coach Naima Baldachieva took it upon herself to keep Osipenko in the game in Leningrad. "Do you understand that you will be finished if you continue like this?" "Yes. . . . Who cares?" This was at a time when the ballerina felt like she wanted to stop dancing altogether, but Baldachieva never stopped pushing. "You don't have the right to leave ballet."

Baldachieva's primary responsibility was the women of the Kirov corps de ballet; her brother Takhir was also a coach of importance there. Baldachieva attributed an improvement in Osipenko's dancing to her beginning to teach the previous autumn. She went to a meeting of the Art Soviet, the artists' council, and requested permission to rehearse Osipenko in the role of Gamzatti. Osipenko herself was apathetic, if not hostile, to the idea of returning to a role that she had always found technically daunting, but she submitted to Baldachieva's initiative. On the night of the performance in June

1967, Baldachieva picked her up and brought her to the theater. "Get yourself together. Everything will be OK. Try to do what you have to do."

But Osipenko recalled that the performance was "torture, total, complete torture." She imagined that the entire company was judging her woefully inadequate. She almost felt as if she was going to hyperventilate; to keep herself calm, she identified the dancers to herself one by one as they walked past her on stage. "Why did I need to do this?" she asked Baldachieva after it was over. Baldachieva didn't compliment the performance, saying only "You did well by overcoming yourself and getting on stage." But, "Oh, my God, it was terrible," Sergeyev and Rachinsky told her.

Critic Clive Barnes was visiting Leningrad from London to review the Festival of White Nights. He sent word to Osipenko that he wanted to meet with her. By this point, the idea of a foreign visitor seeking her out made her nervous. Not too long before, Serge Lifar had visited Leningrad and watched classes on Rossi Street. He spotted her on the balcony of the main studio there. "Alla! Alla!" he called, as he took off his fur coat and put it in the nonplussed Sergeyev's hands. "I thought, My career is over."

Nevertheless, she decided to invite Barnes to dinner at a Caucasian restaurant, along with a Russian journalist, Valentina Veronova, who could translate. Barnes gave her compliments about her Gamzatti, but the performance had been so traumatic that even two days later she could barely remember it. Barnes asked her why she didn't go abroad with the Kirov. She was not forthcoming. "I listened with one ear and let it go out the other, but in my heart it was very painful.

"Why did he ask me in a restaurant?" she decried thirty years later. "Why didn't he write it down, put the question in an American newspaper: 'Why isn't Alla Osipenko allowed to go abroad?'" But here Osipenko was not being entirely fair. Barnes *had* commented on the situation, although it would have been easy for her never to have known about it. Reporting in the September 1967 issue of Britain's *Dance and Dancers*, he wrote that she was "now probably the grandest of the Kirov ballerinas, although if this festival is anything to go on, she does not now enjoy great opportunities to show her qualities." But he wrote glowingly about the Gamzatti as well as a Lilac Fairy he'd also seen her dance that same month.

Tatiana Legat, Soloviev's widow, showed me footage she'd taken during a *Bayadère* that could very well be the same performance that Osipenko recalled and Barnes reviewed. Just as he records, Soloviev was Solor and Fedicheva was Nikiya. If this is indeed the same performance, the entire incident becomes doubly sad. These brief scraps of film, which comprise multiple short takes, show Osipenko dancing a Gamzatti the likes of which I've never seen. How she handled the technical demands of her pas d'action variation and coda we can't know, since Legat was concentrating on her husband's performance. But in the footage of their entrée and adagio, her limbs manifest that "ecstatic infinity," which Fernau Hall mentioned in his review of her 1961 *Swan Lake* in London. Her jump, which she said never recovered from her injury, is nevertheless sizable, even opposite the stratospheric Soloviev.

Osipenko was afraid to be too nasty as Gamzatti, since she is a princess and thus subject to the demands of politesse. Perhaps her own upbringing influenced her insistence on noble reserve at all times. "I always made a line for myself not to cross." Nevertheless, it is clear with the glance she gives Soloviev's Solor after Nikiya's poisoning that as far as Osipenko's Gamzatti is concerned, her word is law. That makes his defiance bolder when he doesn't leave with her, as he does in some productions, but instead mourns over Nikiya's body as the curtain falls.

Other figures of importance in the Western ballet world tried to extend Osipenko opportunities. Pierre Lacotte was in Leningrad with his wife, Paris Opera ballerina Ghislaine Thesmar. Thesmar asked Osipenko why she hadn't accepted invitations to dance in France that Osipenko never even knew had been extended to her. On another occasion, Violette Verdy came to visit Leningrad. She watched classes at the school, obtained Osipenko's phone number, and called her. "How many children do you have?" she asked. "One." Verdy informed her that every time Paris impresarios had requested her they were told that she was pregnant.

Lacotte told Osipenko that he wanted to choreograph a ballet at the Kirov especially for her, on the theme of Beauty and the Beast. He was even willing to waive a fee. "Who do I ask?" He knew that her situation was problematic. All she could advise was that he speak to the Kirov management; but Lacotte was turned down.

Youly Algaroff, a Frenchman of Russian descent, was a dancer-turned-impresario. Visiting Leningrad with a friend, he was toured around the city by Osipenko. At that time the Yousoupov palace on the Moika canal, where Rasputin had been killed in 1916, was closed to the public. But Algaroff wanted to see the basement apartment where the conspirators had fed him a poisoned meal. Osipenko spoke to the mansion's caretaker. He refused the request: if she wanted to come alone that would be acceptable, but bringing a foreigner was another story entirely.

At that time, the mansion was officially undergoing repairs, but Osipenko suspected foreigners were being warned away because the authorities were actually searching for jewels that the Yusupovs, one of Imperial Russia's wealthiest families, might have hidden before fleeing in 1917. When the city's wealthy took flight, many imagined that the Bolshevik takeover would be brief and planned on an imminent return to their homes. Secreted in the walls of the Gastiny Dvor, the enormous old shopping arcade on Nevsky, valuables had been uncovered, planted by the family that owned it before the Revolution.

Algaroff invited Osipenko to dance the *Spartacus* adagio at the Avignon Festival. But the Kirov told him that Osipenko was unavailable and that instead they would send Fedicheva. At the time, Osipenko had no idea what had happened. When she didn't hear from Algaroff she thought that he had changed his mind.

Together with the Kirov's Budarin, Fedicheva, and Vikulov, Osipenko was allowed to go to Israel as a guest artist with the Maly to dance Nikiya in the *Bayadère* Shades. She was again invited by the Maly to dance *Swan Lake* with them on a tour to West Berlin. Rachinsky insisted, however, that she was too busy, although all she had scheduled at the Kirov was a single performance. Maly director Gennady Suhanov went back once more to Rachinsky and promised to fly her back to Leningrad especially for the performance, but Rachinsky still refused to release her. When she complained to the KGB, they told her she had nothing to complain about: "Alla, you *were* in Berlin!"

Customarily, the Kirov season opened with Glinka's opera *Ivan Susanin*, followed the next night by *Swan Lake*. Opening the season meant that a ballerina had to return early from vacation. "Nobody wanted it," Osipenko recalled. She danced the first *Swan Lake* several times but it wasn't a big honor or excitement for her. Once it had been Makarova who was originally scheduled to open the season. "Osipenko!" Makarova called gaily when they ran into each other on Nevsky Prospect. "You will dance opening night." "Why?" Osipenko asked. "*You're* dancing." "No, I'm not that foolish!"

During these years she again was sent on small tours to the Middle East. On one trip a capable local impresario took them to Egypt, Syria, and Lebanon. They performed outdoors as part of the annual arts festival at Balbec in Lebanon, which was very popular with tourists. In Alexandria, they were scheduled for two weeks. Every ticket was sold. The impresario decided to extend the run for two more weeks. He also owned a clip joint, and during their stay, the Russians lived with the hostesses in the house they shared. They became friendly, conversing in English or French. The women came to watch their rehearsals. They found Boris Bregvadze very attractive. At night they left to go to work. Sometimes Osipenko and her colleagues went to watch them ply their trade. Several young men in the Russian delegation went out with them.

But few tickets were sold once the run was extended. Everyone who wanted to see them had already done so. Years later she went back to Alexandria. One morning, going out for breakfast, she ran into the very same impresario. "You are Alla Osipenko, who came with the Kirov Ballet and failed here?" "Yes." "Because of you I went bankrupt."

19

Her Fate

IN 1966, OSIPENKO had gone to Perm to dance two *Swan Lake*s and a concert with the Kirov's Sergei Vikulov. Soon after the first *Swan Lake*, Sergeyev called her from Leningrad: Vikulov was needed to fly back immediately to replace someone in *Cinderella*. The Kirov would be sending a new partner to Perm. "Don't do it," she pleaded. She was comfortable dancing with Vikulov and it wasn't so easy for her to adjust to a new partner. Eleventh-hour substitutions were difficult for anyone. She started crying. "We will send you a very good partner," Sergeyev assured her, "a new, young boy, John Markovsky." "I don't need any John, any Markovsky!" she wailed. "Let me keep Serioza." Finally Sergeyev told her, "I will call my secretary, and if he hasn't gone yet we will do something."

High as his self-regard was, and as skillful a partner as he was, Vikulov was nevertheless somewhat baffled at finding himself indispensable. "Why are you so disappointed? John is a handsome young man." Markovsky had graduated from the Riga School in 1962, had danced locally then gone to Vaganova for a year of further study. He had just joined the Kirov. "I don't want him!" Osipenko insisted. Shortly thereafter, Sergeyev called back. "I did my best but there's nothing I can do. The plane didn't get off so John went by train and he will be in Perm soon."

"This was my fate," Osipenko said to me. She was destined to form with Markovsky her most important partnership, but their subsequent marriage would ultimately prove disastrous.

Back in Leningrad, she danced *The Pearl* first with Soloviev and then Markovsky. Following the medium-height, blond Soloviev, the tall and dark Markovsky made a stronger impression on her as a romantic stage presence, an ideal hero. He was a long-limbed, rugged yet princely figure. It was Baldachieva who suggested to Osipenko that she should start dancing regularly with him. Baldachieva's husband Abderakhman Kumitsnikov was coaching Markovsky.

Markovsky and Osipenko started to rehearse together on their own time, in the evenings, without a pianist. It was going back to the beginning for her, working through all the major classical pas de deux and analyzing them. "To rehearse like that is for children; you have to have the character for it," she said. "Sometimes I thought, Why do I need this? If it had been somebody else I would have stopped it." But she found herself revitalized. She felt that Markovsky's height forced her to be taller, whereas a shorter partner could make her feel small. Her technique became better and she gained new confidence. "We breathed together. This was only with him." And she was personally revitalized as well. "We fell in love so it became more joyful."

Eventually she left Ufeet for Markovsky, but not without considerable confusion and ambivalence. Ufeet treated her wonderfully and she was sure that he loved her. Markovsky was twelve years younger than she. When she told him she had been onstage with Zubkovsky, Pushkin, and other historic figures, he said, "Maybe you danced with Petipa also." She shared her conflict with her mother. Osipenko was surprised when Nina didn't discourage her romance with Markovsky and even seemed to approve it: "Live for yourself for a little bit," she said. Osipenko had become close to Ufeet's family and wondered if they would ever speak to her again. By April 2000, Ufeet was dead and his brother Vladimir now lived in Brooklyn with his family. I saw her soon after she'd gone to visit them and she was pleased that they had treated her like a relative. (Osipenko happily gave me Vladimir's phone number, but he declined to be interviewed, saying only, "Alla was not simple.")

Although Markovsky was the partner she might have been searching for all her career, the total package was problematic, more so than she at first realized. Neither Osipenko nor her mother "could have imagined that John had such a personality," she said. "He had a very bad temper. He was probably often depressed; he sometimes wouldn't talk to anybody for a week." Following perestroika, émigré author Solomon Volkov asked to meet her in St. Petersburg. They spent the entire day talking. Finally he asked, "Alla, could you tell me please: why did you marry John Markovsky?"

"Why do you ask?"

"Because I lived in Riga and I knew him since he was a boy. When you looked at him he had such a gloomy, heavy look. You could just run away after one look."

But had she known, she would still have gone ahead: the artistic gratification she experienced was worth the emotional price she paid. When

Baldachieva died in the 1980s, Osipenko came to the Kirov for the viewing, which was held as was traditional for important company personnel in the lobby behind the czar's box. She spoke to Baldachieva's remains through tears: "Thank you so much; maybe my life with John together wasn't great as husband and wife, but he was great for my dancing life. You helped me."

Swan Lake was central to her repertory, the full-length classical role she danced most frequently. Markovsky's partnering confirmed her belief that perhaps the image created by the Prince was even more important than the Swan Queen's. Around this time she saw the Paris Opera's Claire Motte and Jean-Pierre Bonnefoux dance *Swan Lake* as guests with the Kirov. Osipenko didn't think that Motte's somewhat muscular physique and broad shoulders were right for the role. "But when you saw the Prince next to her, what he was doing was amazing. Bonnefoux was so thoughtful toward her, so attentive, that the way he danced made her look beautiful and feminine."

Osipenko wanted Black and White acts to coalesce on a through line of physical beauty. "They accused me of being cold, just thinking of the visuals." Was her interpretation too aesthetic, even emotionally empty—as some believed? "It's a very hard question," she said to me. Ultra-emotional in real life, on stage she again didn't feel that she needed to project a great deal of overt emotion. And yet she was certain that opposite Markovsky her Swan Queen was infused with new tragedy because "I had a partner I could do anything I wanted with."

She had proceeded from the concept of the Swan Queen that Vaganova had imparted when rehearsing her graduation performance in 1950. Odette's pride and autonomy were primary. "Plisetskaya, Makarova, Moiseyeva wanted the Prince to love them," Osipenko said. "They put a lot of pressure on him to love them. I thought it wasn't right." She wanted to tell him how hard her plight was, how she longed to be a woman again, but miming her tragic history to the Prince she wanted to express resignation more than an appeal for help or a tale of woe. "Obviously the swan had been under the spell for quite a while before Siegfried discovers her. She's accepted it as part of her fate." Shielding Siegfried from von Rothbart, she was not pleading for clemency but defying the sorcerer. A moment that was particularly significant for her was when Siegfried sees Odette for the first time and their eyes connect—then the trembling of her soul is in her legs. Osipenko opined to me that that initial encounter wasn't being performed with sufficient drama today. "It's not love at first glance, but the presence of obstacles to be overcome. She's not in love immediately. It was said that I was cold. I said, 'OK, but I have to be cold at this moment.'"

Thinking about the role, she pondered the behavior and movement of swans. Studying the actual species of bird offered a perspective on their relevant traits: if one partner died, the other followed soon after. But there were dissimilarities between ornithology and the creature of balletic fantasy. Swans' legs are short but the ballet is usually cast with a long-legged ballerina—perhaps to complement and evoke the grace of the swans' wings, their glide across the water.

Some of what she did was unorthodox in Leningrad and thus controversial. Osipenko was reprimanded for hiding from the Prince when she stood with her arms wrapped around her, for looking ahead with aloofness instead of peeking under her arms at him when he made his appeal to her. She was reprimanded for using the shorter Cecchetti attitude in her act 2 entrance and variation, but she felt this position engraved the poses with more presence and aided a sustained balance. She retained the elongated Vaganova attitude to spin out the lines of the adagio.

Osipenko found *Swan Lake* the most difficult of all the classical ballets in her repertory because so much of the role's choreography was supported by her left leg, as is indeed much classical choreography. (I once watched Violette Verdy rehearse for the Balanchine Foundation Verdy's old role in Balanchine's *La Source* with New York City Ballet's Sterling Hyltin. "I wish they would choreograph a ballet for the right leg," Verdy quipped.)

"I don't want to do this!" Osipenko would think to herself before making her first entrance. "Dammit!" By the time she had to bourrée across the stage and into the wings for her act 2 woman-returning-to-swan exit, her feet were exhausted. Not only couldn't she bourrée as swiftly as she thought the passage demanded, but she often didn't think she'd get to the wings without falling off pointe. "Please Osipenko, finish it!" colleagues encouraged her from the wings. "Be strong! Don't fall down!"

When the Kirov made a studio film of *Swan Lake* in 1968, Markovsky was cast not with Osipenko but with Elena Evteyeva. But Osipenko's White Swan adagio with him was nevertheless preserved in a film made in 1974, and it is revelatory. Osipenko is a mistress of melismata, stretching musical and visual time with her sustaining, diminishing phrases above and beyond the metric accents. "I was always late," she had said about Vaganova's class. Yet she doesn't ooze; she preserves a crisp tempo and a taut rhythm. As pliant as her back is, as gossamer the suspension of her long legs, one never believes that she has surrendered to Siegfried completely. Osipenko's Swan Queen remains irrevocably isolated.

Black Swan with John Markovsky.
Photo courtesy Alla Osipenko.

Although the Black Swan is still more difficult technically, Osipenko found the role more open to interpretative possibilities because of its perpetual dynamic of attract and repel, Odile forever enticing Siegfried but never letting him get too close. The diabolical moment when Odile mimics Odette added another layer of duplicity, and yet, once more, as with her

Gamzatti, "I really was afraid in the Black Swan to be very evil." She thought when she entered she actually looked a lot like Odette. She tested to see if he was going to betray her. "A test for a prince." During their pas de deux she would have long pauses where she tried to "say" to him: "Look: I'm different. Think about it: maybe I'm not Odette. But don't betray her." Rather than a response to Siegfried's outstretched arm, Osipenko's développé à la seconde at the end of their adagio was a command. "The prince didn't invite me; I invited the prince: 'This is the last chance I'm giving you to understand who I am.'"

At one point she wanted a new costume to create some additional contrast between Odette and Odile, where her arms would be covered, again heeding some criticism that they weren't expressive enough. Virsaladze was almost ready to create a new costume for her, but she dropped the idea once word got out and the Kirov consensus again was that she'd lost her mind.

One night in 1967 she came to the Kirov to see Markovsky dance Romeo opposite Menchyonok's Juliet. Valery Panov was dancing Mercutio. She admired Panov as a dancer but was "always afraid of him," perhaps seeing a cautionary reflection of her own behavior. "He was too open. He always did what he wanted to do." After the performance, he suddenly invited her to drive with him to the apartment of an artist friend, where they could relax and talk. "No, no, I'm afraid of you," she said. "I don't want to go, and besides I'm already having an affair with John."

"Let's be serious," he said. He didn't want an assignation. What he wanted was for her to leave the Soviet Union with him and begin a partnership in the West. He had yet to meet Galina Ragozina, with whom he eventually was permitted to leave after a long and globally publicized attempt by the Soviets to prevent their departure, or to prevent hers by using the fact that Panov was Jewish as a wedge to drive them apart.

Osipenko preferred to enjoy such furloughs as she was allowed. In March and April 1968, she went on a tour to England, Ireland, Scotland, and Holland with a small group of dancers from different cities in the Soviet Union. She replaced somebody else at the last moment. She thought her inclusion had been permitted because they were visiting small cities in which a defection would have been difficult. Among her colleagues were a number of others who were rarely allowed to tour: "It was very strange."

Semyonov partnered her and they danced the typical mishmash of a Soviet highlights tour. They were assigned the grand pas de deux from *Sleeping Beauty*, something she would never have danced at the Kirov, but for her variation she danced Aurora's Vision scene solo. Also on some of the programs she danced Sergeyev's act 3 Lilac Fairy variation as well, just as she did at home. For her it was "wonderful" to dance anything abroad, familiar role or not. She always experienced a freedom onstage that was unknown to her at home with its attendant tensions.

Prior to their departure, Osipenko went to Moscow to rehearse with Galina Ulanova, who was to accompany them on the first half of the tour. Osipenko anticipated that working with the great former ballerina would be a revelation, that it would unlock some new quality in her. But nothing like that happened. Osipenko didn't think that the class Ulanova taught was anything special. In rehearsal, Ulanova gave her some compliments and some small corrections.

Ulanova was "a very silent woman," Osipenko recalled. She certainly didn't say much on that trip. Osipenko rarely saw her laugh. When they boarded buses to take them from one stop to another, the first seat was reserved for Ulanova. On one three-hour bus ride, Osipenko recalled, Ulanova said not one single word to anyone. Sitting absorbed in her own thoughts, Ulanova suggested a symbol, an icon.

Also dancing on the bill were the Bolshoi's Raissa Struchkova and her husband, Alexander Lapauri. They customarily performed Vasily Vainonen's *Mashkovsky Waltz,* an inevitable showstopper in the Soviet Union and a trademark concert piece for them. It was short, and at home the applause might last a half hour while they performed as many encores as Lapauri's back would tolerate. But in the West encores were frowned upon. Nevertheless, they still wanted the gratification of a repeat performance, and so, as he left the stage Lapauri would keep his hand visible on the curtain to incite a demand for their reappearance. It worked exactly as intended.

On the tour, Osipenko also danced the *Legend of Love* monologue from act 2 and adagio from act 3. Somewhere in Ireland the public wouldn't stop applauding until the conductor asked them to repeat it. After that Struchkova, whose status at the Bolshoi apparently made her de facto director of the small group, forbade encores by anyone, saying that time was being wasted. But still she repeated the Waltz.

Osipenko found Dublin very interesting, the city itself as well as its surrounding spring-blooming countryside, which she visited as the guest of a Russian professor who taught language and literature, a direct descendant of a Russian general who had distinguished himself in the 1812 war with Napoleon. His wife was a member of Irish nobility and they lived in a castle. He showed Osipenko wonderful miniatures that were part of his inheritance. He wanted to give them to the Russian embassy and asked if they would allow it. He was even entertaining the idea of returning to Russia and teaching at Moscow University.

"God forbid, don't do it," she told him. "People have forgotten already about Russian language as you understand it." She warned him too that he would be exchanging his castle for a two-room apartment. His wife eventually persuaded him not to go back.

In Leningrad, Osipenko had been in regular contact with Nureyev's sister Rosa since his defection. But it would have been dangerous for them to see each other. Rosa suspected that the KGB was on her trail and everybody who was in contact with her was followed. They were also each convinced that their phones were being tapped. Whenever Osipenko phoned her she asked, "Do you need sausages?" as a code word. Before Osipenko had left Leningrad to begin this tour, Rosa had given her a letter and asked her to mail it to Nureyev in Britain, which she did.

On April 1, their interpreter came to her and said, "Allitchka, Nureyev is waiting for you downstairs." "Thank you very much, Anna Maximovna, nobody's congratulated me yet on April first." She was still incredulous even after she realized that this was no prank. Osipenko ran to Semyonov. "Vladik, what do I do? It's a nightmare."

"I don't know," he said. "We can't hide."

Osipenko knew that a true Soviet would have refused to see Nureyev, and that would have been the prudent tactic for a Russian of any stripe. But nonetheless she ventured downstairs. The sight of Nureyev standing on the stage was "a horrible shock." He was six feet away but she dared not go any closer. Conversation was awkward; they talked at, rather than to each other.

"Hello," they each said. He asked her why she had worn a wig onstage, which was customary at the Kirov for both men and women, but, as Nureyev told her, "Now in the West nobody does that anymore."

"Vladik and I will dance the *Legend of Love* duet," she told him. "You'll be sorry that you don't have a chance anymore of dancing it."

"I've gotten over it," he said.

"Your sister and your niece are OK," she told him.

"My niece?" he asked. She thought in retrospect that he had forgotten the Russian word *plimanitza*. Osipenko mentioned Rosa's daughter by name and he said, "Aaah . . . Goolah!," recalling her diminutive. Suddenly Osipenko saw that he was looking beyond her, then abruptly he turned and ran away. She looked behind her and saw a KGB officer, who closely resembled another who had been with them in Paris in 1961. "Don't worry; he ran away, it's O.K," Osipenko explained.

"You can't do this," he told her. "You can't talk to him."

"I just came to the stage to do something and I saw him. You saw how big the distance was between us."

"What did you talk about?

"About art, about dancing."

"No, I heard you talked about Goolah, and about his sister."

"I just told him that they are OK."

"Now I am finished," she thought to herself once again, as she had so many times before. It wasn't true; it had never entirely been true before, but every indiscretion, no matter how minor, was of course duly noted, reported, and remembered.

20

Cleopatra

OSIPENKO TOLD THE Kirov that she wanted to dance *Swan Lake* only with Markovsky and made excuses when they tried to give her other partners who were temporarily under-engaged. But her gratification with her new partnership didn't lessen the satisfaction of a brief professional reunion at the Kirov with Nikita Dolgshin in 1968. They had danced *Chopiniana* together in 1961, during his fourth year with the company. But he had become a special bête noir of Sergeyev's and soon he left the company. After Dolgushin had spent six years dancing around the Soviet Union, Sergeyev allowed him back to dance *Giselle* with Makarova, and *Legend of Love* opposite Osipenko as Mekhmene-Banu.

Dolugshin was technically limited, but Osipenko admired the way he would perform three pirouettes and stop with elan. "If he did a double tour he started and ended with elegance, in a perfect fifth position." In the third act of *Legend of Love,* Mekhmene-Banu dreams that she is beautiful again and that her frustrated love for Ferkhad has been reciprocated. Together Osipenko and Dolugushin "brought such intensity and tragic pathos" to their dream encounter, Gennady Smakov writes in *The Great Russian Dancers*, that "it is truly disheartening that this partnership was never allowed to develop further." Dolgushin was told that his interpretations were "too Western" for the Kirov—a standard epithet that persists at the Kirov into the current neonationalistic era. Dolgushin moved across town to the Maly. But he and Osipenko were destined to resume their work together at a much later date.

She liked seeing on stage heroic characters who fought to preserve the integrity of their emotions, their self-pride, who could dare even to destroy themselves rather than sacrifice their emotional convictions: Romeo and Juliet, Tristan and Isolde. But more personal to Osipenko's life and career was Cleopatra, whom she portrayed in an evening-length ballet choreographed by Igor Tchernichov for the Maly in 1968. After joining the Kirov in 1956, Tchernichov had become one of her favorite partners. A knee injury had prompted him to begin choreographing.

Interviewed about the ballet, Osipenko was once asked about political relations between Rome and Egypt. "But it's a ballet about love!" she insisted. She read some historical material as well as Shakespeare's play, but it was Alexander Blok's 1907 poem "Cleopatra" that "I felt caught the essence of her. I believe that with Anthony she didn't think of politics. Perhaps with Caesar." But with Antony—"I think it was very emotional; she was very much a woman. Maybe," Osipenko laughed, "the spirit of Cleopatra wasn't really in me!"

The score by Edward Lazarov, a student of Khachaturian, did not please Tchernichov and his wife Elena, who worked as his assistant. They rearranged it liberally, much to Lazarov's understandable displeasure. Nor was Markovsky their first choice to dance Antony. Osipenko, however, pleaded with them and with Igor Belsky, then artistic director of the Maly, to let her dance opposite him.

Markovsky was neither a virtuoso dancer nor had he performed much contemporary work. Tchernichova recalls in her memoirs that she would have preferred Osipenko to work with another principal dancer who was on the permanent roster. They pointed him out to Osipenko, who was undeterred. And it would have been hard for anyone to deny that, as Tchernichova writes, Markovsky was a "great partner and he and Alla always looked superb paired together." After rehearsals, Osipenko and Markovsky talked and drank with both Tchernichovs in the bar of the Maly Theater, or in the hotel Europa across Arts Square from the theater. "It was a great period of our lives," Osipenko recalled.

After the ballet's premiere in July 1968 Kurgapkina, one of many Kirov colleagues who attended, commented, "If Alla won $100,000, then Markovsky won a million." Her remark became something of a catchphrase in the Kirov.

Osipenko herself alternated as Cleopatra with the Maly's leading young ballerina, Valentina Moukhanova. "We were very good friends," Moukhanova recalled. "We discussed everything." Osipenko appreciated that Moukhanova was going to give a different, but equally valid, performance. Watching Moukhanova she saw a fierce energy that she thought her own performance was lacking. Once again, it was difficult for her to be harsh onstage. But observing Moukhanova released some of her inhibitions: "I thought I could really progress, could do a lot more."

For a second-act duet that followed Antony's return from Rome and his marriage to Fulvia, Osipenko chose not to wear the red sheath that Moukhanova did, but instead a pale costume under which she wore a skin-colored jersey bra and bikini. When the scene began, Osipenko stood still in a pose, the stage lights shining directly on her transparent second skin. At her opening the audience was shocked. Yet again "they were saying, 'Osipenko has gone crazy,'" she recalled—this time not without some amusement and satisfaction that for a moment they thought she had actually dared to go onstage nude.

Tchernichov's choreography required almost nothing in the way of conventional ballet acting but instead unfolded in a series of knottier and more intricate solos and duets than she had ever danced previously. "The choreography was very abstract," Osipenko recalled, but this time no one could nor did accuse her of not being sufficiently emotional. Here "the choreography spoke for itself." If she stood in a pose, she understood why. She knew the background of the character; it all made sense. It was easy to project the character through that particular choreography. "My body just automatically projected the emotion." And given that the work was newly minted, there were no interpretative orthodoxies to observe or be perceived as falling short of.

For Boris Bregvadze, her characterization was certainly martial enough: "In no other ballet was she so dynamic. She was very strong and cold and passionate. Her shape was without comparison: she was like Egyptian statuary. Her Cleopatra was formidable, a masterpiece."

During Osipenko's last weeks in Hartford, in the spring of 2000, she told me about visiting a small Russian jewelry store there, where she admired a ring and necklace. "I'm afraid to ask how much it costs," she told the vendor. He directed her to the catalogue; the ring was called Cleopatra. Her decision was made, since via Tchernichov's ballet, "Cleopatra is a big part of my life."

It was during the late 1960s that she also danced *Raymonda* again at the Kirov, opposite Markovsky. It had been years since her last performance. "I loved this ballet but because of the politics of the company I never danced it." Ten years earlier, when she'd made her debut in the role, it had been the property of Shelest, Dudinskaya, and Zubkovskaya. Now it was most frequently danced by Kolpakova, occasionally by Makarova or Komleva.

Osipenko enjoyed dancing Petipa's 1898 *Raymonda* because of the duality contained within the heroine: she fears the attentions of Saracen Abderakhman but is pulled to him in her dreams. "I was friendly with Raymonda," she said. It seemed inevitable to bring to it what she had absorbed from the starkly modernistic passion and tragedy of *Legend of Love*

With John Markovsky in *Antony and Cleopatra*.
Photo by Nina Alovert.

and *Antony and Cleopatra*. Specifically, her attitude to de Brienne's slaughter of Abderakhman in act 2 wasn't complacent. "Something terrible had happened, and her soul had been impacted." In the act 3 wedding celebration, she was no longer inexperienced or simply joyous; a suggestion of something tragic and unresolved was to remain. This particular tint in her interpretation was commented on in print by critic Marina Ilyacheva. Indeed, after one performance opposite Kutznetsov's Saracen, Osipenko's coach Elena Lukom told her, "Alla, I sometimes don't understand if you like Rakhman more than Jean de Brienne."

Osipenko liked every piece in the ballet, every variation. Raymonda's act 1 dance with the scarf sent her by Jean de Brienne was particularly interesting. She was told by Lukom, who had very likely danced in *Raymonda*'s children's ensembles during Petipa's lifetime, that she should play with the scarf as if engaging in dialogue. The scarf itself, too, had to seem to be speaking. A token of de Brienne's love, Raymonda was to enclose herself in it as if it were something warm, but the illusion was romantic rather than erotic. Osipenko felt as much connection with the scarf as if there had been a real person there. To her it was the most important prop she ever worked with.

In every ballet "I thought first about what was inside, then about my legs." Perhaps it was how she identified with a role that determined how capable those legs became; dancers will say that technical capacity is above all a function of mental assurance. Osipenko believes that *Raymonda* is the hardest of all full-length classical ballets for the ballerina. In the first act alone there are several variations, while over the course of the ballet Raymonda dances multiple adagios and codas. And yet Osipenko didn't experience the same nerves she did dancing *Swan Lake*. "I never made technical mistakes in *Raymonda*," she claimed. "Either the character helped me, or the technique, or my body fit."

Essential to the language of this ballet is the flavor of the Hungarian Czardas, the traditional folk dance that also made its way to the court ballroom. It frequently figures in the celebratory divertissements in Petipa ballets. The Czardas makes its own appearance in *Raymonda* act 3, but it also is threaded with classical vocabulary that Raymonda dances throughout the act, beginning with the Grand Pas Hongrois, an entrance and adagio for Raymonda, de Brienne, and a small ensemble. Traces of the Czardas are present in their twisting shoulders and cocked heads, the way the flick of their palm behind their head harmonizes with the hand resting on the opposite hip.

Raymonda
Photo by Nina Alovert.

Osipenko once demonstrated to me something from the ballet *Paquita*—which incorporates Spanish dance in much the same way—to clarify that Vaganova didn't want overly emphatic accents of character dance to prevail over classical style in these fusions made by Petipa. She wanted the line between classical and character kept clear. This is the way Osipenko approached the Grand Pas Hongrois when she filmed it with Vladilen Semyonov in 1960, part of a Soviet television tribute to Petipa, hosted by Dudinskaya—a performance of unsurpassed elegance.

OSIPENKO HAD FREQUENTLY been at loggerheads with Kirov head Pyotr Rachinsky since he had taken over the theater following Nureyev's defection. She became aware, however, that a personal accommodation with him might have been possible, given that his roving eye was hardly assuaged by his affair with Kaleria Fedicheva. On a tour of Kirov principal dancers to the German Democratic Republic in 1968 she danced duets from *The Stone Flower* and *Swan Lake*. She was given a room in a large hotel suite, from which she observed that at night the eastern sector was almost totally dark, while West Berlin was lit up like Manhattan. Around 1 A.M. she heard a knock at the door of the suite. Rachinsky stood in his pajamas: "We're neighbors." He suggested they have supper together. She left immediately and went over to the Russian embassy, where some of the other Kirov dancers were staying. It was near the Berlin Wall, and that evening the divided population shouted at each other or threw messages across.

In 1970, Rachinsky sent her and Markovsky to dance at a large festival in far-off Siberia, featuring performers from all over the republics. After the concert, the dancers were invited to eat on the shores of Lake Baikal, where homes for government bigwigs were nestled. The dancers were being put up in cabins. Rachinsky evinced a desire to make amends—on his own terms. "There's no one like you," he told Osipenko over a celebratory shish kebob. "Your legs are the most beautiful in the world."

"Yes," she replied, "but these beautiful legs haven't danced in the world for ten years already."

"Now, your life will change completely," Rachinsky said. "Believe me, it will change completely."

The party broke up around 2 A.M., and Osipenko went to her cabin. There she found Rachinsky waiting with a spread of food and champagne. "Is this my house or your house?" she asked. "No, it's yours. We are the only two people here. You and me." She said good night to him and left. She went to Markovsky's cabin and told him about it; he suggested that they enjoy the beautiful night and the lake. The moon over the lake was full, enabling Osipenko to spot Rachinsky spying on them. The next morning, he didn't deign to greet her.

For two years in the late 1960s, the Kirov opera house was being renovated and a new wing was attached that contained additional studios for the ballet, which until then did most of its rehearsing on Rossi Street. During the renovation, the Kirov danced at many Palaces of Culture around the city. The stages were enormous but not built with ballet in mind, while the auditoriums were often several times as big as the 1,600-seat Mariinsky. "Nobody wanted to dance under these conditions," Osipenko said, "but we had to do it." She had to do it more than some of her fellow ballerinas, who were allowed more trips abroad, but it did mean that she was frequently on stage in what were to be her final years in the Kirov.

Before the renovation, all stage machinery had been worked by hand-controlled winches. After the remodeling, everything was mechanized and all that was required was the push of a button. On the first night of the theater's reopening, Osipenko danced the Lilac Fairy. She was required to rise up out of a trap door to make her act 1 entrance but the machinery jammed. The stage floor couldn't open. She alerted Sasha Kondratiev, the stage manager, who told her to jump off the trap and instead run up to the wings of the stage and enter from there. She did. Onstage, she was moving, while the trap had belatedly begun opening, and she was forced to leap over it. When it was time for curtain calls, the button that was to release the curtain also jammed. All told, it was an unnerving evening.

In the summer of 1969, Osipenko spent six weeks touring resort cities with Markovsky on a concert program in which they alternated in pas de deux with Kurgapkina and Valentin Onoshkov. Each couple changed while the other danced, but Kurgapkina always closed the program in a rousing pas de deux that would allow her to reel off thirty-two fouettés.

They were in the city of Feodosia, on the Black Sea in the Crimea, when Nina sent her a telegram that her great-aunt Anna had died in Leningrad. Nikolai Zubkovsky, Kurgapkina's husband at the time, was also along. His drinking had been a problem for years, and keeping track of what he was doing was an ongoing concern of Kurgapkina's. Nevertheless, it was he who provided Osipenko with emotional support, accompanying her after a performance to the telegraph office to telephone Nina in Leningrad, since there wasn't a phone where they were staying. "I am alone with the body, please come and help me," Nina implored. But the administrator couldn't release her because their concerts had been announced and he didn't have a replacement.

When her grandmother Maria had died two years earlier, she had left her a pair of Fabergé earrings, a wedding present from her husband. Now Osipenko sold the earrings to buy a half share in the country house of Irina Kolpakova and Vladilen Semyonov. They owned the bottom two floors of the dacha, built late in the 1920s in the woods near the Gulf of Finland. Now the two top floors had become available.

In 1970, Osipenko again traveled with the Kirov to Japan. It had been ten years since her first visit. In Tokyo, a small store she and her Kirov colleagues had patronized in 1960 had now expanded dramatically. On the walls were autographed pictures they had presented to the owner a decade earlier. She thought it had given the store cachet. A decade earlier it took them eight or nine hours to go by train from Tokyo to Osaka. Now the same train trip took only three hours.

In Tokyo, Osipenko and several other leading dancers were invited to visit a fashionable boutique, where Osipenko tried on some pantsuits that were, however, prohibitively expensive for her even though on sale. She decided to buy something cheaper, as did all the visiting dancers present. But when she opened her package back in her hotel room, she saw one of the suits she'd tried on. "You see they changed the clothes," she told Markovsky. "Something is not right." She imagined the police would soon arrive, accusing them of theft and provoking an international incident. "I was thinking like a Komsomol," Osipenko recalled to me wryly—a testament to the impact of incessant propaganda even on a mind that was inclined to disbelief. (Over the years there had been several shoplifting arrests of Soviet dancers abroad.)

She had a performance that night, but she hurried back to the store, where she was greeted with "Osipenko-san, Osipenko-san . . ." "It's OK," the staff assured her. "We saw that you liked it. We didn't understand why you didn't buy it, so we decided to just make it our present to you."

In Tokyo, Osipenko and a Kirov delegation went to party at a house for geishas, where the residents performed the traditional tea ceremony. Patrons to whom the geishas were particularly attached were reportedly invited into a separate room, a study. As the Kirov visitors were expressing their thanks and taking their leave, Sergeyev made a show of reluctance. "Why? We have to go to the study." Dudinskaya "laughed," Osipenko recalled. "She understood that he would never go there—not with her around!"

They made excursions to many beautiful sites, none more memorable than a visit to mineral baths in the mountains. Two Japanese picked up Markovsky and Osipenko after rehearsal; another group of dancers had gone earlier. They took a two-hour bus ride, driving higher and higher into the mountains.

When they arrived they saw many different bathing pools. Everything was silent. They went into a small pavilion. They were invited to place their shoes on the tatami mats. Still thinking like a Komsomol, Osipenko remarked to Markovsky, "Now they will kill us in the chamber."

They bathed in a lake fed by the base of a waterfall. The water was hot and cold in layers. They put on kimonos, were handed their own clothes, and shown into an adjacent room. There were Sergeyev, Dudinskaya, Soloviev, Legat, Vikulov, his wife Tatiana Udalenkova, Rachinsky, and two agents of the KGB. All were also clad in kimonos. No one was talking and all looked frightened. "Oi, thank God you are here!" Somehow they hadn't realized that work was detaining Osipenko and Markovsky; and were worried that they might even have defected. One KGB agent expressed his relief by calling for sake all around. Dinner followed. They were given apartments in which to rest. "Alka, you can't imagine how Dudinskaya looked getting into the water!" Legat told her when they were alone. The shore was slippery and occasioned the improbable sight of the indomitable ex-prima ballerina crawling nude into the pond.

In *Cinderella* in Japan, Osipenko and Makarova were paired as stepsisters to Gabriela Komleva's heroine. Both "sisters" had long faces that looked somewhat similar. At one point in the ballet, Iraida Utretskaya as the stepmother was sitting on the armchair engulfed in an enormous crinoline under which both stepsisters were to hide. Osipenko somehow missed her cue; she sat under the skirt whispering, "Natasha! . . . Nat-a-lia?!" Suddenly Makarova came to her side and pulled open the skirt: "You fool, why are you sitting here so long? Come out!"

At each performance they improvised many jokes together: "one day this, one day that." At one performance, Makarova yanked at Komleva's forearm; Osipenko tugged at one of her ringlets and it promptly came off in her hand. The displeasure Komleva vented once the curtain fell was accepted as their due by the two conspirators. Sergeyev, however, told them he'd enjoyed it.

In 1967, she had watched Mikhail Baryshnikov's graduation exam on Rossi Street from the balcony of the school's main studio. "Misha surprised us all. It was fantastic." He was small and very young looking, and few in the theater had taken notice of him up to that point.

In January 1970, she enjoyed dancing the Lilac Fairy to Baryshnikov's first Prince Désiré. She had danced with many different Désirés, transporting each to the sleeping Aurora while vested in psychological immersion: "I would think to myself, Do you think he is going to be a good Prince?" Her role required her to be a beacon of seniority, wisdom, and omnipotence, but shepherding Konstantin Sergeyev years earlier, "I felt subordinate. Sergeyev was Sergeyev." With Soloviev, on the other hand, she enjoyed a different collegiality: "we were friends together." But "the innocence that Misha brought into it—I was older, he was younger—" fit the storyline. Baryshnikov had more of a little boy's eagerness and playfulness, as he requested the Lilac Fairy to please show him the vision of Aurora. It was a less stately, more intimate connection than she had felt from most of her Prince Desirés. "With Misha I was more frivolous." Once a critic noticed that she was different and said that her performance had improved with Baryshnikov.

Like many young men, he had not been a strong partner when he first joined the company. But his rise at the Kirov was made possible in part by older, high-ranking ballerinas who wanted to dance with him, who were willing to endure whatever difficulties ensued, and to tutor him. "I was much less experienced than all of them," Baryshnikov recalled. "They were my university."

Sergeyev had spent much of 1970 choreographing a new, one-act *Hamlet*. It was a fraught production—nobody seemed to want to dance it. Both Baryshnikov and Soloviev each rehearsed the title role; eventually Soloviev bowed out and Baryshnikov followed after dancing a few performances. Finally the role was taken by Panov as well as Dolgushin, who returned again to the Kirov solely to dance this role. Sergeyev had originally cast Osipenko

With Mikhail Baryshnikov in *The Sleeping Beauty*, 1970.
Photo by Nina Alovert.

Rehearsing Konstantin Sergeyev's *Hamlet* with Sergeyev and
Anatoly Sepagov, 1970.
Photo courtesy Alla Osipenko.

as Gertrude. She learned the part but felt that Sergeyev had really designed it
with Dudinskaya in mind and that the choreography was all wrong for her. "I
don't feel right in this role," she finally told him. "There's not enough adagio,
and that is my forte." She asked Sergeyev to release her. "It will be worse for
you if you don't do it," Sergeyev warned her; however his days as director were
numbered, for it was on Sergeyev's watch that Makarova defected in London
in September.

21

Return to London

THE KIROV'S SIX-WEEK London season at the Royal Festival Hall was scheduled to open in late July 1970. Kaleria Fedicheva had been scheduled to go, but on a tour to Australia a year earlier she had had an affair with an Australian impresario, Michael Edgley, who subsequently visited her in Leningrad. Rachinsky remained loyal, insisting that she be allowed to go to London, but no other authority was as tolerant. A week before the company was due to leave, he invited Osipenko to his office. "For many years you weren't allowed to go abroad and now you can—we've decided to let you go." Markovsky had not been scheduled to go either, but now he was also going to be included, principally to partner her. Usually husbands and wives weren't allowed to travel abroad together; instead, one spouse was kept in Russia as hostage. Exceptions were sometimes made, however, if parents or children remained in Russia. Osipenko came home from her appointment with Rachinsky. "You see," she told Markovsky, "when they needed us they took us."

It was a long, important season, and there was no point in standing on ceremony or injured pride, to nurse wounds left by years of exclusion. That had been her response a couple of years earlier, when she had actually turned down a ten-day tour to Austria, where she would have replaced a ballerina who was injured. "It's like when you throw a bone to a dog," she complained about the earlier offer. "I thought, am I just a little girl for them?" She declined to go on that tour.

Now she received an invitation to the district Party headquarters, where she was told that it wouldn't be legal for her and Markovsky to room together on tour. How could she consider Markovsky her husband when her passport hadn't been stamped with a marriage registration? She explained that they had been living together for several years. "What is your opinion?" she asked. "What is better?" They could either travel as a couple and live in one hotel room, or live in different rooms but spend the nights together. "Which is better for Russian prestige?"

"Let us think about it."

The next day at the theater she was summoned to the Kirov's KGB office and told to claim that Markovsky was indeed her legal husband, but to add in parentheses, "The marriage is not yet registered."

While they were in London, they jointly purchased a Russian Volga car. But after it was shipped to Leningrad following their return and they wanted to register the vehicle jointly, they were again told it was impossible. At that point they legalized their union at the Nevsky Prospect Registry.

Once again it was easier for her to perform on a foreign stage. Throughout that London season "Alla danced wonderfully," Kirov character dancer Nikolai Ostaltsov recalled. On the opening night of the season, she and Markovsky performed the Black Swan pas de deux. In her variation, she turned a triple pirouette—"I surprised myself," and, apparently, other people has well. "Alla, it didn't look like you," Dudinskaya told her.

Victor Hochhauser, the English impresario presenting the Kirov, met Osipenko in a backstage elevator. Her reviews had been so glowing for the gala program that he was now insisting that she dance *Swan Lake*, act 2, on the opening night of the second program. The Kirov had no choice but to comply, although Osipenko thought they would have preferred to cast Makarova.

Curtain call, London 1970. Left to right: Osipenko, Sizova, Baryshnikov, Makarova, Soloviev.

Photo by Rosemary Winckley.

On the third program the Kirov presented that season, Osipenko danced Lavrovsky's *Walpurgisnacht*. It was a "terrible ballet," she laughed, but "so much fun to dance," one reason being that it was technically easy. It was one of the opera ballets she customarily danced in Leningrad, where the Kirov opera was fortunate to have the full resources of the ballet company at its disposal, since most Russian operas contain a ballet. Also in her repertory was the Persian dance in Mussorgsky's *Khovanschina*. Choreographed by Lopukhov, it was "a very beautiful dance, a very beautiful costume. A very beautiful scene; all the ballerinas danced it with pleasure." And there was also the Polonaise in Glinka's *Ivan Susanin*, which had been Dudinskaya's favorite way to begin the season.

The Kirov danced *Walpurgisnacht* as a separate piece on tour, but in Leningrad it was performed only in the context of Gounod's entire *Faust,* and so it meant a very late evening: coming in the opera's fifth act, the twenty-five-minute-long ballet didn't begin until midnight. Writing in *Dance and Dancers*, John Percival also suggested that the timbre of Leningrad reserve relative to Moscow's assertiveness, which may have been accentuated in Osipenko's case, was again a performance determinant. She was "less playful than Bolshoi casts have generally been. Whether you find this more or less sexy is a matter of taste." But Osipenko herself didn't feel constrained. For her, *Walpurgisnacht* was "a breeze. . . . I was very relaxed," enjoying the way Markovsky twirled her high in the air.

Visiting the West gave her exposure to a wider spectrum of dance activity than she saw at home. Together with some colleagues, Osipenko went to watch a class in Martha Graham technique at the London Contemporary Dance School. "It was absolutely incredible," she recalled. "We had never ever seen anything like this. We were so impressed."

Indian dancer Ram Gopal was frequently present during the Kirov's season. In the wings after one performance, he gestured to Osipenko to come closer. He looked around cautiously. "I want to give you a present," he told her, "but I am afraid to do it where everybody can see because you might have some problems." He handed her an Indian topaz ring as well as a diamond stickpin that was intended for Markovsky. He also gave Osipenko a Venetian crystal rose that he said had once been Pavlova's. She subsequently donated the items to the Theater Museum in Leningrad.

As always, success and special attention for Osipenko brought repercussions. Sergeyev suddenly informed her that she was cast in the corps de ballet of noblewomen in act 1 of *Giselle*. Osipenko told him in that case she was buying her own ticket back to Leningrad the next day. Sergeyev explained

Rehearsing in London, 1970.
Photo courtesy Alla Osipenko.

that Hochhauser fiscal guarantee increased according to how many principal dancers were on stage in each performance, which was true. He said also
that Osipenko would alternate in her cameo with Kolpakova, Makarova, or
Sizova. That turned out not to be true.

When Kolpakova danced *Giselle*, Osipenko duly appeared in the act 1
crowd, wearing a picture hat and standing in profile so that no one in the audience would recognize her. Principal character dancers Anatoly Gridin and
Konstantin Rassadin were on stage in the ensemble with her. They had already
agreed in Russia to participate. But the men of the corps de ballet improvised
what Osipenko interpreted as an apology for their administration: during the
performance they sank to their knees and presented her with posies of daisies.

"We were ashamed and very embarrassed watching," recalled Tatiana
Legat, who sat in the audience. "On the one hand, they certainly didn't
have enough dancers, and they needed someone. But they could have asked

someone else." Osipenko received a letter from an admirer after the performance in which there was a drawing of her in profile; "It's a catastrophe for the Kirov Ballet that the great ballerina of *Stone Flower. . ."* was now reduced to being one of the crowd.

When *Giselle* was next performed, Osipenko found that it was she, not Kolpakova, Makarova, or Sizova, who was again cast in the entourage. Her ex-husband Anatoly Nisnevich came up to her and told her that he'd just overheard a conversation between Sergeyev and a dancer who occupied a unique position: he was dancer, KGB agent, and assistant director. "He had the right stripes," Osipenko recalled tartly. "But we promised her that she would alternate; tonight it would be Kolpakova," he said. "No, it's OK," was Sergeyev's answer. "She will have to put up with it."

Osipenko was actually willing at that point to turn around and go home, but she didn't want to leave Markovsky in London by himself. His life in the company wasn't easy. In London he was partnering her, but he was still officially in the corps de ballet and was paid as a corps dancer. Instead, she simply sent the costume back to the wardrobe room. Someone unknown took her place in *Giselle*. No other ballerina took this place in the ensemble during the London season.

On August 27, the Kirov premiered another divertissement program, in which she and Markovsky danced the act 3 *Stone Flower* duet, Danila's leave-taking from the Mistress. It was, Mary Clarke wrote in the *Dancing Times*, "dramatically nonsense out of context but does allow Osipenko to show her extraordinary, serpentine suppleness and fantastic extensions."

"They're watching me like hawks," Baryshnikov told Osipenko in London. It was widely suspected that his phenomenal success during the season could spark his defection. Unwittingly, however, he acted as decoy for Makarova's defection on the night of September 3, 1970. The following evening, Osipenko and Markovsky were planning to go to dinner at the home of a couple of wealthy admirers. The KGB said that no one from the company would be allowed to go anywhere. Osipenko turned on her jailers. Hadn't Nureyev and Makarova been enough? Did they want her to get so angry that she stayed in England, too? Was another scandal what they were looking for? Finally she and Markovsky were allowed to step into the waiting limousine, a fancy car with power windows. "We thought, this is what Makarova is going to get by defecting."

They were out until four in the morning. Their hosts asked if they wanted to know for sure whether Makarova defected. They went over to a newspaper office. Osipenko was startled to see Makarova on the front page wearing one of Osipenko's own suits; the two ballerinas wore the same dress size and earlier in the season had traded outfits.

When they returned to the Strand Palace hotel, KGB agents were waiting in the lobby. They told them that Rachinsky wanted them to come to his room; when she walked in Osipenko saw friends and colleagues she had never realized were so intimately in league with the KGB. They wanted to hear what Osipenko knew about the how and why of Makarova's defection. But she was as taken by surprise as the rest of the company.

The KGB asked her to write a postcard to Makarova, remonstrating with her for her decision and asking her to reconsider. She complied willingly, indeed enthusiastically. In Makarova's 1979 autobiography, she quotes from Osipenko's communication: "It is impossible to believe what has happened. . . . Your soul is Russian. It will not survive what you are doing."

"I thought it would make her change her mind," Osipenko recalled to me. "I was so shocked. I didn't want her to defect. I worried about her because she didn't have the character that she has now, the strength of personality. She was very flighty."

The London season closed only days later, the final performance concluding with *Sleeping Beauty*, act 3, with Kolpakova as Aurora, Soloviev as Desire, and Osipenko as the Lilac Fairy. Osipenko and I discussed photos taken by Rosemary Winckley of the curtain calls on that closing night. In one her smile was rather aloof and melancholy: "You could see it on my face"—her sadness at Makarova's defection. One shot showed Sergeyev bringing forward Kolpakova and Osipenko to accept the acclaim of the audience. "I thought, Why are you holding my hand? Leave me alone."

The company continued its tour in Holland. Dancing her own scheduled performances as well as those that would have been Makarova's, she danced the same repertory as in London. The authorities "left me alone. I was happy." Reflecting on London, and the incident with the *Giselle* costume, "I thought, I fought for myself and gained something from it." As a friend of Makarova, however, Osipenko was more vulnerable than ever to the new round of reprisals that began.

She assumed that she would be dancing *Swan Lake* in Romania, where the company was headed after Holland. She had made a hit there earlier in her career. A certain Romanian operetta star would invite her to his performances; when he was presented flowers on stage, he would toss them to her in her box. But now in Bucharest, people were asking her, "Why aren't you dancing *Swan Lake*?" Indeed she wasn't scheduled to dance anything at all in Bucharest. She was stunned.

During a press conference there, Rachinsky had introduced all the principals present except her. Baryshnikov shot up and said, "And you forgot to mention Alla, our prima ballerina." "Oh, I didn't mention your name?" Rachinsky twittered. "I'm so sorry." The journalists present suddenly turned their attention to her, sensing the hint of discord. At press conferences Sergeyev customarily fielded questions; here he was asked why she had disappeared for ten years. (In London too, she said that he had been asked the same thing in a similar situation.) Now she turned to Sergeyev: "Please," she said under her breath, "don't tell them that I was pregnant."

"We needed her more in Leningrad than abroad," Sergeyev announced.

The Kirov summoned Moiseyeva, who hadn't been included on the tour and had gone on vacation. Markovsky went to Sergeyev and said he couldn't partner her because his back hurt. This was malingering on his part, perceived as a gesture of loyalty to Osipenko: "Everybody was saying to him, 'You will pay for it; you will pay for it!'"

"I tried not to talk to anybody, just to do my job," Osipenko said, which at this point meant no more than coming to class in the morning. "I didn't see anything around me. I had had enough."

In Markovsky's place, Vikulov was asked to partner Moiseyeva and agreed. That night, Osipenko didn't go to the performance but instead to a party given by one of her local admirers. Moiseyeva was out of shape and the opening went badly; Vikulov had trouble lifting her. To make matters worse, the performance had been televised and patrons started returning tickets to the Kirov's season.

The Kirov's next stop in Romania was the city of Cluj-Napoca where it was announced that finally Osipenko and Markovsky would be dancing *Swan Lake*. Rachinsky told her that she would dance the matinee. Sensing that she had, at least for the moment, the upper hand, she refused. He agreed to give her an evening performance. Into that performance she poured her anguish and her relief at dancing the ballet again. The theater had a wonderful stage, and she was familiar with it from previous visits. It was the rare time that she had danced *Swan Lake* to her own satisfaction. Angelina Karbarova, with whom she'd gone to the Prague competition two decades earlier, told her that she had never danced better. "It was like a victory," Osipenko recalled. "I wanted to show everybody who I was." After the performance fans lifted her up and carried her to her nearby hotel.

But back in her hotel room, she sat with Markovsky, unable even to speak. She was both numb with upset at the administration and at the same time shocked that they could still precipitate this degree of response from her.

"You know, I think I'd rather resign," she said to him. If they had been able to put her into the corps de ballet in London, she anticipated being forced to retire when they returned to Leningrad, as had happened when Alla Shelest walked into the theater to find a sign congratulating her on her imminent departure. It would be better to preempt being dismissed. Markovsky agreed. "If you would like to resign, just do it right now. Don't wait until they force you."

The next day, she submitted her resignation. In the evening several administration members showed up unannounced at her door. "We're asking you not to." "No, if I've decided, that's it. End of conversation."

"No, no, no, please don't do it abroad." It clicked to her that they did not want a political scandal. Rachinsky refused to accept her resignation. She told him that the next time the Kirov harassed her would be the last time.

PART THREE

22

Resigning

FRIENDS URGED OSIPENKO not to drive her car if she was nervous or agitated, but for her, driving fast was therapeutic. It took her forty minutes to drive from Leningrad to her dacha, just half the time it took a neighbor. The route to her house took her along a beautiful road that led into Finland, lined with pine trees, birch trees, and berry bogs. It was dotted with rest homes and dachas, and motor speed was restricted. But the police were indulgent. Once a policeman stopped her and asked what speed she'd been traveling at. "Medium speed." He corrected her: "We couldn't reach you even at *our* speed."

Once she was driving on a small back road from her dacha to visit Tatiana Vecheslova, who lived nearby. The sunset preoccupied her until she was jolted out of her reverie when her car flipped over several times and wound up in a pond. Covered with green algae, Osipenko emerged like the creature from the black lagoon. But both she and the bottle of vodka she was bringing Vecheslova were unharmed. A truck came and pulled the car out. The body was totaled, but the engine was fine. She sold the damaged car to someone who knew how to rebuild it.

Very often she used her time on the road to reach a decision. The major decision she now made in the spring of 1971 was to finally leave the Kirov for good. Makarova's defection led to Sergeyev's dismissal as artistic director of the Kirov. He and Dudinskaya were re-assigned to direct the school, where Dudinskaya had taught since Vaganova's death. Vladilen Semynov, nearing the end of his dance career on the Kirov stage, was named acting artistic director of the ballet. But for Osipenko, nothing had changed there for her. That season, the choreographic team Natalia Kasatkina and Vladimir Vasiliev asked her to dance the She-Devil in the comic *Creation of the World* that they were creating for the Kirov, in which Kolpakova, Baryshnikov, and Panov were also starring. But the administration overruled their casting and put Fedicheva into the role instead.

The company was planning a return visit to Japan. Osipenko was to be taken, but not Markovsky. "They were afraid we would defect from Japan." Osipenko balked when Semyonov told her that she would be starting a new partnership with a member of the corps de ballet. Osipenko asked instead that Semyonov dance with her.

Semyonov and she had graduated together and danced together frequently in the past. He was a danseur of elegance and lyricism who, in Osipenko's estimation, went from an indifferent partner to an expert one after dancing with Alicia Alonso when she made a guest appearance in Russia in 1958.

Semyonov had a gentle touch and long, elegant fingers. "He had an intellectual face. His features were those of a cultured man. You felt his politeness, his culture on the stage. Probably I liked dancing with him because we were total opposites. When I was very emotional I felt calmness coming out of him and I felt very secure."

However, this time Semyonov told Osipenko he would have to go home and think about it. The next day he told her, "Alla, we decided that I won't dance in Japan." Osipenko found that refusal unforgivable and insisted that her resignation now finally be processed. She refused to speak to either Semyonov or his wife Irina Kolpakova for fifteen years.

Delegations from the Kirov and the Party urged Markovsky to persuade her to stay, but he told them that his wife was so miserable that she was crying herself to sleep. Friends started calling: "Why are you doing it? You're crazy. Where will you find another theater like this?" She told a friend, Kirov character dancer Irina Gensler, that they had all kept silent for too long about abuses committed in the company. The resignation of a single dancer didn't mean anything, but a multiple or even mass walkout could precipitate a scandal that might result in some reforms. Gensler informed her that the company was too excited about being able to see Japan again to consider such a thing.

Any kind of collective action against authorities, of the kind that she and her fellow dancers had waged in 1962, was rare and improbable, given that each dancer was grateful for any privilege allotted amid a national climate of restriction. But the resignation of a star dancer did make its own, unwelcome statement. The Kirov administration "hated me for what I did," Osipenko claimed. It was customary for retired dancers to retain their backstage passes and thus be allowed to come and go as they pleased, whether or not they had transitioned to rehearsal staff. Her pass, however, was now confiscated.

An official notice, literally an "order," in the parlance of theatrical bureaucracy, was posted backstage. "Due to the fact that People's Artist of the Russian Federation Alla Osipenko is retiring, we now have a position open and will be looking for somebody else to fill it." This was also aberrational, undoubtedly intended as a reprimand. Senior ballerinas were considered singular, and outside replacements were not recruited. Succession and advancement came only from within the ranks, supplied by the school. Help wanted ads were not customarily posted.

Osipenko's farewell was a *Stone Flower* that was filmed for television. The theater was bought out by the television company, and it was announced on the radio that anyone who wanted to attend would be admitted free. At the last minute, however, Rachinsky ordered all the doors locked. From backstage, Osipenko heard people clamoring outside the theater, would-be spectators pounding on the doors until the police were called. No audience was allowed in. Osipenko danced to a battery of television cameras but a nearly empty theater. Almost all her sister ballerinas, however, were there to watch. "I was nervous; my performance was reserved."

There's no doubt that the incident with Semyonov had precipitated her leave-taking. But talking to her about it on several occasions, I felt that there was more to it than that. Osipenko recalled discussing retirement for years before she actually left. The standard term of civil service for ballet dancers was twenty years, but principal dancers could usually stay longer. Kolpakova, Kurgapkina, and Zubkovskaya had each said they would retire after twenty years, but each danced well past age thirty-eight. Osipenko recalled telling her colleagues that she intended to leave the Kirov after her twenty years were up, but rather than stop dancing, she would enjoy trying her abilities in another repertory, another troupe. The fall of 1970 had marked her twentieth anniversary. At that time, she remembered what she'd said earlier, and "I was ready to leave." Of course that readiness was also probably triggered by her problems with the Kirov that fall as it made its way eastward after Makarova's defection in London.

But was it really her decision? "She thought that she left [of her own accord]," Bregvadze told me, "but the situation was another story." According to him, Markovsky had first submitted his own resignation and it was she who followed him. In London the previous summer, another dancer overheard Markovsky threatening the administration that he would defect. Osipenko said that Markovsky had wanted to leave, independent of her own decision. He felt stifled by the Kirov bureaucracy and was frustrated by the difficulty of doing anything new, which would have been beneficial to his development and position. He was in demand as a partner by ballerinas besides Osipenko, but technically Markovsky wasn't on the same level as a Baryshnikov. Both men were from Riga, but they were not friendly. Markovsky "couldn't find his place in the theater."

Leaving the Kirov together was almost like a mutual mini-defection; they could only hope it would turn out to be a rebirth for each of them.

23

A New Beginning

FOR A WHILE Osipenko and Markovsky were adrift. "I had no job, no money, nothing. Nobody even wanted to know us." She pawned things to pay her living expenses. Markovsky started to talk about leaving the country. Their doldrums were relieved when Leonid Jacobson asked them to join the new company he had been allowed to form. For years he had worked at the Kirov but faced resistance from both theater administration and Party. "Alla, how long will you stay in this shit?" he had sometimes said to her while she was still with the Kirov. Now, for some reason, his was to be the first dance company in the Soviet Union dedicated to the work of a single choreographer.

The new company had around fifty dancers. The government was sponsoring it, of course, but hardly to the tune of anything like the lavish stipend given the Kirov. "It was so little money, almost for free," Osipenko said about her salary. But Jacobson promised, "We will go abroad. We will see the whole world and the world will see us."

Working with him was not easy. She had known him since she was a girl and was still a teenager when he made his first piece for her. At forty she still felt like a girl in his presence. "Keep quiet and do as I tell you," he often said to her. "Sometimes I tried to argue, but I knew I wasn't brave enough to contradict him."

"Who are you?" he demanded. "The time will come when you will disappear and I will disappear. You will be completely forgotten but my name will be known."

They danced for a different public than had attended her Kirov performance. There were many tourists, and some were seeing ballet for the very first time. "The public was like 'the second degree.'" Jacobson impressed upon her the all-too-pertinent, if not absolute, truth that "The public is foolish. It doesn't understand anything. We have to prove to everybody that we are right and what we do is art, high-class art."

She frequently danced two diametrically different short pieces: *Taglioni's Flight,* which he created especially for her, and *The Minotaur and the Nymph,* a reworking of a piece that he'd made a decade earlier, a continuation of his Rodin theme, again with unpointed feet. Of the two, she much preferred the latter, whereas Jacobson's tribute to the Romantic era's Marie Taglioni prompted in her a desire to scream "No more Romantic ballet!" She felt that Jacobson was giving her a role really designed with Makarova in mind. "I didn't have the style. I couldn't do it." Her coach Marina Shamshova quipped that Jacobson tried to turn a wolf into Little Red Riding Hood. But contrary to their protestations, the video evidence is persuasive. Performing to Mozart, she is in flight almost every second, supported by four partners, never permitted to descend from the empyrean realm.

In *The Minotaur and the Nymph,* Osipenko and Markovsky danced a duet of bestiality and ravishment to music by Alban Berg. It naturally prompted accusations of proscribed "erotica," an epithet potentially fatal to its chance to be seen. "Alla, how can you dance this?" the KGB asked. She tried to turn the tables. "It's not erotica. It all depends on your point of view. An immoral person would see immoral things. You have spoiled the purity of it." What it really was, she claimed, was a fight between Feminine and Masculine. "Each wants to be the winner. There is no eroticism here, no pornography. For me it's a fight for survival. It *is* Socialist Realism." She and Jacobson cowed the bureaucrats into pretending that they understood a deeper message. It was allowed to be performed and subsequently filmed—a fight for survival, a zero-sum battle for dominance. Moments of real physical risk make this duet spectacular. Locked in mutual antagonism, she and Markovsky grasped hands but strained away from each other, suspended in isometric equilibrium. When they broke their hold, she once went sprawling. At times she is active, catapulting herself at him; at times she resists passively, all but limp in his grasp.

A decade after Nureyev's defection, ex-Kirov general director Georgi Korkin had reestablished himself in the arts management hierarchy. He was invited back to the Communist Party and became director of the Leningrad Concert Bureau. The Jacobson troupe was now under his aegis, and he was helpful to Osipenko on more than one occasion. But Jacobson's company was never allowed to expand the way they had all hoped. For one thing, he was a Jew; for another, the entire enterprise was probably too unorthodox not to be kept at arm's length by the authorities. Indeed its existence may have been a form of tokenism, a gesture of tolerance largely for show. The company was not permitted to go abroad; instead, their touring was confined to small cities around the Soviet Union. Occasionally they had a season at one of Leningrad's Palaces of Culture, but "we never danced at a good theater." For some reason, "we weren't allowed to go to Moscow." They went to Kiev. They went to Georgia, which for her was as exotic as Europe. In Georgia "the hospitality is wonderful. You come there and feel you are in Paris." But Markovsky began to seem frantic, afraid that they were now trapped in the USSR forever. She urged him to be patient, while they looked for such additional work as was available.

Maya Plisetskaya invited them to join her own small company of about fifteen dancers that she led sometimes on tours around the USSR. But phone discussions about possible repertory made it plain that two divas were going to be one too many. Plisetskaya assured Osipenko that she would be able to dance anything she wanted, but took exception when Osipenko proposed Jacobson's *Minotaur*. "No, no, no. Anything except that." Osipenko claimed that was because "it was very successful and she was afraid I would have too much success." The result was that "I said, 'Ciao, Maya.'" In Osipenko's telling, however, her sister diva had desired and pursued the last word: "Later she sent other people to talk to John, to invite him to the company, but he refused." But she and Markovsky went with the Bolshoi's Mikhail Bank, when he toured his own small group around Russia.

In 1972, the class of girls she'd taught at Vaganova graduated. Dudinskaya chastised her for excluding fouetté turns at the graduation exam. "What is it? You don't teach your students to do fouettés? I understand the group is a weak group, but why can't your girls do fouettés? It's included in the program; you have to do it. You didn't show us what they can do." In Dudinskaya's class all the girls could do fouettés, although Dudinskaya herself hadn't been good at them. "Good or bad, but everybody did it," recalled Osipenko. "One girl, Lena Galieva, even did 164."

Osipenko gave as good as she got. "Yes, Natalia Mikhailovna, I taught them only six years; it's an experimental group. I studied with you for eleven years, and you didn't teach me fouettés." It wasn't an exceptionally talented group, but all her students received offers of work from provincial theaters while one danced in Leningrad's Maly.

Once more, and for the last time, Valery Panov approached her about leaving the Soviet Union when he came to watch a performance by the Jacobson company. Since he'd proposed defection to her five or so years earlier, he had married Galina Ragozina. They were now "refuseniks" trying to obtain permission to emigrate to Israel. Baroness Batsheva de Rothschild, a patroness of Martha Graham, was a staunch friend and supporter, Panov told her. Rothschild had promised to help him when he made it to Israel. Osipenko and Markovsky could leave with Ragozina and Panov, and with Rothschild's support start anew in the West. Once again, however, Osipenko demurred because of the family ties that bound her to home.

Her father Evgeni had miraculously survived both Soviet prison and the Eastern Front. Nor had he been vanquished by a heart attack in the mid-1960s. He never told her anything about prison, "maybe because people who were in the camps don't like to revisit them." She regularly visited him with her son and Markovsky. "He was a very talkative person. He liked life. He liked to laugh. When we visited him it was like a party." However, in the early 1970s, a tumor was discovered in one of his kidneys. The doctors explained to her that he needed surgery, but because his heart was weak they didn't think he would survive an operation.

Visiting him in the hospital, she realized how much she took after him physically as well as facially. They shared the same blue-gray eyes. She saw his still-shapely legs and recalled a moment more than thirty-five years earlier when she had been in her parents' room where she saw him nude from the back.

It was time for her to go to a rehearsal. A nephew of her father came to replace her at his bedside. That night Markovsky woke her up: "What happened to you? What are you doing?" She was gesturing as if trying to clear away some impediment. "My father was just here," she said groggily. "Maybe I dreamed it. He came and asked me to give him some water." She went back to sleep and when she got up she called Evgeni's second wife Katya to ask how he was. "Your father is dead," she was told. Osipenko asked what time it had happened. It was the same time that Markovsky had awakened her. Now she called her mother, who also asked what time he had died. "Two A.M.," Osipenko told her. "That's impossible," Nina replied. Usually Nina slept soundly. This night she couldn't sleep and got up to smoke a cigarette. Just around the time Evgeni had died, she became sleepy again. Katya organized a small party in Evgeni's memory, as was traditional in Russia. "He was lucky that he had you," Nina told her successor. "If he had had me, he wouldn't have lived this long."

24

Baryshnikov

IN 1972, TWO years after Osipenko's *Lilac Fairy* had piloted Baryshnikov to the sleeping Aurora in his *Beauty* debut, she danced with him again in *The Tale of Serf Nikish*, a forty-five-minute ballet created for television by Kirill Laskari. His ballet fell somewhere between the Icarus and Firebird legends. The Kirov's Elena Evteyeva was Baryshnikov's earthly love, while Osipenko danced some sort of mythical bird he pursued.

During the filming, she and Baryshnikov discussed Yuri Soloviev. Osipenko felt that the Kirov was now taking him for granted even though he was only in his early thirties and still in his technical prime. And he had refused repeatedly to join the Party. The situation was a delicate one: Baryshnikov and Soloviev were friends, but now Kolpakova had exchanged Soloviev for Baryshnikov as her regular partner. "You see what happened to Soloviev?" Osipenko cautioned. "Don't forget that the same thing can happen to you." Baryshnikov assured her that yes, he did understand.

A year later, Baryshnikov was being allotted a Creative Evening of his own at the Kirov, where he would choose and cast the program himself. Three new ballets were to be performed when the Evening was brought to the Kirov stage in February 1974. Baryshnikov had just turned twenty-six. It was an honor for him to be extended his own Evening, a concession to the fact that he was now the Kirov's brightest young star, and part of the administration's attempt to deflect his defection, which was widely considered only a matter of time. But Baryshnikov could not exact from the dancers he chose the type of commitment he wanted. They were aware, perhaps, that the performance was unlikely ever to be repeated, while the choreography was difficult and unfamiliar. The administration's attitude was also perhaps ambivalent.

Baryshnikov was to dance the Prodigal in a new *Prodigal Son* created a short time earlier by Estonian choreographer Mai Murdmaa. The Kirov's

Valentina Gannibalova was originally scheduled to dance the Siren, until she and Baryshnikov quarreled in rehearsals and she left the cast. Baryshnikov now asked Osipenko to be his Siren. No, Osipenko told him, she had made a promise to herself never to dance again at the Kirov. He exhorted her to get back out on the Kirov stage and prove to everyone there that she was still alive, well, and having a wonderful career on her own.

She agreed, and Baryshnikov's treatment of her made it as easy as it could possibly have been. As always, her partner's attitude to her made her willing to overlook any problems. They worked together tirelessly. Baryshnikov was not a strong partner when he began dancing, and she was taller than the partners with whom he was usually paired. His inexperience made it something of a risk for her. She considered it his first experience of the intricacies of partnering in contemporary ballet: "a lot of over the head, through the legs."

"He didn't do badly," she said. Osipenko was touched by his eagerness to meet the challenge. He was willing to stretch onto three-quarter point to overcome the difference in heights. Osipenko was pleased at the critical response describing their duet as "'that kind of a pas de deux that only Osipenko could do.' They called it 'a chiropractic pas de deux.'"

The gaps in their ages and experience gave this mating of Prodigal and Siren a special authenticity. Indeed, on the basis of the duets in *Serf Nikish* this was a partnership that could work very well provided the spectator was given a dramatic pretext to rationalize disparities in height and age.

Baryshnikov told her he was tired of working at the Kirov. The company atmosphere was now considerably ruder than it had been only a couple of years earlier. "There were a lot of Communists and they were sure that they were secure," Osipenko recalled. At one *Prodigal Son* rehearsal, a Kirov dancer had kicked Baryshnikov as he lay on the floor. "How can it happen?" she asked Baryshnikov. "You're just not used to it," he said.

Mai Murdmaa had the greatest admiration for both Osipenko and Baryshnikov, but she was not entirely satisfied with their performance. "The dancers needed to understand that every movement was like symbols," she recalled to me in 1999. "Every movement is not realistic movement." But Baryshnikov was prone to act the steps. "We had a different approach," Murdmaa said. "And the same happened with Alla, too."

Murdmaa's *Prodigal* had first been danced in the state opera house in Talinn, capital of Estonia, where Murdmaa later became ballet director. Despite the fact that the dancers there were not of the caliber of Baryshnikov and Osipenko, "they understand all contemporary meaning. More abstract."

Realization came to her later, however, in 1974: "I didn't understand much what was different, only that it was exciting to do it for the Kirov, and Misha and everyone danced so well!"

Baryshnikov "made a great success," Osipenko recalled about this Evening. He was "completely different" in Murdmaa's *Daphnis and Chloe* than he was in *Prodigal Son*. In addition, he danced Georgi Alexidze's *Les Petits Riens* opposite Kolpakova.

Psychologically it was not easy for Osipenko to step back on the Kirov stage—"I had a lot of bad memories"—but she felt to some degree vindicated by the experience. At the dress rehearsal, she appeared on stage in her unitard costume. "I looked fantastic," Osipenko told me baldly. The orchestra put down their instruments and applauded. When their rehearsal began going into overtime, conductor Robert Luther announced to the orchestra, "Alla needs twenty minutes, so what is it going to be? Are you going to leave or stay for Alla?" They stayed.

At the post-performance party, she was shocked, however, when two Kirov principal men told Baryshnikov to his face that he was a good dancer but a bad actor. They didn't understand why he had gone to the trouble of putting on the Evening. "It was unbelievable, but it happened," she recalled. She rose up and replied: "You have to understand that he is only twenty-six. He only started his progression. This is a start. He has to acquire a little bit more experience."

Baryshnikov himself listened but didn't say a word. "We continued to drink vodka," Osipenko recalled. But his disappointment over the way the company had responded to his Evening led to a period of depression that contributed to his decision to defect five months later.

She saw him not long before he left Russia. Very late one night, he had called and asked her to come over. She arrived with a group of friends bearing vodka and hors d'oeuvres. He told her that he was exhausted by his struggles at the Kirov and they talked about starting a small company together. Murdmaa would choreograph a new *Phaedra* for Baryshnikov, Osipenko, and Markovsky and they would tour it around the USSR.

Perhaps Baryshnikov came to understand the degree to which the country's political situation was paralyzed. "We thought when Brezhnev left it would be better, but Misha understood it would always be the same," a Kirov dancer recalled. Of course, after Brezhnev's death in 1982 and Gorbachev's election, things did liberalize considerably. But by then the country had been ruled by Brezhnev for seventeen years.

25

Rupture

ASKOLD MAKAROV, RETIRED from dancing at the Kirov, had turned his sights to such entrepreneurship as was possible in the USSR. In 1974 he invited Osipenko to take part in a tour to the Far East and North Africa that he was organizing. He was recruiting dancers from the Kirov, from the Maly, from Jacobson's company. She surmised that his invitation to her had raised eyebrows in officialdom, for he told her that he had pledged his Party membership card that if allowed to go with his group she would not defect.

After class, she rehearsed with Jacobson in the early afternoon. From 3:00 to 6:00 she rehearsed for Makarov's tour on the roof theater of the Kirov. Two separate programs were being put together, and all told she was scheduled to dance *Swan Lake* act 2, Lopukhov's *Ice Maiden* duet, Jacobson's *Minotaur and the Nymph*, Chabukiani's Gluck adagio, and Lavrovsky's *Walpurgisnacht*. Sometimes she rehearsed again with Jacobson in the evenings. Still, he "hated me" for going off on her own. "Why are you dancing these things?" he demanded. She reminded him that she was dancing his ballet as well. He was pleased, but still not mollified, envious because his own group was not allowed to go abroad.

Osipenko's ex-husband Anatoly Nisnevich had since married Osipenko's old friend Nina Smirnova. Smirnova brought their young son Maxim to one rehearsal, where he seemed intent on following Osipenko around. Finally Maxim said, "Will you come with me, please?" "Why?" "I would like to introduce you to my father." "Let me do it some other time," she quipped to the amusement of those who overheard.

Working with Jacobson one afternoon, Osipenko was exhausted and felt some pain in her legs. She asked Jacobson to let her take it easy. "I don't care if you're going abroad," he told her; she still had to rehearse for him full out. Later that night she was to perform her entire tour repertory for a foreign impresario who was considering presenting them abroad. He had only one day to spend in Leningrad. By the time it was nearly midnight, all that was left for her to do was *Walpurgisnacht*, but he assured her that he'd seen enough to convince him. "No, no, no, no," Makarov insisted. "We want to show you this also. Alla, can you do it now?" No problem, she told him. As she said to me, "A performer can never say no."

Walpurgisnacht went smoothly until it was time for a fish dive into Markovsky's arms. She heard a ripping sound, and everyone around her heard it, too. She didn't feel any pain, but when she looked down she saw that the ribbons on her left pointe shoe had gone slack. She told Markovsky to pick her up, not to let her put any weight on her leg. She couldn't straighten it anyhow. He carried her off stage. Consternation in the roof theater ensued. Several of the men brought her to the elevator and out through the Kirov lobby. On the way she encountered the impresario. "I'm sorry; I didn't want you to dance *Walpurgisnacht*. I would have taken the group abroad, but I can't without you." Markovsky carried her to their car.

Her calf was withered, helpless. She was afraid to touch it. She was forty-two and understood that her career had probably just ended. "And I understood that I needed a drink." She suggested that they go to the Europa hotel and buy a bottle of champagne: "We'll say farewell to my ballet dancing." He started the car. Suddenly, Inna Zubkovskaya opened the car door. "Alka, what happened to you?" "You see I have no Achilles tendon. Sit down with us and let's go to drink champagne." There was no need, Zubkovskaya said, pulling out of her handbag her own stash of all-purpose Russian palliatives. Zubkovskaya's daughter Katya was dancing on the tour and had phoned her mother, telling her what had happened to Osipenko.

They went back to Osipenko's apartment, where they drank Zubkovskaya's vodka and the champagne purchased en route. Suddenly the bell rang, and there was Makarov and his wife, retired Kirov ballerina Ninel Petrova, together with a number of colleagues and their own magnum of champagne. The next morning she went to her doctor and announced, "I am finished with my ballet dancing." He couldn't get her leg to straighten. He recommended surgery.

On the night before her operation she talked by phone to her doctor over the babble of background noises from yet another party in progress in her apartment. "Don't drink too much because the anesthesia won't work," the physician cautioned. After surgery, her leg was in a cast for two and a half months. In the hospital she read, she wrote poetry, and she entertained many visitors who took her mind off her situation. The consensus of opinion was that she would never come back to the ballet stage. One morning Nisnevich came and asked her to return her costumes. She was going to be replaced. She told him she wasn't ready to relinquish them until they actually found someone else. Later that same day Makarov and Petrova visited, and conveyed a different message. "We know your character," Makarov said, "and we know that you will go with us even if you have to use crutches, because you know he won't take us without you."

After her cast was removed, she still required crutches. She was brought to stay at the apartment of her teacher, Marina Shamshova, because the building had an elevator. In the shower she saw how atrophied her left leg had become. Better to go to her dacha to recuperate, she thought. She still couldn't straighten her leg, but she had to start to walk again somehow. Markovsky made her special wooden shoes, like Japanese pattens, and, now with crutches, she tried to walk to the lake nearby. Normally it took ten minutes, but now it took no less than one and a half hours. She began training again by trying to bend her injured leg while executing tendus with her right. Markovsky kept cutting the shoes down lower. When she was ready to support her injured leg entirely on the ground she went back to class with Shamshova.

Her right leg was functioning normally, despite the extra compensatory pressure that an injury made inevitable. But her left leg was still spindly and weak, and it is the left leg that absorbed most of the strain of this adagio. Nevertheless, she danced both the adagio and coda in rehearsal on the Kirov's roof stage. The corps around her was trembling with trepidation and when it was over they applauded. Only later, after the tour was in progress, did she start dancing the White Swan variation as well, changing it slightly to make it less taxing on her injured leg.

Preparations for the tour were stymied not only by mishap but tragedy. Sergeyev's son Nikolai was scheduled to dance with them. Nikolai was "a very good fellow," Osipenko recalled. "Not a good dancer, but hard working. Everybody liked him" and they accepted that he was given more to do at the Kirov than his talents warranted. "Maybe Makarov hired him just because he wanted to do a favor to his father." Nikolai's wife, Svetlana Yefremova, a talented young ballerina at the Kirov, was also included.

Early one morning, Nikolai attended an all-night party celebrating the end of the ballet season. Yefremova went home to bed. Sergeyev turned his attentions to a recent graduate from Rossi Street who had just joined Jacobson's company. He overcame her reluctance to accompany him on a jaunt to Komarova, where his father and Dudinskaya kept their dacha. He was sleepy or drunk and his driving was so fast and erratic that the police began following them. In Sestroretsk, a cordon of fire engines lined up to block his path, but Nikolai failed to put on his brakes. Both he and his guest were killed. He was replaced on Makarov's tour by the Kirov's Oleg Sokolov.

The six-week tour was scheduled to begin in Morocco, but political turmoil made it inadvisable. Therefore, they had ten days free until their next engagement in Tunis. Makarov called Tunis and wangled an arrangement whereby a "Mediterranean" four-star beach resort agreed to put up the dancers in exchange for two performances. They were given chips to use as currency within the confines of the resort, amid its beaches and swimming pools, casino, and topless waitresses. At meal times, long buffet tables were piled outdoors with everything imaginable to eat and drink, in overwhelming abundance. She was startled and appalled by the amount of food discarded after each meal.

They ventured to the Far East, to Malaysia, New Zealand, Singapore, and the Philippines, and were then able to fulfill their engagement in Casablanca after all. One Sunday they were invited by the Russian embassy to rest at its villa. She was playing volleyball when a girlfriend signaled her to come over. "Alla, please, don't tell anyone," but Baryshnikov had defected in Canada.

Despite her girlfriend's admonition, Osipenko immediately looked for Markovsky and shared the news. She had no doubt that Baryshnikov was making the right decision. "We all thought, 'Thank God.' I was sure that after a couple of years the same thing was going to happen to Misha that happened to Soloviev. In the Soviet Union it was like a rule, a tradition that there is no person who can't be replaced." She knew this, too, of course "very well from my own experience."

She and Markovsky now sat in stunned silence. "We have to stay here," he said. The American embassy was right next door. They could request asylum then and there. No more doors were open to them in Russia. Nureyev, Makarova, and now Baryshnikov had left; this was their chance to seize, and perhaps their last one. "No, John, we can't do it. Vanya is twelve already. We can't do it. But you can make your own decision."

"OK. I'll go. Bye-bye."

"Where are you going?"

"I'm going to the American Embassy. I'm asking you for the last time: will you go with me or not?

"No, John, no." He walked away. She sat on the beach for what in retrospect she thought might have been three minutes or might have been an entire hour. She thought about Makarov and his pledged Party card. "You can't leave like this," she wanted to tell Markovsky. She thought that she had to alert somebody. She tried to stand but her feet were paralyzed. Suddenly Markovsky's voice brought her to herself. "Do you think that I could leave without you?"

"Yes, I believed it; I thought that you would do it."

He told her he'd been joking. She herself wasn't sure what had made him return. She understood that it wouldn't have been easy for him to start a new life and career without her.

That evening, the shock of Baryshnikov's defection precipitated a great deal of drinking by all. Somehow their colleagues knew, too, about Markovsky's threatened defection. But she was relieved that she had not, in fact, alerted anyone.

Back in Leningrad, Jacobson, now seventy, started to revive old pieces. He wanted her to again dance *Meditation*, which he had made for her when she was sixteen. She hadn't danced it in years, perhaps a decade. That wasn't what she wanted to do. "I can't repeat again what I did so many years ago," she protested. "I came to you to do new things, not go back."

Much more adult was a new ballet he began to rehearse to music by Leonard Bernstein. "This is your biography," he told her, "Markovsky's biography, everybody's biography." It was a portrait of a difficult, volatile relationship. She was interested in the piece. But he was putting steps on each beat and there was no time to breathe, to rest. "Please, I just had an operation," she pleaded. "I cannot do it, not because I don't want to, but because it's very difficult for me." She needed more time to get back into the kind of shape necessary. Jacobson was affronted. "What? OK, I don't need cripples in my company." She walked out to their car and cried. Neither Jacobson nor Osipenko knew that he was already fatally ill from cancer, but they never spoke again. He died less than a year later, in October 1975.

By now Igor Belsky had replaced Vladilen Semyonov as the Kirov's artistic director. Rachinsky had been fired. Maxim Krassdin took his place as general director. Krassdin asked Osipenko to come see him and extended an invitation to return permanently to the Kirov.

"Maxim," she replied, "be very careful about inviting me. How long have you worked here? You may not want to be here after six months. It's very difficult work in this situation." "Everybody loves you," he assured her. "Why are you so suspicious?" Osipenko advised him to wait until her return went before the theater's Art Soviet, the council comprised of important artists at the theater whose deliberations were supposed to be taken into consideration by the administration. Osipenko's friend Olga Zabotkina was adamantly in favor. Kolpakova concurred, but frequent partner Vadim Budarin was lukewarm. "She is already retirement age," Budarin said. "We don't have to take her. But of course we want her to come back." But there was a stipulation: that she return without Markovsky. "We have people much better than Markovsky now in the theater."

Despite their by now exclusive partnership, Osipenko was persuaded to at least sample what a return on her own might be like. She started rehearsing *Stone Flower* with Budarin, with whom she had danced her farewell *Stone Flower* three years earlier. They worked for a couple of weeks. Rehearsals went well. On the day of the performance, however, he called in sick. Osipenko suspected sabotage. She asked Belsky with whom she would dance that night's performance. He offered Evgeni Scherbakov, with whom she had danced *Stone Flower* at the Kirov in the past.

Scherbakov was a superb partner. Filmed for television in *Legend of Love*, they look exquisite together. However, she told Belsky that she was pulling out. She had in all likelihood been sabotaged, but it's impossible not to consider as well that in this case, as undoubtedly in others, she had sabotaged herself. As it turned out, within a year, Krassdin suffered a severe heart attack and resigned his position.

She said to herself that her own breach with the Kirov was irrevocable, but it was perhaps the right place for Markovsky. Time was running out for her as a dancer, but he was twelve years younger. And it was possible that eventually something would change there. She spoke to Belsky about the possibility of Markovsky being re-hired, even if it meant starting again in the corps de ballet. But despite her urgings, Markovsky himself had no more interest in returning to the Kirov than she did.

26

Roaming

SINCE LEAVING THE Kirov in 1971, Osipenko had continued dancing *Swan Lake* at the Maly theater. Her coach Marina Shamshova had always urged her to inject more overt emotion into her performance. Only now, however, did she counter Osipenko's fear that too much display would look sloppy, assuring the ballerina that the way her body looked would prevent her expression from ever seeming excessive. It was at that point, Osipenko claimed, that she broke through her career-long complex. The Maly was another of the city's lovely old theaters, twenty years older even than the Kirov, catercornered from the Russian Museum and the Philharmonic on Arts Square off Nevsky Prospect. Osipenko called it "a kinder place to finish out my career in classical ballet." Then-current Kirov director Igor Belsky had directed the Maly when Osipenko danced *Antony and Cleopatra* there in the late 1960s. The Maly was now directed by Oleg Vinogradov, who again succeeded Belsky when he became Kirov director in 1977. Compared to the Kirov, the Maly was an experimental stage, and so it was acceptable to simplify parts of the hallowed choreography that Osipenko had always found onerous in both White and Black acts of *Swan Lake*. These were adjustments that she wouldn't have been allowed—or wouldn't have allowed herself—to make at the Kirov. In addition, the stage was smaller than the Kirov's, and the space limitations meant that she had to do fewer bourrées in the White Swan exit. In some places, indeed, she now walked where at the Kirov she had been required to bourrée. In the White Swan coda, she performed passés in place of entrechat quatre. Most of the choreography was supported by the ballerina's left leg, but she now permitted herself some relief by switching some supporting positions to the right.

She made the role less technically daunting, while at the same time she believed that years of being partnered by Markovsky had made her technically stronger. Certainly, watching the supported finger pirouettes in the film she made with Markovsky of the White Swan adagio in 1974, one would never suspect how difficult pirouettes had been for her.

She felt emotionally freer than ever before in what she was convinced was her greatest classical role. It was all the more surprising for me to learn that she had never particularly liked the ballet's score. She much preferred Tchaikovsky's Sixth Symphony, his 1812 Overture, and symphonic poem *Francesca da Rimini*. "The first time that the *Swan Lake* music attracted me was when I saw Matthew Bourne's production." Bourne's *Swan Lake,* featuring an all-male flock of swans and a homosexual love match, had come to Broadway for an extended run in 1998. It was Bourne, she thought, who was the first to truly "read" and understand the music. "Tchaikovsky has composed a tragic ending: they died, both of them. Bourne showed it was a real tragedy."

Some ballerinas, ending their careers, left the stage with galas; some without fanfare. Zubkovskaya, for example, had impulsively decided that a *Swan Lake* she was scheduled to dance in 1969 would be her final performance after more than a quarter century with the Kirov. The company was dancing at one of the Palaces of Culture where it had moved while the old theater was being renovated. In class that morning Zubkovskaya looked sad.

That night Markovsky and Osipenko were giving a private performance—which they sometimes did to earn extra money—hosted by a club like the artists'-only V.T.O. After their performance, she suggested that they catch the final act of Zubkovskaya's. Along the way, she bought a bouquet to give her. By the time they got to the Palace of Culture, the final act had just begun, and the most difficult parts of the ballet were over. In the wings, Osipenko asked Zubkovskaya how it had gone. "It seemed OK to me." Osipenko handed her the bouquet and wished her "Good luck." "Alka, how did you know that this was my last performance?" "I don't know how, but I felt it." Zubkovskaya only announced it following the performance.

Similarly, it was after a particularly successful *Swan Lake* at the Maly that Osipenko decided to retire the ballet from her repertory. Visitors backstage told her it was her best *Swan Lake* ever. "It's too late—I'm not doing it any more," she said. The technical adjustments she'd made so far seemed to her aesthetically defensible; she did not want to continue to a point where she was forced by age to make more severe compromises.

In the spring of 1975, Vinogradov invited her to his office. "I know that your twenty-fifth anniversary is coming up." He proposed two gala performances in honor of the occasion: *Antony and Cleopatra* at the Maly and a concert at the Rimsky-Korsakov Conservatory. At the concert she danced two items new to her repertory: Spartacus's leave-taking duet from a recent version of the ballet that Igor Tchernichov had choreographed, and a restoration of the pas de deux from Petipa's *Le Talisman*. Lidia Tyuntina set it on her and Markovsky. "I was trapped in my seat for forty minutes!" Zubkovskya complained about the crowds that stayed to cheer when she came back to congratulate Osipenko after the performance. Together they went on to a party.

Osipenko's departure with Markovsky from Jacobson's company put them into limbo, however. "We left the company and we went nowhere," she said. "Nowhere" meant in fact nearly every corner of the Soviet Union after they signed with the Leningrad Concert Bureau as a freelance duo. "We were dancing for kopeks, touring to horrible places." Their concert repertory of duets consisted of Jacobson's *Nymph*, Chabukiani's Gluck, the White Swan, and the *Talisman* pas de deux. They also performed a forty-minute reduction of *Antony and Cleopatra* that roused audiences to "vociferous hysteria," according to British ballet historian and critic John Gregory, a frequent visitor to the USSR during these years.

In addition they danced a pas de deux to music from Adam's score for *Giselle* that Markovsky himself choreographed. "Very beautiful music," Osipenko recalled, "but it's not part of the ballet, just in the composer's notes." They also danced this in concerts at Leningrad's Philharmonic.

Osipenko's son Ivan informally called their itinerant concert program the "Theater of Two Actors." (In Russia, "actor," is used generically the way "performer" is here.) Touring this way was "just so difficult, physically and emotionally," Osipenko recalled. But, she said, "for a dancer there are no bad theaters. I danced on any stage as well as I could. I never allowed myself to make a *haltura*," a performance that gives the audience less than they deserve. "That's why my conflicts started with John." She insisted that they both had to dance with their full strength and their full heart. "In every city there can be people who understand theater and dancing."

In the summer of 1975 they were touring the south of Russia as guests with a group put together with the Bolshoi Ballet. It was gratifying when Makhmud Esambayev, the renowned solo performer, who lived in Chechnya, came to see their performance and told them afterward, "It was a pleasure to see that you two danced as well as if you were in Moscow or Leningrad."

When their names were announced to the audience on their concert tours, hers would be preceded by "People's Artist of the Russian Federation." Aware that Markovsky resented not being given any official honors, she finally requested that her own title not be mentioned either. Often, on the night they opened in a new city, the announcement of their names would be greeted with silence as they were unknown to the audience. Many of their tour stops were so remote "that they could have announced even Plisetskaya and nobody would have known who she was." The next night, however, word of their performance would have spread or repeat spectators would be in the audience, for their names would be greeted with applause. "Do you hear it?" she asked Markovsky. "This is your title. People love you for who you are and not for your title and not for mine. As long as people need us for *us* we have the title."

Not that Osipenko herself, like virtually all Russian performers, was not proud and covetous of state honors. She had never been given the highest accolades—"of the Soviet Union." But years later, when the USSR collapsed in 1991, "I thought, I've won, because the Soviet Union doesn't exist anymore," but her awards—"Honored Artist" and then "People's Artist" from the Russian Federation—were still germane.

Nevertheless, she too felt in the mid-1970s as though she was succumbing. "I was tired. I didn't believe in things. I was empty inside." It was perhaps her psychological malaise that prevented one potentially extraordinary project from happening. Tchernichov asked her to dance *Giselle* with Markovsky in Kuybyshev, where he was now artistic director. "Alla, we'll make a completely new version about a modern woman, modern relations." But this didn't happen. Osipenko at that moment didn't feel she was capable of such a venture. She couldn't forget that she'd been told at the Kirov that she wasn't right for Giselle, despite the fact that this would have been a completely new retelling, tailored to her own balletic persona.

At the end of 1976, Osipenko saw Yuri Soloviev for the last time. He and Kolpakova were using a studio at the Maly theater to rehearse for an upcoming Kirov performance. Earlier that year the two had been guest artists at the Maly, creating a new duet by young choreographer Leonid Lebedev. Soloviev danced a page tragically in love with his royal mistress, who cut his own throat when denied her affections.

Now Osipenko asked Soloviev why he looked so sad. "I am so tired of everything," he told her. "Tired or not tired, but maybe you have to try to change your life. Try something else." Perhaps he should join the Maly full-time. There he could continue to dance interesting new work created especially for him. "I'm too tired to start anything again." The emptiness in his eyes was more disturbing than if he had been sobbing. The next month, Soloviev's friend and classmate Sasha Chavrov appeared at Osipenko's apartment, asked for a drink, and described what he had discovered at Soloviev's dacha. Ten years after Soloviev's apparent suicide, Osipenko told his friend Lisa Whitaker that for her it remained "a weeping wound."

27

Boris Eifman

OSIPENKO EXPECTED THAT somehow their fortunes would eventually improve. Indeed they finally did. Thirty-year-old choreographer Boris Eifman approached them. The Kirov had already shown two of his pieces. Now he had been asked by the Ministry of Culture to start a new company that would be specifically designed to appeal to younger audiences. He wanted Osipenko and Markovsky to join his Leningrad New Ballet. "I wanted to bring new audiences to my theater," Eifman recalled. "I didn't want to bring the ballet people. I wanted to bring young people who had never seen *Swan Lake*."

He, of course had seen *Swan Lake* and had seen Osipenko dance her classic repertory at the Kirov, as well as Cleopatra at the Maly and her repertory with Jacobson. "I was amazed by her." At the Kirov, she struck him as something quite different from her surroundings: a complete creature of the twentieth century, albeit with a body that could exemplify centuries of textbook ideals. Less ingratiating onstage than her sister ballerinas, she was "a queen of the dance and a very strong individual." She was sometimes angular, not emotionally effusive—seemingly closer to Balanchine than to Petipa.

He called her and she invited him to visit. Her apartment was very beautiful, filled with antique furniture; at the same time there was something "distorted" about it, as if it wasn't being given the attention it deserved. She and Markovsky seemed somewhat lost. Over vodka in their kitchen, Eifman extended his invitation. Although Osipenko didn't know much about his work, "she was a woman in love with experiment."

As an introduction, he wanted them to dance *Antony and Cleopatra* again with his company, with rehearsals scheduled to begin in a month. He told them also about a twenty-five-minute ballet, the first that he'd choreographed, *Interrupted Song*, about revolution in South America. He wasn't sure that they'd like it, however; he thought that it would be perfect for Markovsky but less suited to her.

Osipenko and Markovsky vetoed *Antony and Cleopatra*. They had just taken it on the road for two years, and if Eifman was beginning something innovative, they didn't see how he could start with something that was almost a decade old. "Let's start with something new"—if not by Eifman himself, then by Mai Murdmaa, who had choreographed the *Prodigal Son* that Osipenko had danced with Baryshnikov. She and Markovsky had seen Murdmaa's choreography to Bartok's *The Miraculous Mandarin* performed in Talinn, but it was unknown in Russia. Osipenko and Markovsky offered Murdmaa 600 rubles for the rights to the ballet. She accepted the offer, but said she wanted to do further work on the ballet to tailor it to them. She lived at their apartment while she revised it.

But the first ballet they danced did turn out to be *Interrupted Song*. "It was very difficult to dance because the choreography was so unusual," Osipenko recalled. "It was very much like samba." When she first saw it danced by Eifman's younger performers, she decided it would be impossible for her, but she and Markovsky rehearsed and rehearsed together. "It was much easier for John. It's one thing when a girl is flouncing around but it's not easy when you're a forty-five-year-old woman."

They rehearsed in the Estrada theater on the Moika canal near Nevsky Prospect. During the twilight of the Romanovs, the space had been a lavish restaurant called "The Bear" that her grandfather Borovikovksy had frequented. "Oh, what a pity," Osipenko would sometimes say to herself, that here where her grandfather used to throw money around all she could do now was sweat.

Most of the company were raw recruits who weren't happy about the appearance in their midst of leading dancers from the world of classical ballet. There was palpable resentment that the ex-Kirov couple might turn the new company into a personal showcase. Finally they were ready to rehearse the ballet with the entire company. "We were so tired and we were very nervous." Markovsky was white. "Probably I was blue." Eifman was also white: if "People's Artist" Osipenko turned out not to dance his work to his satisfaction, it could have been very awkward. Osipenko and Markovsky realized that, too. There was pin-drop silence as they ran through it from beginning to end without stopping. When they finished there was silence and then, after a second, applause. "From that moment we became friends with the whole group."

Now Eifman made for Osipenko and Markovsky a duet, *Two Voices*, which was set to the primal-scream, fuzz-box distortions of American rock group Pink Floyd, the type of music that remained officially prohibited. Yet included in the duet were quotations from their Kirov repertory, from *Raymonda*, Grigorovich's *Legend of Love* and *Stone Flower*, as well as Tchernichov's *Cleopatra*. It was something of a portrait of their volatile private relationship as well; frequently throughout the duet, they were sprawled on top of each other. Salted throughout the work were the spectacular lifts and entanglements for which they were renowned.

It was fascinating to see the piece given its Manhattan premiere in 2007, thirty years after Osipenko and Markovsky had first performed it. Eifman's company had made its US debut in 1998 and quickly won a wide following, particularly among New York's Russian émigrés. *Two Voices* was applauded the moment it began, presumably from spectators who had seen it in their native country.

Two Voices and its soundtrack were also meaningful to Osipenko as an attempt at mutual understanding of her son and his generation. Now fifteen, Ivan had become something of a problem child. She had enrolled him in the Vaganova Academy but he had absolutely no interest in ballet, a rejection that Osipenko tended to take personally. Next she placed him in an academic school established for the children of French diplomats.

Two Voices with John Markovsky, 1977.
Photo by Anatoly Pronin.

Like Jacobson's company, Eifman's reported to the Leningrad Concert Bureau, which was headed by Yuri Sadonikov after Korkin died. Certainly, a heightened appreciation of the subleties of art had not been effected by the transition; Sadonikov had been in charge of requisitioning building maintenance supplies at the Kirov. Eifman's troupe was performing at the 4,000-seat Octobersky concert hall in Leningrad when word came through that in their upcoming debut in Moscow, performance of *Two Voices* would not be allowed. Osipenko, assigned to interface with the government representatives as the company's senior member, was confronted with the now-familiar accusations of erotica, pornography, and, this time, infection by foreign rock music as well—elements that should have pleased those who'd tasked Eifman with the mandate to bring younger audiences to ballet. In that case, she told them, if *Two Voices* wasn't taken to Moscow, she wasn't going at all. The Bureau administrators replied by informing her that if she refused to go, they were just going to close the company. And if they went but danced *Two Voices* after it had been forbidden, the company would also be closed.

Osipenko reported back to her colleagues, who were unanimous in their insistence that if *Two Voices* wasn't allowed to go to Moscow, nobody would go. Instead they would strike. Osipenko turned around and delivered their ultimatum to the authorities. Negotiations delayed the performance at Octobersky for almost a half hour. Finally the government team announced that they had decided to relent, but "if there will be one review about you running around naked on stage we will have to close the company."

It was and would remain a matter of pride for Osipenko that she had been able to find a dancing future beyond classical ballet. At a tribute to Vaganova in the early 1980s, Osipenko made sure to add that had Vaganova been alive, "I think she would be very happy that I had the opportunity to build on her training and what she gave me, and I was able to change my style and do other things."

28

Letting Go

LIVING WITH HER mother was often difficult for Osipenko, but more difficult still for Markovsky. There never was any question about who was head of the household. "She demanded we live by her rules," Osipenko recalled. Friction was inevitable. Nina wanted everyone in the apartment to sit down at dinner together like a conventional family, but the nature of Osipenko's and Markovsky's work made this impossible. And that family unit was all the interactive involvement that Nina seemed able to embrace; she wasn't much interested in contact with the outside world. If her daughter announced that she was inviting people over on a weeknight, Nina would object. "Why on earth do we have guests tonight? It's just a normal day."

"John, Mama, and I were each totally different people," Osipenko said. "We couldn't find a common ground at all." She was torn by wanting to please them as well as her son. Nina, who had once encouraged her liaison with Markovsky, now chided her: "If you had married Ufeet, Vanya would have been brought up differently, you would be calmer, you wouldn't have such a life."

Markovsky and she danced together sometimes when they weren't even speaking. They would avoid looking at each other, but still make an emotional, a nerve contact, their performances together reflecting years of professional collaboration rather than the proximate reality of personal estrangement. At one point, around 1979, she came to believe that "our situation was completely hopeless," and she was ready to make a new beginning entirely.

"I want to tell you why I became a pauper at the end of my career," Osipenko announced to me one day. She described a friend who worked at the French embassy in Leningrad. The man helped Ivan with his French, while she helped his daughter with Russian. He planned to return to France. As a diplomat, he could take whatever he wanted out of the country. Markovsky decided that this would be a way to emigrate to Israel without having to leave everything they owned behind in Russia.

They intended, of course, to take Osipenko's mother and son. Nina told them that she would never leave Russia. Markovsky, however, assured Osipenko that "When everything will be ready, your mother will agree to go with us." Markovsky made an inventory of the jewelry, artwork, and antique furniture retained from the pre-Revolutionary heyday of the Borovikovskys. It was packed and shipped and left the USSR with their friend. She cried when he cut one of her favorite paintings into four pieces so that it could be transported. All told, what went with the French diplomat was worth at the time, Osipenko said, a minimum of $100,000.

It was agreed that the Frenchman would sell some of the things and store the rest until they arrived. He was to pass along the proceeds to Leonid Jacobson's widow Irina, who had emigrated to Israel following Jacobson's death. Osipenko and Markovsky had said they would need $5,000 cash to start anew in Israel.

An invitation for Osipenko, Markovsky, Ivan, and Nina was sent to a KGB official. "But he got it and we didn't." Osipenko's friend was subsequently posted to Tunis. Over the years he did send $5,000 in installments to Osipenko in Russia. About what had happened to the rest of her valuables, "I don't know anything," she told me. But a friend of hers said that he had been in the man's house and that there were many Russian pictures there, "so maybe they're mine." Osipenko told me this story matter-of-factly. By that time she had had to face many more devastating travails and losses.

Eventually, her relationship with Markovsky deteriorated to the point at which people close to her advised her to separate. "If he is here in our house I will leave," her son said. "Make him leave or I will." Nevertheless, "I couldn't do it for a long time. I felt that I had to be with him only. With no other partner did I have such a union as we had. I didn't have enough will to make a decision."

"I think she was happy only when she was dancing with him," Eifman said, and she was trying as hard as she could to postpone the inevitable. Perhaps she realized that as a life partner Markovsky was not worthy of her; if so, that seemed to Eifman to make her even more committed to him. Markovsky was "very talented, very beautiful," Eifman recalled. But also, "He was very difficult to work with." He had developed by now a visible contempt toward his profession and his involvement with it.

Eifman "took suppressed feelings and allowed them to be expressed," she said. He made a ballet from Dostoyevsky's *The Idiot* in which the turbulence of

Osipenko's and Markovsky's own marriage could be sublimated into the fatal relationship of Nastasia Philipovna and Parfyon Rogozhin. Choreographer and ballerina frequently discussed Dostoyevsky and his novel: "She was very smart, very educated." At forty-nine, her technique was frayed, but her dramatic expression was overpowering: "She kept the audience in huge tension every time she came on stage," freely channeling her own torment. "Every time I live part of my life in this part," she told Eifman.

Finally, there was *Requiem*, set to the adagio from Beethoven's Seventh Symphony. It was "a very tragic ballet for me," she said. Performing it was, again, for her something in the way of a self-portrait, and one that she was reluctant to fulfill. Indeed, it took months of persuasion by Eifman before she would agree to dance it. She did it first at a special celebration for coal miners, where the workers received awards and were then treated to a performance. By the time Osipenko appeared on stage, the audience "had already had a lot of Bloody Marys."

"Imagine the scene," she told me. "I'm sitting on stage in this as-if-nude costume and crossing myself. All of a sudden I start to rise to my full height. They see me looking totally naked and they start screaming." In this piece she mostly danced alone, with only a short duo with Markovsky. "I don't remember how we danced," she said, since this particular audience not only screamed throughout the piece but screamed for an encore. But it was hardly the type of reception appropriate for the mood of the work.

She was now saying good-bye to the stage, to Markovsky: "Good-bye everything." Having decided finally to divorce, Osipenko felt as though she was on the verge of a breakdown. She checked into the city's finest psychiatric clinic, called the Fifteenth Line, after the street on which it was situated. There she was given insulin treatments for a week. "It helped." One day she was told that someone was waiting for her downstairs. It turned out to be Markovsky. They talked for a while, long enough for her to become so agitated that as soon as he had left she immediately requested a sedative. A Dr. Rosenblatt, the physician treating her, had passed by and overheard them in the lobby. He called her to his office. "Who was there? Who were you talking to?" "My former husband." "Do you realize that he's mentally ill? He's very sick, but if he ever asked me to treat him I would never do it. I could not help him. I advise you never to have anything to do with him."

When Eifman came to visit, he was greeted by her with some wariness. "To what do I owe the pleasure of seeing you?" she asked. "I need to talk to you because I would love you to come back to the company." "But do you understand that I cannot dance with anybody else?" But Eifman had a tempting offer to convey. The Bolshoi's Maris Liepa had called from Moscow, saying he'd heard that Osipenko had separated from Markovsky, and that he wanted to dance with her.

She had danced with the Bolshoi star once before, in *Swan Lake*, when he'd appeared as a guest with the Kirov. He had been scheduled to dance both *Legend of Love* and *Swan Lake* with Fedicheva, but she canceled *Swan Lake*. A day before the performance, the Kirov told her that Liepa had requested her as a substitute. She agreed to go on stage with him after just one rehearsal early on the day of the performance. Their *Swan Lake* turned out to be "nothing spectacular, but nothing bad," and they found each other agreeable. And so yes, she told Eifman, she would try working with Liepa.

Soon after, he came to Leningrad, succeeding Markovsky in *The Idiot* as well as *Requiem*. She left her clinic every day to rehearse with him. Liepa "felt hopeless," Osipenko recalled. "He said, 'I don't understand how you work.'" Artistically there was an unbridgeable gulf in temperament between them. The stage was a refuge for the Leningraders where they could sublimate and escape their personal problems. While leading dancers in both the Kirov and the Bolshoi lived better than most Russians, the life of a Bolshoi star like Liepa was much more comfortable than for any comparable ballet star in Leningrad. The Kremlin naturally favored the Moscow company. Salaries were higher, tours more frequent. "It was like two different spirits, attitudes, worlds meeting on the stage," Osipenko said about her appearances opposite Liepa.

Their partnership didn't turn into something permanent, but "he was very kind to me. He saved me. He just cherished me. He knew how to court a woman." Before the performance he would bring her a rose; after he would take her to dinner. On weekends they drove out to the country or took excursions on a boat owned by a friend of his.

Nina was anxious that Osipenko now realize that ballet was a lost cause. She had always pushed her to ballet and back to ballet, but never imagined that at fifty her daughter would still be dancing, despite the infirmities of pain, injury—she was beginning to suffer from arthritis in both hips—the inevitable depredations of age. "She thought that I was crazy," Osipenko said. The dancer finally "understood that I had to leave the stage."

One night she dreamed that she was living in a castle. She saw a young, beautiful woman walking from the gates. The visitor came closer and she saw that it was Anna Pavlova. Osipenko tried to embrace the legendary ballerina, but she had no body; rather, her body was like glass. "I died when I was fifty," Pavlova told her, "so at fifty you have to stop your career." Osipenko thought about it all the next day. That night she dreamed the same dream once again. The next she made her decision and wrote Eifman a resignation letter.

Two decades after she'd left Eifman, she remained not pleased with the way he treated her legacy in the company. "Boris is so *naglay*," she said, using the Russian adjective connoting something between impudence and insolence. So closely did she identify with the works he'd made for her that she went so far as to insist to me that it was his "duty" to retire those works. "He staged them with my life, my blood."

Above all, she felt proprietary about Eifman's *Two Voices*. It was "all about me. It was my autobiography, and he shouldn't have given it to someone else." It was eventually danced by Liepa's daughter Ilse after she joined Eifman's company. "When she started dancing nobody could understand what it was all about." In the program, Eifman had always stipulated that it was "Dedicated to Alla Osipenko." She expected him to at least now write "It was dedicated to Alla Osipenko, and is now danced by—." He didn't do it, and it wasn't an entirely realistic or fair expectation. But there was no mistaking how meaningful it had been to her.

"While I was fighting for my position I was still very strong," Osipenko said. "I didn't care where it was, what theater; as long as I could perform and dance I felt alive." But now, without income, career, or husband, the traumas of the prior twenty years returned in force. She didn't work for two years after her final performance with Eifman in 1981. "Nobody called me," she said. "I was forgotten," she claimed. Finally her mother told her that she had spoken to a research institute nearby that was looking for a concierge. "Maybe you will go there to work. They said, 'OK, let her come to us. She is a person with education and culture, so we want her.'"

Osipenko balked. "Why not?" her mother asked. "You are already fifty. You're no longer a dancer; your career is finished. Be what you are and keep silent. Work as a guard and come home and watch TV. This will be your life." Looking back, Osipenko believed that Nina was sincere if insensitive. But at the time she was incredulous. "Mama, you don't know me. I am your daughter, but you don't know me, you don't understand me. I can't do such a thing; you can't ask me to." She would rather "die or just be a drunk" than spend her days hanging up other people's coats.

"When my mother was old, she would say, 'You have your own life; Vanya has his own life. I'm all by myself.' Now I'm sitting here, and I'm really by myself," Osipenko complained through tears in Hartford. "For my mom, I was right there next to her. She didn't work after forty-five. I worked. She lived on my money." When they argued, Osipenko would sometimes leave for a day or two, but "my mom always knew that I would come back and I would apologize. Now, when I'm sixty-six," she told me in the spring of 1999, "I'm all by myself, absolutely."

After her last performance with Eifman in 1981, for two years she taught private ballet classes to ballet students. In 1983, she contemplated a return to ballet at the invitation of Georgi Alexidze, who had created *Syrinx* for her in 1966. He was going to choreograph *Sarabande*, a duet about Don Juan, to Gluck for Nikita Dolgushin and Osipenko. She rehearsed extensively, but one day her arthritis simply prevented her from continuing any further. She bent down and could not straighten up again. She was taken to the hospital, although eventually she was able to perform the piece.

A year later, Nikita Dolgushin persuaded her to dance a piece that he wanted to choreograph, eventually titled *Andante Sostenuto*, that would be something of a joint biography of the two them. She took class every day and in addition, twice daily she went through a special exercise regimen originally devised by Filippo Taglioni back in the Romantic era and recommended to her by Dolgushin. In two months she was ready for the stage. But of course any type of rigorous dance was only going to become more and more difficult. One year younger than Osipenko, Kolpakova was still dancing full-length ballets at the Kirov, but Osipenko's feet had always been weaker and her arthritis could not be ignored. Five years later, she underwent dual hip replacements. However, her career as performer was hardly over; indeed, it continues to this day.

29

Maternal Duty

"IN 1986 MY son and his friends were arrested," Osipenko said to me one day in February 2000. Her declaration came more or less out of the blue. Nevertheless, it was something I had learned from others and had of course wanted to hear about from her. But as it turned out, before I could broach the subject, she did so herself.

Now twenty-four, Ivan had studied acting but not pursued it. He had never had the benefit of a consistent and definitive parental chain of command. His father, Gennady Voropayev, was not very involved in his upbringing. Markovsky had tried to a certain degree to be a father to his stepson. By her own decision, Osipenko's mother was at least as much of a parental figure as Osipenko herself. Both indulged him. If one authority figure denied him something, Ivan was prone to appeal that verdict with another parent or parent surrogate until he got whatever he wanted. Osipenko was too preoccupied with her career and its many attendant vicissitudes to do as much as she later wished that she had.

A friend of Ivan's named Fedotchenko was trying to raise money to make possible his emigration to the West. Fedotchenko spoke six languages in addition to Russian. He had wanted to enter the Patrice Lumumba University in Moscow but wasn't admitted due to the fact that a relative, a general, had been arrested and shot, "an enemy of the people." The stigma still stuck to his own profile in officialdom. Fedotchenko never mentioned his parents. Osipenko wondered if they too had been victims of state persecution.

Fedotchenko had devised a scheme in which he purchased dollars and foreign currency and sold them to Russians: "one dollar for four rubles," Osipenko explained. At this time in the Soviet Union, it remained illegal to have even a dollar in one's possession, but it was only with dollars at shops catering to foreigners that certain things could be purchased. Ivan became

Osipenko with her mother and son.
Photo courtesy Alla Osipenko.

part of the enterprise, and so did "A," the third member of the band, the son of two of Osipenko's former colleagues. He and Ivan had been friends since childhood, when they were both enrolled at Vaganova. Together with his parents, he lived in the building next door to the one that housed Osipenko's apartment.

The young men had sold dollars to two Mongolian students at the Rimsky-Korsakov Conservatory. In Leningrad there was only one shop, Beryozka, where dollars were accepted. The store was of course controlled by the KGB. The two students were arrested when they tried to shop there, and they informed the authorities who it was that had sold them the dollars.

In early November 1986, Ivan and A were arrested at a restaurant on the Neva that was frequently the scene of police sweeps. Fedotchenko had arrived with them, but he was in the toilet when he saw the police checking documents. He jumped out the toilet window and escaped.

The next day he called Osipenko's apartment. "May I talk to Vanya?" "Vanya's not at home." "Where is Vanya?" "He is not at home. He will not be at home for a long time." She repeated the information several times to let him know that Vanya had been arrested. Fedotchenko fled to Moscow, where he was arrested at the train station. Someone had betrayed him to the police. Osipenko thought he would have done better to flee to an obscure city, where it would have been harder to trace him. And in that case, without Fedotchenko, the mastermind of the scheme, in their custody, the authorities' case against Ivan might have been dropped.

She dreaded telling her mother about Ivan, but she was able to stall because Nina had been hospitalized with a minor stroke. For six weeks she told Nina that Ivan was in the south resting, but Nina could sense that something was amiss. "I've had bad dreams," Nina told her. "You're lying to me. He couldn't have left knowing I was sick in the hospital." The doctors wanted to send her home. Osipenko asked them to keep her a little bit longer and explained the reason. They agreed and she remained ten extra days. Finally Osipenko told her the truth. Nina accepted it: "OK, we have to be strong."

She wanted to send her mother to a rehabilitation center. She couldn't pay attention to her at home, so preoccupied was she by her son's situation. "No, I will go home!" Nina insisted. "I don't want any rehabilitation center!" The winter was very severe—"almost like 1942." (The first winter of the Leningrad siege had been one of the most brutal in the city's history.) Nina's room was drafty because it had a balcony, so Osipenko moved her mother into Ivan's room.

Nina insisted on involving herself in the case. She visited various offices; she looked for a lawyer for Ivan. She also consulted law books containing statutes dating back to the Stalin era. "This is an awful crime," Nina announced. "He will be shot." On the books the sentence for currency exchange, financial manipulation, was seven to fifteen years, or death. "Stop reading these books!" Osipenko screamed at her mother. "Stop telling me Vanya will be shot!"

The Kirov's Irina Gensler came to visit Osipenko, representing a number of her old friends in the company. "We want to help you. Find out how much you have to give as a bribe. We will get the money." Osipenko was grateful for their generosity, but declined. "I thought that if he had committed a crime he was supposed to be in jail. I didn't know that it was as complicated and bad as it was." She was afraid, too, that she herself would be arrested for bribery and it would make Ivan's situation worse. But, as it turned out, her two Kirov colleagues were able to attain her son's release after six weeks in jail by making a sizable bribe to the district attorney of Leningrad. Later, the attorney was fired for a pattern of graft. When she found out about the bribe, Osipenko drank a little vodka and called them. "Why didn't you tell me about it? We could have done it together. Why did you forget about me?" They apologized but after that avoided meeting her. "Are you not ashamed?" she asked A when she saw him on the street.

On December 27, 1986, Nina suffered another stroke at home and was taken by ambulance to the hospital, unable to speak. To earn money, Osipenko was again giving private lessons. The following evening, the doctor called and said, "She feels much better and she's started to talk." Osipenko went to the hospital but her mother's condition still didn't permit her to visit. The next day she was told by phone that Nina had asked for some water with lemon, and that she could now see her daughter. She urged Nina to stay calm. "I am sure that Vanya will come home soon." Nina made an angry face, as if she knew that her daughter was lying to her. A day later, Osipenko came home from a class she had taught, called the hospital, and was told that Nina had died quietly.

Osipenko had no money to bury her. They had pawned a number of valuables that could be redeemed and sold. But her mother had signed the receipt. A friend went to the hospital and persuaded the doctors to sign a statement that Nina was deceased. Osipenko needed 400 rubles to redeem her things. Friends had pooled together 350. They went to the pawnbroker with her mother's pocketbook containing the receipts. She looked at her mother's bag: tucked under the fabric was a 50 ruble note, just the amount she needed. Among the items she redeemed was a beautiful Japanese tea set, which she eventually gave as a present to the lawyer who represented her son.

She was at home when the mother of one of her students brought money that she had gathered from the parents of the ten or so girls that Osipenko was teaching privately. They understood her situation and offered it as an advance on the lessons; later they insisted on paying her again when tuition for the lessons would have been due. Her friend Natalia Bourmanova made all the cemetery arrangements for Nina's burial.

Osipenko wanted to make one last conciliatory gesture to her mother, who hadn't been able to see Ivan in her final weeks. She talked to the police investigator in charge of Ivan's case to ask if she could even bring her mother's body to the prison and let Vanya say good-bye to her. The answer was no, but the investigator told her to keep phoning and she would try to do something. Osipenko called her frequently. By now it was January 3: "It's the holidays. There's nobody here. I can't do anything." In that case, was Ivan allowed to write a letter to Nina? "I want to put it in the casket." The investigator agreed to that and said that she would come to the church on the day of the service and hand Osipenko the letter.

"Mama looked so young and beautiful in the casket," Osipenko recalled. "Calmed down." Despite Communist disfavor, the church remained a vital institution. Elderly women were frequent visitors, attending all events that took place. "Alla, she looks like a countess," they told Osipenko. Many Kirov dancers also came to the church service, including Kolpakova, with whom she had not spoken since 1971. "We're old now," Irina said, "and we can talk."

Nina was buried in the same cemetery where Osipenko's father, grandmother, and great-aunt were also interred. Not by anyone's design, Nina's grave plot happened to be adjacent to her ex-husband's. "My father had waited for her."

The service ended a little bit later than it was supposed to. Osipenko saw the investigator sitting on the frost-covered steps on the church. She had Ivan's letter with her and told Osipenko, "You have to read the letter in my presence." They opened the casket. Osipenko read it, in accordance with the belief of the Russian Orthodox Church that the dead can hear for a matter of days, ranging from nine to forty, after death. They dropped it into the casket and closed it once again.

The investigator said that Ivan had been in tears when she told him that he couldn't come with her to the church because there were no guards working who could accompany them. Sometime later, Ivan railed to Osipenko about the way he'd been treated in prison. "Not everybody is so bad," she said. "This woman helped me; she brought me your letter." "Yes, she did," Ivan told her, "but after that she interrogated me for twenty-four hours straight." Apparently she hoped that Nina's death would make the distraught, as well as exhausted, young man more likely to disclose information.

On the advice of the lawyer Osipenko had secured, she collected character references to aid the defense, to explain that by virtue of being Osipenko's son, Ivan could not be as sordid as the prosecution would be sure to paint him. Her lawyer insisted she ask Dudinskaya and Sergeyev for references. Having to humble herself before them was one of the last things she wanted to do, but she forced herself. They immediately did as she requested. "Everyone knows that Osipenko is a wonderful ballet dancer. Her whole life is in ballet," they wrote. "You must help her in her difficult situation." During the course of the trial Ivan's essential goodness was sure to be revealed. Their letters asked for mercy.

But was it possible, her lawyer wanted to know, to ask someone even more famous? Makhmud Esambayev was at that moment performing his solo concert in Leningrad. Osipenko had been on good terms with him for thirty years. He was celebrated throughout the USSR for his national dance performances but had started in ballet, admired it passionately, and wanted to be part of it. He had been Rothbart in the 1968 film that the Kirov had made of *Swan Lake*, in which Markovsky danced Prince Siegfried.

Esambayev had a tiny waistline that he liked to compare to hers, whenever the two met, every year or two. "Alla, let's see who's thinner." Since her retirement she had taken to assuring him: "Makhmud, you're thinner. I'm already out of shape." He was chief of a society defending children and mothers from familial abuse, Osipenko recalled. "He was a kind person." She came to his hotel one morning, where he entertained her in luxury befitting the potentates of his native Chechnya. His dressing gown was silk. On the table were many different native foods as well as cognac, a lavish table prepared for perpetual open house. She explained what she needed and he set down immediately to write an appropriate letter.

Osipenko attended the multiple court hearings in which her son as well as Fedotchenko were tried. A was present in court as a witness, dressed to look pitiful and using crutches as if he were injured. He had had knee trouble, but Osipenko knew that he was already dancing on stage once again. "The judge said, 'Are you not ashamed to be here just as a visitor, and your friend is here like a criminal? You did the same thing as he, maybe even worse, but you are free and he is arrested.'" Fedotchenko, however, said that only he was guilty, implicating neither Ivan nor A, receiving a sentence of three years in prison and two years at labor in the Urals. Ivan was given one and a half years in prison, to be followed by a work term of an additional year and a half.

In Natalia Zozulina's biography of Osipenko, there is a picture of Osipenko with her mother a couple of years before Nina's death. A much larger version of the same photo hung in Osipenko's bedroom in Hartford. Apart from size, there was one notable difference: her son was included in her copy of the picture. But because of his incarceration, he was a non-person even in the culture of the late-Soviet period. Osipenko was furious when she saw proofs of the book and realized that her son had been airbrushed out. "It was nonsense," she complained. "I said, 'Stop the book,'" with which she had so far cooperated. "I don't want it!" Zozulina and the book's editor told her that while the first edition was already in production, there would be a second edition in which they would change it. Osipenko relented, although she later learned that in prison her son had seen the first edition. "Joel," she said to me, "if your book appears, please put this photo in."

Fedotchenko contacted her and said that he needed 800 rubles to pay off the right person so that he would not be assigned to heavy manual labor when he was sent to the Urals. Prisoners who logged forests, for instance, often died from cold and hunger. If he had the right bribe, he might only have to do something like drive a delivery truck. He asked her to send money to him in the camp, and she did.

Six months later, however, Fedotchenko arrived at her doorstep in Leningrad. "How did you get here?" He told her that he was on some kind of furlough. It sounded dubious. She suspected that he had somehow escaped. Her suspicion was confirmed later when she learned that he had killed himself. She surmised that he thought recapture was just a matter of time and would mean spending an indefinite period in jail.

After Ivan had served one and a half years in prison, the work facility where he had been sent was closed and inmates sent to different parts of the country. It was possible that he'd go to Siberia, but just as possible that he would be relocated to Leningrad itself. Osipenko knew a secretary at the "Fifth Department" of the KGB who helped get her an appointment with the department manager. She told the manager that she had only one child and she might need his assistance. Would they please not send him very far away? His response was to chide her for "too much noise about this process!" That was all she needed. "If you don't want to help me," she told him, "I have some contact with journalists and they will prove that A was freed for a bribe. I'll find people who will start researching it." She was told to come back the next day, and when she did she heard a somewhat different story.

"I'm sorry we can't leave him in Leningrad, this is for the most severe criminals, but he will be sent to Pavlovsk," in the suburbs, about thirty minutes by subway from the center of Leningrad. She was overjoyed. "Thank you; I will not complain; I will not write to anybody. Thank you very much." She rented a room in Pavlovsk to be near him. One summer she stayed there for a month rather than go to her dacha. He was allowed to come to her place for lunch sometimes during the week. On the weekends he could go back with her to Leningrad.

30

Perestroika

"SOME PEOPLE MET it with hopes," Osipenko said about the Russian response to perestroika, "but some people were indifferent, too tired already. They were sure that nothing good could happen in this country." She herself "didn't feel that there would be changes, improvements. I thought that nothing could be changed in this society."

Yet there was no denying that the political upheavals allowed for radically expanded options, making possible independent business arrangements as well as unrestricted foreign travel for the first time since the end of the Soviets' New Economic Policy in 1928. Dancers benefited as much as any other sector. In the past, proceeds from foreign engagements went primarily to the government, but now dancers could negotiate their own contracts and pocket the money they had brokered.

"At the same time," Osipenko felt that "these people changed. They got worse. Greedier, of course." She told me with bemusement a story she'd heard about two Kirov stars who in 2000 had given their casual agreement, made by telephone, to dance at a gala in New York. Not long before the gala, however, they informed the producer that their fee would be $5,000 apiece. Told that that was impossible, they announced that in that case they were not coming, and they didn't. "We couldn't even think of such things," Osipenko said. If she and her colleagues were given the chance to go abroad, for any fee whatsoever, "it was happiness."

Osipenko herself was able to benefit immediately from the lifting of restrictions. In 1988, she went to London to assist Makarova, who was staging *La Bayadère* for the Royal Ballet. Makarova told her that she'd buy her a round-trip ticket with a return through any country she liked. Osipenko picked Italy. She worked in London for two weeks, sharing an apartment with her interpreter, Anna Maximovna, who had translated for her the last time she'd visited the United Kingdom, in 1970. "If you want to slap my behind, you have to give me a dollar," Anna was fond of saying, "Why? Because I sat on Lenin's knees, many, many years ago." Her father had been a member of the British Communist Party in England. As an infant, Lenin had dandled her, during one of his visits to London. "If we don't have enough money for our supper, I'll be able to make money like that," Anna Maximovna joked.

Starring with the Stratford ensemble in the late 1960s, Dorothy Tutin and Paul Scofield had played a run of *Romeo and Juliet* in Leningrad. Osipenko had loved their performance and went back to see it a number of times. "I want you to make the acquaintance of my good friend," Anna told Osipenko, "a very good actress," who lived near her. Osipenko was startled when it turned out to be Tutin. She was also flattered to learn that Tutin had seen her on stage as well, when Osipenko danced *The Stone Flower* in London in 1961. It was gratifying, too, as she walked down the aisle at a performance or left the Covent Garden stage door, to find herself recognized by balletomanes.

Teaching in Florence soon after, Osipenko was reunited with Rudolf Nureyev. Together they shared nostalgic recollections. He told her that she needed now to stay in the West and work. He had been artistic director of the Paris Opera Ballet since 1983. He extended her an invitation to teach class at the Opera, despite her claiming to him that she didn't think she had any special talent for teaching.

With Ivan, greeting Makarova at the airport; 1989.
Photo courtesy Alla Osipenko.

Over the years Nureyev sent her many gifts; she felt he was acknowledging what she had lost because of his defection. Now once more, Nureyev "changed my life" by beginning her teaching career in the West. He arranged for her to arrive in Paris on her fifty-seventh birthday, June 16, 1989. That night he hosted a birthday dinner in his apartment to which he invited balletomanes and critics who had seen her performances in Paris years earlier. She stayed with his volunteer secretary and close friend Douce Francois, a woman of independent means.

Nureyev asked whether her relationship with Attilio Labis had continued beyond 1961. She explained that it hadn't. "It's good," Nureyev replied, "because he always sweated too much."

She toured the school with a group that included the Kirov's Gabriella Komleva. They were steered to a studio in which they would observe a class. Osipenko asked who was teaching. She was told that it was Christine Vlassi, the wife of Labis. After all that had transpired nearly three decades earlier, she preferred to wait outside. The rest of the group went in. All of a sudden their guide appeared in the hallway. "Come in! Come in!" "Why?" "The first thing she asked was, 'Is Alla Osipenko with you?'"

"How are you?" Mme. Labis asked. "Fine, thank you. How are you?" "Fine. I've been Labis's wife a long, long time. We have two children. And what about you?" "I have one child." "Have you see Attilio?" "No." But subsequently she did bump into him in an elevator at the opera house. He rested his head against hers. "We loved each other once," he explained to the other dancers riding with them. Yes, she agreed, they had.

These were years of exchanges and reconciliations between the former Soviet Union and its expatriates. In November 1989, Nureyev returned to the Kirov stage to dance two performances as James in *La Sylphide*. He arrived on November 12, five days before the first performance, and Osipenko went to Pulkovo airport to meet him. Soon after he started rehearsing, fifty-one-year-old Nureyev sprained a muscle and requested that instead of James he perform the pantomime role that Fleming Flindt had made for him in a ballet based on Gogol's "The Overcoat." But Kirov artistic director Oleg Vinogradov, who had been Nureyev's classmate on Rossi Street, insisted that he perform as originally planned.

"Now we'll see how these cunts who denounced me on a tribune will come to kiss my ass," Nureyev announced. The door opened and two of the culpable appeared, but warm greetings were exchanged all around. Nevertheless, Nureyev's ribald comments throughout rehearsals shocked even salty Ninel Kurgapkina, who had been his partner and friend. She now was coach for his young Sylph, Zhanna Ayupova. Certainly Ayupova and many of her contemporaries in the corps de ballet were unnerved. "Now you will see how this old ass will dance," he told them as he paused before beginning his act 2 variation at a stage rehearsal.

In attendance for his return to the Kirov were company dancers of all generations, including several ballerinas he had partnered during his three years with the Kirov. Osipenko joined them in the first row of the orchestra section, where retired Kirov stars were traditionally seated. James was a role that hardly showed him to advantage. Indeed, Nureyev had continued to dance lead classical roles against every consideration of present capacity as well as prudent maintenance of his own image and legend. People who had seen him in his youth were dismayed at his present condition. Many who had never seen him dance couldn't fathom the reason for his renown. But at the same time he was accepted as a near-mythical figure who was continuing to break rules and make up new ones at his discretion.

Professionally, Osipenko had never been a particular fan, although by now she'd watched many videos of him during his Western career and thought that he had developed tremendously from the dancer she'd known in Russia. She watched the *Sylphide* performance abstractly, brooding on the irony of history that had brought him back too late to the stage to which he had been destined and entitled. She thought it a terrible thing that his career hadn't been able to unfold there.

Behind his bravado, Nureyev seemed "very sad and lonely," Osipenko recalled. In Leningrad they sat down to a joint television interview. "People say you are rich," the host mentioned to him, "you have houses, farms." "Yes, I am very rich," he replied. "I even have an island. But what is sad is that nobody is waiting for me. Only the stage is waiting for me. That's why I will be on stage as long as I can."

"Rudi really loved her," Violette Verdy said. Osipenko had proven popular with the Paris Opera dancers and the theater might have been a comfortable berth for her. But Nureyev was at that moment involved in tumultuous contract negotiations with Pierre Bergé, the new Opera president. Nureyev called Bergé's bluff by resigning immediately after he returned to Paris from Leningrad. He hoped to be invited to return but this never happened. He continued to coach his own productions at the Opera, however, and was planning to stage a new *La Bayadère*. In Florence he had asked Osipenko to procure for him a copy of the original piano rehearsal score cloistered in the Leningrad theater archives. Osipenko petitioned them on his behalf and they agreed to loan it to her for two days only. It contained notes by both composer

Minkus and choreographer Petipa. She went to photocopy it at an office several days before Nureyev's return to Leningrad and passed it along to him when he arrived. Nureyev's production reached the Opera stage in October 1992, three months before his death.

"I DON'T WANT somebody to tell me that my pupils are very bad," Osipenko said. "For me, hearing it all the time, it's just not a pleasure at all." She was relating this apropos her experience in 1992 of returning to the Kirov to coach Yulia Makhalina in her old role in Grigorovich's *Legend of Love*.

Ballet is a ruthlessly competitive field, but an enormous company like the Kirov, blessed with an overabundance of talent, is inevitably going to be more cutthroat than most environments. Making the atmosphere even more factional was a new development since the days when Osipenko had danced there. In the 1960s, most if not all coaches worked with a number of different dancers, depending on what ballet they were dancing. Now coaches often assumed entire control of the dancer's rehearsal schedule. Some devoted all their time to a single dancer. Each coach relentlessly touted his or her charge to all who would listen and frequently had only the most scathing putdowns to issue about any dancer who was a potential or actual rival to theirs. It became inordinately important to the coaches that their pupils dance as many performances of as many roles as possible, particularly when increased foreign touring made overseas travel more accessible. Increasingly, the veteran Kirov dancers-turned-coaches came to view their remaining in the game a matter that rested entirely on the progress of a few dancers. Any notion of esprit de corps within the company was certainly diminished.

Osipenko said that, "I could never tell a student, 'You're the best; nobody's better than you.' I would just say, 'Just do what you do.'" But working at the Kirov, it became necessary, as she said, "to have such a mentality, that you're the best, you represent the best, your pupils are the best—and you just spit at everybody else." Anyone working with less than that degree of self-confidence or bravado would find herself at a distinct disadvantage, as Osipenko was to discover.

Photographer Nina Alovert, who had emigrated in 1976, now was a frequent visitor to Leningrad. She was an admirer of both Makhalina and Osipenko, and it was Alovert who asked Osipenko to work with Makhalina. As Grigorovich himself confirmed, he had choreographed the role of Mekhmene-Banu originally for Osipenko. But after she sprained a muscle, the role was danced at the premiere by Zubkovskaya, followed by Moiseyeva. Osipenko only assumed the role several years later. She danced her version, which departed in points of detail from what other ballerinas were doing. It was this choreography that she now taught Makhalina. At that time, Zubkovskaya taught at the school, while Moiseyeva coached at the theater, as did any number of Osipenko's contemporaries. "They were not happy with my version." Even old friend Zubkovskaya seemed to be carping from the sidelines. "All the other women were saying, 'Oh, here she came, and said that everything should be different.'"

"They just needed to talk," Osipenko claimed, but nevertheless it became necessary to address the controversy. She told Makhalina: "I'm showing you how Grigorovitch taught me, the way he choreographed it for me. If you want, do it this way. If you don't, it's up to you." Makhalina and her friends and family, including Vinogradov, threw a party for her, which she appreciated. But "I just damned everything, because it was such a horrible experience."

In 1995, she watched the Vaganova Competition, in which senior students at the school competed. She was invited to attend by former colleague Igor Belsky, who was now the school's director. Veronika Part was a member of Zubkovskaya's senior class, one year away from graduation. Part competed but didn't win any of the handful of awards. Osipenko's response was to ask Belsky, "Why don't you create a new prize for individuality?" If the jurors hadn't deemed Part fit for citation according to the established criteria, it nevertheless should have been clear that she was unusual. "Just give her a little something, to make her happy, to make her feel different." It didn't happen, but as Part recalled, Osipenko told her, "Don't worry, you have a big future." Part joined the company a year later. Sometime afterward, Osipenko went there to watch a performance of *Giselle*. When Moyna appeared in act 2, she said, "Who is this girl? Who is this beautiful girl?" It was the very same Veronika Part.

Rehearsing *The Legend of Love* with Yulia Makhalina, 1992.
Photo by Nina Alovert.

The Kirov's two-week season at the Metropolitan Opera in the summer of 1999 was momentous. The company's caliber was a dazzling contrast to its condition during its last New York season four years earlier. One Saturday, Osipenko came in from Hartford to watch them dance a matinee *Giselle*, bringing with her a Russian girl she was teaching privately. It was a pleasure to see the Kirov dance, Osipenko said to me, more so than it had been in quite some time. It was a special pleasure for her to watch Maya Dumchenko, who danced Giselle that afternoon. As a girl, Dumchenko had been Osipenko's pupil for several years. She had originally studied for one year in Perm before her parents brought her to Leningrad. They asked Osipenko to prepare Maya to take the entrance exam to Vaganova. However, the school rejected her because of a spinal curvature that the examining doctor predicted would cause problems down the line. Osipenko continued to teach Dumchenko herself and also lobbied for the school to admit her. In her opinion, Dumchenko's scoliosis was no more pronounced than that of many others who successfully studied there. The condition sometimes righted itself in adolescence. As it turned out the doctor was right: Dumchenko was plagued with injury throughout her career, but as it also turned out, Osipenko too was correct: Dumchenko became one of the Kirov's finest ballerinas.

In New York after that *Giselle* matinee, Osipenko went to congratulate Dumchenko in her dressing room, in the process bumping into Moiseyeva and Kurgapkina backstage. Current star Uliana Lopatkina came running after her: "Alla Evgenyevna! I've always wanted to meet you!" After Osipenko moved back to St. Petersburg in 2000, she continued to attend performances at the Kirov, but as of today, there has not, unfortunately, been any real rapprochement between her and her old company.

31

America at Last

OSIPENKO WAS TEACHING in Florence when Baryshnikov arrived there to perform in the spring of 1994 at the Maggio Musicale. They, too, had a warm reunion. He told her to get in touch with him if she ever was in the United States. "I will never be in America," she replied. But a year later she made her first, long-belated visit to the United States, starting a new life in Hartford, Connecticut.

In Florence, Osipenko had become friendly with Franco De Vita, a ballet teacher who owned a small school there. He was invited by Kirk Peterson, who had become director of the Hartford Ballet in 1993, to join the school and company faculty, and he recommended Osipenko to Peterson.

Not being allowed to dance in America with the Kirov in 1961 and 1964 had been one of her greatest professional frustrations, and she accepted Peterson's offer eagerly. It seemed, however, that neither she nor the Hartford administration had entirely considered the question of what it would take her, at age sixty-three, to embark on a new life in a foreign country where the language was unknown to her. Hartford is a suburban city with its own cultural amenities, but nothing on the order of the European capitals to which she was accustomed. There was a large Russian community there, but most were merchants rather than the artists and intelligentsia she had been surrounded by in Leningrad.

Furthermore, she was wading into a more difficult working atmosphere than she had imagined. Peterson was putting his own team in place and their teaching syllabus was different from hers. Peterson was in fact opposed to the aesthetic Osipenko represented, as much as he admired her personally. He believed that Soviet ballet, including or even particularly due to Vaganova's teachings, had robbed the Russians of their French- and Italian-based foundation. He and the teachers he hired—De Vita, Raymond Lukens, Maria Youskevitch—instead took the Italian school systematized by Enrico Cecchetti as their orientation.

After Osipenko arrived in Hartford, company sponsors held a party for her and presented her with new kitchen utensils, beddings: "everything for the house. Everything that I needed was given to me," she recalled. She was responsible for her own living expenses, but an apartment was found for her in a high-rise building that the Hartford Ballet used for its staff. Her immediate sensation was complete disorientation. Once she asked where to find a particular store. She was directed to a nearby corner, but "I left and I immediately got lost. I sat on a bench and I started to cry like a young girl." She didn't know what to do; she didn't know her own address. She didn't even know the telephone number. "I thought, Why was the KGB always following me? I don't even know where to go!"

Jean-Pierre Bonnefoux, who had met Osipenko in Paris in 1961, was now director of the Charlotte Ballet in North Carolina as well as the summer dance program at the Chautauqua arts community in New York State. When he came to Hartford on an audition tour, he was reunited with Osipenko after decades. "I didn't even know she was there—the shock!"

"One of the most beautiful days for me was to see her teach," Bonnefoux recalled. "I loved the steps. She brought all her tradition and artistry and allure and the refinement that was there."

She had a welcome neighbor in the person of Yaroslav Fadeyev, a young dancer from the Kirov who had just joined the Hartford Ballet. His mother, Svetlana, had been a ballerina at the Maly and a friend of Osipenko, who had helped him find his new position in Hartford. His apartment was on the third floor, hers on the eleventh. Fadeyev's mother had instructed him to treat Osipenko's welfare as his personal responsibility.

Also in the picture was Igor and Elena Tchernichova's son Alexei and his wife Andrea. Alexei was a decade older than Fadeyev; he, too, had known Osipenko since childhood, when she had starred in his father's *Antony and Cleopatra*. He was living in New Milford and teaching at the Nutmeg Ballet in Torrington.

Osipenko was of different minds about paradoxes in the American national character. In America, "I like when I'm passing people and they say, 'Hi! Good Morning!' In one way Russian people are very closed. No one says hello to each other in a city." But she also said, as did other Russians of her generation, that the bonds of friendship went deeper in Russia. "If you're in trouble and you need help at any time of day or night, they're there to help." Osipenko believed that generosity here was a more calculated quid pro quo: "Favors, you have to return the favor."

There were days when she was missing from classes and was incommunicado in general. This was something that would be more easily tolerated in the Soviet arts world than in its US counterpart, which was chronically underfunded and could not easily absorb any extra expense or inconvenience. Yet her vagaries were tolerated here. People would bring over food; if she didn't answer the door they would hang a care package on the doorknob and call to see if she'd gotten it. She was certainly grateful that she hadn't been fired, that the school and company staff realized her worth and were "waiting for me to get better."

She had arrived with what I could only call an absurdly idealized vision of the United States, shared by many of her fellow citizens. The more anti-US propaganda the government spewed, the more many Soviets were convinced that America had to be a bastion of everything pure and just. Nevertheless, it seemed incredible sometimes that a woman of her years and experience could have entertained such naiveté. She once told me that a student of hers was going to a ballet competition. Someone familiar with the competition had told her not to worry, not to bother: "Everybody knows who will be the first, number two, number three."

"It's exactly the same as it is in Russia," Osipenko complained. "It is all about who bought whom. Well before the competition the results are already known." But wasn't that a factor of universal human nature, I asked her. She could only admit that it was; nevertheless, "it was such a disappointment for me. We thought America was a free country and so in America everything was beautiful, wonderful—no corruption."

Osipenko was for a long time somewhat marginalized within the Hartford school and company, which only exacerbated the problems she had in acclimating. She taught only students; rarely did she teach company class.

It certainly was true that the Cecchetti and Russian systems were distinctly different. (I find it difficult to use "Russian" interchangeably with "Vaganova." She has been dead since 1951 and discretionary elements were just as essential to her work as any existence of a rigidly delineated "system.") Undoubtedly the Russian ballet language is more flowing and expansive, bigger, perhaps at the expense of some detail, the lines lengthened. Vaganova herself had been taught by Cecchetti when he lived in Russia and incorporated some of his class into hers. But the Italianate elements—speed and flashing batterie above all—had faded out of her system due to the different emphases of successive generations.

Osipenko herself was loyal to her ex-teacher's memory and to her work, but she was not a zealot and did not look at anything uncritically. Indeed, she would refer to what was now being taught on Rossi Street as the "so-called Vaganova system today," which she believed had eroded some of the important emphases of Vaganova herself. It was Osipenko's opinion that not

Teaching in Hartford.
Photo by Nina Alovert.

only speed and batterie, but jumps and bourrées were not being given the necessary emphasis that Vaganova had insisted on. A shift had begun when Dudinskaya inherited Vaganova's class after her death; Osipenko believed that Dudinskaya, who was still dancing, let her class be governed too much by her own performing propensities.

Certainly it was shocking to Osipenko that respect for teachers was nothing like what it was in Russia. The first time I interviewed her, the Hartford school had just given a recital. "I found it strange that in the program they put the number, who choreographed it, the music, the dancers, but the teachers were not mentioned. They didn't put under each number that 'This is the class as taught by —.' They do that all over the world."

In Russia it had always been customary in any classroom or studio that when a teacher entered, her pupils stood to greet the teacher. It is mandatory protocol, but it also reflected respect for age, authority, and expertise that is more than deference to power. When Osipenko walked into the studio to begin class on her first day in Hartford, she was astonished when she greeted the class and "nobody answered or looked at me." It happened again the next day. On her third day, she yelled, "Good morning, everybody!" The girls were startled and reciprocated her greeting. Osipenko thanked them profusely. "Nobody has explained to them how they have to behave when a teacher arrives." She was disappointed that she remained "the only teacher they greet. Nobody else demands it from them.

"People say that Russians aren't brought up the way they should be sometimes, but I look at my students, how they behave—is it good behavior to yawn when you talk to a teacher? Now that I am there they don't do things like that openly." But on occasions when parents were allowed to visit and watch their children, "the children would cover their mouths, but their parents would still yawn with the mouths open."

One day at the school there were boxes that needed moving. Osipenko was astonished to see the girls take the initiative, while the boys stood and watched without lifting a finger. She called a halt and insisted that the boys take charge.

In 1996, Osipenko was on stage again, as Giselle's mother Berthe in Peterson's production of *Giselle*. Incredibly, no one in the US dance press seemed to have written about the fact that one of the world's most admired dancers had moved to this country. This was partly the reason I myself didn't know until Elena Tchernichova mentioned it to me in March 1997. Soon after that, I called the Hartford Ballet to set up an interview. For a number of reasons this didn't take place right away. When I called again at the end of July, Youskevitch returned my message and told me that Osipenko had just suffered the greatest tragedy of her life: the death of her son Ivan. He had died from blood poisoning when an ulcer, developed during his stay in prison, had suddenly ruptured. Osipenko had been teaching in the school's summer session but of course she left for St. Petersburg immediately.

Ivan had been in the business of selling used foreign cars. She always did anything she could for him, attributing, I believe, any problems he had to her failures as a mother in his youth. Ivan had married a young actress and left behind a six-year-old son, Danila (named perhaps for the Danila adored by Osipenko's Mistress of the Copper Mountain in *The Stone Flower*). Osipenko returned from St. Petersburg to Hartford in September. I don't remember why it was that I didn't arrange an interview until January. In any case, when I returned for my second interview, I drove her home from the school, where Youskevitch had translated our talk. Osipenko was going to give me photos to use in my *Ballet Review* article. On the way to her apartment, she brought up her son's death. I told her I knew about it and expressed condolences. She remained fluent in French. "*Toute ma vie tragique,*" she said.

Her living situation was depressing. She had moved from the high-rise to a low-rise Deco apartment building on Farmington Avenue that was nice enough, but she lived in the basement. It was reached by a separate door at the back of the building; it had an ignominious feeling, impossible to reconcile with the giant artistic shadow she cast. The apartment was three small rooms. On that visit, she made delicious coffee. She said that she felt very alone in Hartford. She showed me a stack of pictures she'd brought back with her—some of her son as a child, some of her grandson—saying how much they looked alike. I wanted to do something to relieve the gloom. I mentioned Tchernichova's name and she smiled. I asked if I could call her in Philadelphia, where she was then living. Tchernichova was home; I gave Osipenko the phone and they talked—in Russian, of course.

At the end of February 1998, the Brooklyn Academy of Music together with producer David Eden was presenting a program featuring Kirov dancers as well as students from the Vaganova school. A panel discussion on Vaganova herself was planned. I informed the Academy that a celebrated ex-student of Vaganova was living not too far away. They immediately sent Osipenko an invitation to participate.

The panel was moderated by Francis Mason, editor of *Ballet Review.* Featured were Osipenko; Kolpakova; Anna-Marie Holmes, then director of the Boston Ballet, who had studied at Vaganova during the 1960s; and ex-Kirov principal dancer Sergei Berezhnoi, who now worked with Holmes. But the two ex-Vaganova students commanded most of the attention and discussion. The indomitability of each ex-prima ballerina emanated from the conference table they shared. When Kolpakova stood up to demonstrate an element of balletic style, Osipenko responded by staying in her seat and using just one arm to give a devastating caricature of Bolshoi port de bras. It was marvelously entertaining as well as informative. It was never repeated, but it should have been.

Staging a new production of *The Sleeping Beauty* that spring, Peterson now welcomed her participation, although he did not like the 1952 Sergeyev production that Osipenko had danced most of her life. He was including the pantomime that had been excised in Russia but had remained in the Royal Ballet production that ex-Mariinsky regisseur Nikolai Sergeyev had first staged there in 1939. But Osipenko had first danced Lilac at the Kirov prior to Sergeyev's revival, and in any case she was happy to see the pantomime restored. She recalled to me Mikhail Mikhailov's statement that "gesture doesn't diminish the choreography, it broadens it."

As it turned out, she worked a lot with the Hartford dancers on the pantomime, urging them to let it manifest the character of dialogue, to wait for one's partner's response before beginning the next gesture. "Any movement I do on the stage, this is like an inner language." Peterson asked her to make sure to demonstrate as much as possible so that they could learn and take inspiration from the eloquence of her own arms. The program expressed "special thanks" for Osipenko's "invaluable assistance."

Immediately after *Sleeping Beauty* concluded in early May, Peterson was fired as artistic director. Reportedly, the Hartford Ballet was financially at a breaking point. De Vita, Lukens, and Youskevitch were also fired. Osipenko was not fired, but it was rumored that she was not going to return in the fall because there was no money to pay her.

The wings of a theater were "still magical for me," Osipenko said. "I have to push that feeling away. Going backstage to see dancers, she told herself, "Alla, forget that the stage exists." But her own performing career was actually far from over. That summer she enjoyed returning to the St. Petersburg stage as star of an operetta, *The Actor's Life*. As ever, she loved performing above anything else. "When I was asked to participate in this musical, I went with all my heart."

She was playing the role of an elderly performer recalling her life and career. "It was a parallel; it became my autobiography," she explained to me after she did in fact return to Hartford in September. It was staged to a collage of music by Hungarian composer Emmerich Kálmán. She was pleased when admirers who'd watched her from her first days at the Kirov brought her flowers. She didn't speak in the musical, but actresses who came backstage told her, to her satisfaction, that she had "shown us with your body more than can be said with words."

Ex-husbands Voropayev and Markovsky had come to see the show and went backstage. She always found contact with Markovsky upsetting. I think she continued to feel attached to him, responsible for him. She was "more energetic" than he; "I'm just stronger." By now he had fallen on hard times. Sometime later, during the 2000s, she paid a large amount of money, which she'd earned from coaching in Russia after she moved back there, for him to be able to move into a retirement home.

She had agreed to star in *The Actor's Life* with the stipulation that the producers would let her dedicate the show to the memory of her son. "I wanted to give him something, one big thing." This was of course agreed to. "I was very pleased and touched."

32

Artistic Credo

DESPITE THE HARTFORD Ballet's financial difficulties, Osipenko's situation there when she returned from Russia in September 1998 was now "much better," she told me that month. "I have more work, better work, and more respectful work." In addition to her classes at the school, she participated in the Hartford school's arrangement with the University of Hartford's Hartt School's bachelor of fine arts program. With them she rehearsed *Sleeping Beauty*'s act 3 Jewels quartet, and excerpts from the Shades scene of *La Bayadère*. She had moved to a sunnier and bigger apartment, in a modern low-rise building on West Hartford's Boulevard.

For a time, she was going regularly into Manhattan to see her dentist, Dr. Wayne Yee, on East 64th Street. She had given him a videotape of her dancing. After watching it he told her that all her work would now be free. She came to know the Upper East Side, and was enchanted by the Frick museum. "When I came out it was as if it was not America but it was Europe." She observed a stark difference between the complexion of capitalism in the United States and Europe. "Here you see it's open: people work for money, do everything for money. In Europe it's the same, but they have more culture, more intelligence, more respect for art, museums, books, ballet. And you see the difference."

She was, of course, well aware of the degree to which Russia itself was mired in a brutal stage of embryonic capitalism such as had prevailed in the United States a century earlier. The Soviet government had paid for all arts activities; now it was retaining but reducing its subsidies and the new class of entrepreneurs was not inclined to take up the slack.

"I want to teach Russians, New Russians how to give money, how to be generous," she said to me. Her son had visited Hartford in the company of a businessman friend who was "throwing money here and there." She found this so disturbing that she finally told Ivan's friend: "Please don't do it in front of me because I earn money working very hard. The Hartford Ballet needs money very badly. Instead of taking a limo from Hartford to New York and spending $500, it would be better to rent a car, pay $100 and donate something." She told him about a pre-Revolution arts patron, Savva Morozov, a businessman who was also an arts patron. "In Russia everybody knows his name even today." When Ivan and his friend attended a party given by the school, Osipenko announced that his friend was going to give some money. He contributed $300, which was exactly what they needed to make a costume for Balanchine's *Tchaikovsky Pas de Deux*.

A year later Ivan's frie nd called from St. Petersburg. "Alla Evgenyevna, is there any program where it's written that I gave money to the Hartford Ballet?" "Yes," she assured him; there was a list of sponsors and his name was included. He asked if she would be so kind as to forward it to him in St. Petersburg. He wanted to hang it on the wall of his office. "He realized that it was good not only to be a contractor but to donate money and to be mentioned somewhere."

That fall I was working on an article for *Ballet Review* which was both a profile of American Ballet Theatre's Ethan Stiefel and a look at the uphill battle that ballet faced trying to exist in the United States. I asked her—perhaps rhetorically, perhaps not—what justification she would give for ballet's continued existence in America, what she would say to advocate its funding. She parried with a masterful dialectical contradiction: "I don't know why Americans need ballet. I just have no idea. I have no clue!" Her actual intent, however, was to suggest that Americans in fact needed ballet more than they knew, needed it as a cultivating influence, and were sorely wanting by the lack of such an influence. For her, the fragile etiquette of balletic courtliness could not exist without an equivalent attempt at polite deportment by ballet professionals. She continued to find that lacking in the culture around her. She described a teachers' meeting at the school, where guidelines were being established for the way students would be required to dress in class: "no earrings, no bracelets, just very proper and beautiful." But as they talked, "one teacher is having a sandwich, another is sitting with his legs on top of the table."

"Excuse me, is this a dinner or a meeting?" she asked another teacher.

"Do *they* understand why they need ballet?" Osipenko asked me.

But she was a passionate proponent of the art form. One of her students told her that she was never going to pursue ballet as her vocation. Osipenko emphasized that she had to apply herself to it nonetheless. "It will help you in any style that you choose. It's like a fundament of your future dancing. It doesn't matter whether it will be jazz, or anything else. You have to know classicism first. Classicism is beauty, abstraction, what you need to become a dancer. Classicism gives you the form, the shape, the body you need."

To me she cited the example of Zizi Jeanmaire, who spent most of her career in popular entertainment but trained originally in ballet. "She has a classical platform under these things. It gives her the possibility to support her shape until now." A couple of years earlier, Osipenko had watched Jeanmaire, then in her mid-seventies, perform in Paris. "She danced a tango with eight men. It was shocking: her movement was wonderful, like a young woman's."

For me, Osipenko had "an even larger question: does America need art, cinema, theater?" In Hartford she had seen *Titanic*, "a very bad movie." She was dumbfounded that it could have garnered eleven Academy Awards (once again, the idealism of the disaffected Soviet had been dashed). But she was fascinated by what she saw around her: "for three hours, everyone was eating popcorn and drinking Coca-Cola." That summer of 1998, *Titanic* reached St. Petersburg and she decided to take her grandson to see it; the flaws of the film aside, it was still a poignant and absorbing story. "Everyone in the audience was staring at the screen," she recalled. "They didn't lose one word. They were all concentrated, compassionate to what was going on." When Kate Winslet tossed her diamond brooch into the North Atlantic, her grandson asked, "Babushka, did you see how she did it? She did it as if there was no diamond on earth that would be worth a human life."

"Right now, he can feel and see, but when you eat popcorn you miss it." That year Russia was in the throes of financial crisis. "The economic situation is horrible," Osipenko said. "There is no food, no money, but theaters are full. People just absorb everything in art that they can. They will spend their last rubles to go to the theater. They don't know if the Communists will come back or not, but art is a very big part of their life."

There was truth to what she said about American cultural habits, but at times her attitude was unabashedly chauvinistic. Osipenko frequently rented American films and as well as enjoying many of them, she was glad to watch anything because it also helped her pick up English vocabulary. But despite its being set in the mecca of American escapism, she told me that *Leaving Las Vegas*, a film that she loved, wasn't "an American topic. Who dies from drink? Russians."

She believed that art should be healing, a balm for the spirit. Once when Osipenko was in the hospital in Hartford, an acquaintance had brought her a book of Chekhov's short stories. Osipenko found Chekhov's "Ward No. 6," one of his greatest stories, particularly cathartic. The hero is a doctor in a state mental institution who thinks independently, creatively, so much so that he is eventually ostracized by his colleagues until he himself becomes an inmate. Reading it had helped restore her.

Although "I had differences with Boris Eifman," which still chafed twenty years after she'd left his company, she continued to admire the choreographer's work and his belief that "people are tired of machines and they need something spiritual. That's why he creates ballets based on very big material, like Dostoevsky, or *Red Giselle* [on the madness of Olga Spessivtseva], because people need this connection for their souls."

TEACHING DID NOT offer Osipenko the fulfillment of performing, but "I try to do the best I can." Since beginning to teach in 1966, she had explored the way her body functioned as it performed various steps and thought about how best to explain to students the correct way to execute them. "I teach them things that I couldn't do, but now I understand how to. There's a famous Russian saying, 'If the youth knew—if the old could.'" She thought her teaching had become more creative over the years.

Much of her pedagogical philosophy was a rebuttal to what she saw as her own shortcomings as a student. In her estimation she had been lazy in school, "so now I think that you have to do a class with an energy like it's the last class of your life."

She wanted her students to have crisper footwork, more optimum turnout than she had. She wanted them to listen carefully to music. "I wasn't a very good listener, but still, I think the most important thing is to dance with the music than against it." She nevertheless defended her own interpretative approach to music, which may not have been as accurate as Vaganova wanted but had given her dancing a singular luxuriousness. She and I agreed that musicality "means many things." For her, musicality at its most profound was "not the person who precisely follows, and just goes straight on the beat, but the person who sings it with the body and the soul." There was a difference between that and actually being behind the music: "It looks like delay, but it is delay inside the bar."

In 1962, New York City Ballet brought to Leningrad a different vision of musicality than anything that had been conceived in the Kirov. Balanchine wanted an almost anticipatory attack in many steps. His musicality was like "an earthquake. We realized that we would never be able to do it like that." And yet, dancing some of Jacobson's later works, she believed that she had come close.

As much verbal correction as a teacher may provide, ballet students invariably tend to copy what they see in front of them. Osipenko was still able to demonstrate beautifully with her arms and torso and, when supporting herself at the barre, with her legs as well. She believed that in the studio it was "better not to speak English and to show it well, than to know what you're doing and not be able to show. It's better to see it once than to hear it a hundred times."

There were elements in her class that departed from Vaganova's, but "right now I understand that I achieve more success with my pupils when I remember Vaganova's directions, what she taught us." She and her classmates hadn't understood all that their teacher was transmitting. In retrospect, "we were too young. We didn't think about anything." What would have been better, she said, would have been to start with Vaganova sometime after she'd joined the Kirov. Indeed, what would have been ideal, she added, from the standpoint of maximum comprehension and retention, would have been to study with her only toward the very end of her dancing career.

In the summer of 1998, she had been walking through St. Petersburg with her grandson, wearing flat shoes. "Babushka, why are you so small?" Danila asked. "You're so short. Why are you so tall on stage?" She stood five-foot-five and one-quarter inch medium tall for a ballerina of her generation, but had learned in her career how to maximize her height, to lengthen herself further by using the breaths she took to inflate, elongate her muscles. "I didn't understand then that I was using the breath. Right now I understand that you have to use the breath, and I try to teach my students consciously about breath." Perhaps it was something that Vaganova taught, and yet it wasn't something Osipenko took away from her class. She thought that ballerinas who'd gone to work with Vaganova in adulthood could understand. "Dudinskaya was short but on stage she was huge because of her energy. Shelest was also small, but she was very big on stage."

AFTER FIRING PETERSON in May 1998, the Hartford Ballet had reconfigured itself. Direction was now in the hands of Enid Lynn, who had directed the school since 1971, together with Peggy Lyman, who had started in ballet but became a principal dancer with Martha Graham. The company was downsized and renamed Dance Connecticut, and the repertory was now increasingly dominated by jazz and modern dance. By early 2000 there was less and less to interest Osipenko in Hartford.

Her decision to leave and once again be based in Russia was spurred by an incident that occurred early that year. She had been rehearsing the school's students in the corps de ballet passages of *Swan Lake* act 2 for several months to prepare for a recital. One day she arrived at a rehearsal and was told that her students had been sent to another rehearsal. *Swan Lake* had been scratched from the recital program; instead she would rehearse with them again once the recital was behind them. In that case, why bother to rehearse at all? "Just for experience," she was told.

"I said, 'No, I don't want to. I'm not a trainer. I'm a professional.'" She'd been offered a raise in salary to return the following season, but she was convinced that it was time that "I go. *Basta*! I've always done it like that, all my life," she said.

It's possible that New York, the School of American Ballet, and Osipenko herself had each lost a valuable opportunity that might have prolonged her stay in the United States. In late 1999, John Taras told me that he'd wanted to propose to SAB that Osipenko take over the class in Petipa variations that Alexandra Danilova had once taught. It hadn't been given since Danilova retired, not long before her death in 1997. Taras had been at the Brooklyn Academy of Music panel on Vaganova early in 1998 and later that year he'd chatted with Osipenko at a publication party for Diane Solway's biography of Nureyev, for which they had both been interviewed. He told me that he had explored the possibility with her but didn't think she was interested. I asked her about this and it seemed that she hadn't understood that he actually had an offer to make, although each was fluent in French and they could certainly have conversed easily enough.

By that point she was already thinking about moving back to Russia not simply because of professional considerations but for personal reasons as well. "All my strength, all my health I give to American children, and my own grandson is there without my attention."

33

Home Again

UNLIKE MANY PREVIOUS leave-takings in her life, Osipenko's parting from Hartford was amicable. She showed me a letter she had received from ex-company head Kirk Peterson, who was now a coach at American Ballet Theatre. He apologized for the rough time she had had when she arrived in Hartford. "What an inspiration you were to me, to the company and to everyone," he wrote. "Words alone cannot possibly express your impact and your contribution to my efforts. I am eternally grateful to you." School director Lynn threw a farewell party at her home, attended by about forty people, including co-director Lyman, as well as teachers and pianists from the school. Osipenko was given presents, among them gold earrings set with a small diamond that were a gift from Lynn and Lyman. Russian food was served. She made a speech to the guests. Twice, she told them, she had contacted the school's administrators and informed them that she was on the verge of a breakdown and needed to check into a hospital. Lynn as well as Osipenko's fellow teachers had been supportive, willing to replace her in her classes. At other times she had sprained her shoulder, arm, and hand, and the school had also been willing to work around her infirmity. After her son's death they had collected $500 for her grandson. She used that money to open a separate savings account for him. "All the time I had help from them. This was very touching to me and a big surprise to me."

"I knew that Americans were good people," she told the guests, "but I thought that they just liked to ask 'How are you?' without even listening to the answer. But living here for so many years I saw that they are very helpful and did so many good things for me."

Translating for her there was Natasha Isenberg, wife of Osipenko's physician in Hartford. Mrs. Isenberg was a pianist. The next night Osipenko attended another farewell party that Gregory and Natasha Isenberg hosted for members of the Russian community. "I said to them, 'I gave you so many troubles and you come to me like you are happy.' They said, 'It will be boring without you.'"

She intended to return to teach in Hartford during the school's summer sessions. She hadn't discussed details with Lynn, but "I will come," she had assured her. As it turned out, however, she never did return to Hartford. She was scheduled to teach there during the summer of 2001 but came down with a virus. She did subsequently return to the United States to teach in Florida during a couple of summer sessions at Vladimir Issaev's school in Miami.

The Hartford Ballet did not survive even in its repurposing as Dance Connecticut, nor did the school. As of this writing, some of the faculty has been absorbed into the Hartt School at the University of Hartford. As I write there are stirrings of a new ballet enterprise on the former premises of the Hartford Ballet.

"I DON'T LIKE my character," Osipenko said to me during her last weeks in the United States. "I wasn't a good mother; I wasn't a good daughter. Ballet was everything." I was reading Turgenev's *Fathers and Children* and she told me about rereading the book not long before. Her response to it had been quite different than when she had read it as a student. "Now I understand we know almost nothing about our parents, about the people who are not with us now. That's why maybe we don't respect them the way we should." The generation gap had been most relevant to her when she first read the book; now she saw in it an indictment of her own callowness. Looking back, "you find that you were egocentric when you were young. You liked only what you liked, were concerned about yourself, but were less caring to other people."

Osipenko's final assessment—at least, the final one she made to me in Hartford—on who she had been as a performer was both severe and complimentary. "I don't understand why my name was as known as it was. I consider that I wasn't technically capable of doing the lead classical roles. That's why I always fought for a better partner, because he was supposed to help me to be technically stronger." She had been studying videos of herself, as well as of Dudinskaya, Zubkovskya, and Shelest. "They were better ballet dancers than I was," she claimed. What had enabled her to succeed had been above all, in her opinion, the physical attributes she had been born with, although what she did not say was that without training and constant work those attributes would not have projected the way that they had. Watching Jeanmaire on video, her legs attracted Osipenko "like a magnet. Something like that happened with my legs also."

"Now, in the year 2000 I am still alive on the screen. My style from the 1970s still looks contemporary, and not only contemporary but exemplary. Up to now no one has overtaken me." That was a claim with which I could only agree.

In June, Osipenko was going to turn sixty-eight. It would be the fiftieth anniversary of her graduation on Rossi Street. For years her class had had a pact to reconvene at midnight on December 31, 1999, near the monument to Catherine the Great built in the little park behind the Alexandrinsky theater near the Rossi Street school. But she had been in Hartford and didn't know whether they had met. She'd asked ex-husband Voropayev to bring a bottle of champagne to see if people were waiting, but his wife didn't want him to go out late alone on the millennial eve.

In so many ways it was of course an unimaginably different Russia than it had been then, when Stalin still had three more years to live. It was clear, however, even less than six months after Vladimir Putin became Acting President, that the cause of personal liberty in Russia was again headed into recidivism. In March 2000, Osipenko had talked by phone with a friend in St. Petersburg, a writer who described a tightening of restrictions. "People are afraid that the dictatorship will come back. You can't publish an article if they don't like it. They make some obstacles for people who want to go abroad—things that they haven't done for many years already." But for Osipenko, as unfortunately for so many Russians, this had long been hard-wired as a now-and-forever norm of Russian governance.

Her sense of humor, frequently ironic, deprecatory and self-deprecatory, never left her. In Hartford she once told me about a recreational therapy class she'd participated in at a hospital there. A number of patients were assembled in a circle and a physical therapist asked them to toss a ball back and forth. The therapist approached: "How beautiful your movements are! How graceful you are!"

"It's practically my profession," Osipenko had told her.

"I'm going to do nothing before I leave," Osipenko said as she showed me a leak in her ceiling. "Every time I think I should vacuum the apartment, my back starts to hurt!"

On May 21, 2000, I drove to Hartford in the late afternoon for our last interview. With me was Nina Baren, a friend of Osipenko from Leningrad who had emigrated here a decade earlier. Before going to Osipenko's apartment, I drove Baren around Hartford and West Hartford, showing her Bushnell Auditorium, where I'd seen the Hartford Ballet perform Peterson's *Sleeping Beauty*, the Wadsworth Museum, the Hartford Ballet school, the apartment building on Farmington Avenue where Osipenko had lived when I first met her, and the adjacent homes of Mark Twain and Harriet Beecher Stowe farther east on Farmington. After we arrived at Osipenko's place, the three of us talked until after midnight, then parted gaily.

Seeing her on my trips to St. Petersburg, I know that initially she found it difficult to readjust to life in Russia. She was confronted with the reality that there was no longer the common cause of artists, rebels, and intelligentsia she had known before perestroika. Most people were consumed with the relentless pursuit of income, whether for bare subsistence or vast accumulation. But soon she was entrenched once again in the Russian ballet world, first as a coach with Konstantin Tachkin's St. Petersburg Ballet Theatre.

I think she did enjoy coaching; I'm sure that she liked it better than teaching, which is much more arduous: confronting a studio full of students each with her own issues to attend to and trying to build in them a technical foundation. At least in Russia, coaching usually means dealing with dancers who are technically ready. Virtually everyone comes from the state-supported schools, many of which remain excellent even in far-flung outposts of the ex-USSR. (This continued not to be the case, unfortunately, in the United States. When I watched Elena Tchernichova rehearse at American Ballet Theatre during the 1980s, it was surprising to see how often professional dancers were not technically prepared to dance classical solos. She had to do major technical remedial work at the same time that she worked on style and interpretation.)

In the fall of 2007 the Maly theater, where Osipenko had danced many times, was taken over by oligarch Vladimir Kekhman and it reverted to its original nineteenth-century name, the Mikhailovsky. Newly appointed artistic director of the ballet, ex-Kirov star Faruk Ruzimatov, now hired both Osipenko and her old friend and partner Nikita Dolgushin to coach there. That October I watched them rehearse the husband-and-wife team of Anastasia and Denis Matvienko, who had just joined the Mikhailovsky roster. She worked enthusiastically with them, and later shrewdly observed to me that while the husband had reached the limit of his artistic potential, his younger wife still had more capacity to grow. As she had with Tachkin's company, she accompanied the Mikhailovsky on tours around the world. Kekhman had even designated her deputy director for a tour the company took to Venice in 2008.

Over lunch in 2007 she told me that she liked working at the Mikhailovsky, but "the moment any intrigues begin, I leave." A year later, Ruzimatov resigned and was replaced by Moscow's Mikhail Messerer. She quarreled with Messerer when he attempted to make her impose elements of style that she felt were inappropriate for St. Petersburg. As she had so often in her life, she tendered her resignation. Kekhman, however, refused to accept it and continued to remit her salary into her bank account. All the while she had continued to perform from time to time, once in a theater piece based on the film *Harold and Maude* with the Kirov's Anton Lukuvkin.

In 2011, Osipenko suffered a broken hip that necessitated replacing an artificial hip joint installed twenty years earlier to relieve deterioration brought on by arthritis. At the Mikhailovsky, Messerer had been succeeded as artistic director by modern choreographer Nacho Duarto, who nevertheless supported the company's extensive classical repertory. Osipenko found him more congenial than Messerer. She gradually returned to work at the Mikhailovsky and was pleased that the company now sent a car to pick her up and take her back to her apartment. Osipenko lived across the Neva in Petrogradskaya; soon after her return to Russia she had bought a small but comfortable apartment in the building where her daughter-in-law and grandson lived. Subsequently, Duarto left and Messerer returned. (Shades perhaps of Konstantin Sergeyev and the revolving door of Kirov directorship in Osipenko's day!) At age eighty-two as I write, Osipenko is still sharp as a tack. One of her greatest pleasures is her grandson Danila's infant daughter Maria.

In 1999 I asked Inna Zubkovskaya, "How do you think ballet can survive in Russia, with all the economic problems, or survive anywhere in the world?" "Politics doesn't touch ballet!" Zubkovskaya insisted. "Politics goes by itself and ballet by itself. Every day will be our exercises, classes, that's it!"

Perhaps the ex-ballerina was simply saying that politics was a dangerous subject best worth steering away from! Politics had, of course, a great deal to do with ballet in the USSR: the government was ever vigilant, Party membership was useful to a dancer's career. Party member or not, leading dancers cultivated contacts in Moscow who could be helpful. But a certain tunnel vision as espoused by Zubkovskaya was probably necessary to pursue ballet's esoteric culture amid so many tumultuous changes in society. And certainly the aloofness of the ballet aesthetic could provide refuge and stability in a world wracked by change.

How lovely it would be, I think to myself, if relations between our two countries could be as cordial, as mutually respectful, as between Osipenko and myself. There was a wide gap in age, background, experience, and orientation between us, and yet we knew not to drive any difference of opinion toward a flashpoint. Leaving Hartford in 2000, she had similarly been gratified to think that her students had ultimately understood her and that she had understood them.

The world of openness, of mutual acceptance, that she undoubtedly envisioned as she made her way out of Russia in the 1950s had not exactly manifested. Nevertheless, the extent of mutual tolerance that existed, however erratically and imperfectly, was something she couldn't have imagined in the Stalinist USSR of her youth. Again and again Osipenko had forged links with colleagues that transcended national boundaries. She had many blunt individual opinions about productions, companies, and dancers—but no categorical bias. She became a paragon of the Russia, the international world of culture, that could be and might be.

Notes

Interviews only mentioned at the first time of their attribution.

INTRODUCTION

Page 1. "The more abstract," Gennady Smakov, *The Great Russian Dancers,* p. 207.

CHAPTER 3

Page 28. "She was plump," author's interview with Boris Bregvadze, September 2005.

CHAPTER 4

Page 33. "didn't like anything casual," author's interview with Ninel Kurgapkina, November 1997.

Page 34. "Vaganova's closest friends," author's interview with Igor Belsky, April 1999.

Page 34. "could not remember," Vera Krasovskaya, *Vaganova: A Dance Journey from Petersburg to Leningrad,* p. 249.

Page 36. "ideally made for ballet," Krasovskaya, *Vaganova: A Dance Journey from Petersburg to Leningrad,* p. 100.

CHAPTER 5

Page 43. "It makes us feel," Iris Morley, *Soviet Ballet,* p. 17.

Page 43. "Around half," figures cited in Christina Ezrahi, *Swans of the Kremlin: Ballet and Power in Soviet Russia,* p. 88.

Page 44. "picked her leg up," Elena Tchernichova, *Dancing on Water: A Life in Ballet from the Kirov to the ABT,* p. 126.

Page 46. "always nervous," author's interview with Irina Kolpakova, June 1998.

CHAPTER 6

Page 50. "fidgeting," author's interview with Sergei Vikharev, July 1999.

CHAPTER 8

Page 65. "lovely extensions," Clive Barnes, *Dance and Dancers*, September 1956, p. 16.
Page 66. "was described," Valery Panov, *To Dance*, p. 86.

CHAPTER 9

Page 68. "From you," author's interview with Evgeni Scherbakov, August 2001.
Page 68. "your help," Balanchine to Lopukhov, December 1971, MS Thr 411 (1091), Houghton Library, Harvard University.
Page 72. "was the best," Helen Atlas interview with Yuri Grigorovich, June 2009.
Page 73. "neo-Petipan manner," Fernau Hall, *The World of Ballet and Dance*, p. 74.
Page 77. "she was an actress," author's interview with Maya Plisetskaya, September 2001.

CHAPTER 11

Page 83. "very beautiful, very intricate," Tchernichova, *Dancing on Water: A Life in Ballet from the Kirov to the ABT*, p. 89.
Page 85. "with a marked will," Natalia Roslavleva, *Era of the Russian Ballet*, p. 291.

CHAPTER 12

Page 95. "saw Nureyev slip," author's interview with Anna Kisselgoff, January 2015.
Page 96. "a senior master," author's interview with Tatiana Legat, August 2004.
Page 97. "She had a body," author's interview with Violette Verdy, January 2001.
Page 97. "so stunning," author's interview with Jean-Pierre Bonnefoux, June 2014.
Page 97. "was warned," author's interview with Alla Sizova, February 2002.

CHAPTER 13

Page 102. "magnificently," A. H. Franks, *The Dancing Times*, July 1961, p. 601.
Page 103. "The whole season," Fernau Hall, *Ballet Today*, August–September 1961, p. 8.
Page 104. "more cryptic," author's interview with Alexander Soloviev, April 2005.

CHAPTER 14

Page 108. "I was horribly nervous," author's interview with Inna Zubkovskaya, July 1999.

Page 108. "New York did not see," Lillian Moore, *The Dancing Times*, November 1961, p. 85.

CHAPTER 16

Page 123. "unbelievable," author's interview with Roudolf Kharatian, February 2009.
Page 125. "Very internal," author's interview with Mikhail Baryshnikov, May 2010.

CHAPTER 17

Page 133. "magnificent" Smakov, *The Great Russian Dancers,* p. 207.

CHAPTER 18

Page 139. "high on her hips," author's interview with Natalia Bar, April 2014.
Page 141. "probably the grandest," Clive Barnes, *Dance and Dancers,* September, 1967, p. 30.

CHAPTER 20

Page 155. "very good friends," author's interview with Valentina Moukhanova, June 2000.

CHAPTER 21

Page 166. "danced wonderfully," author's interview with Nikolai Ostaltstov, August 2001.
Page 167. "less playful," John Percival, *Dance and Dancers,* October 1970, p. 32.
Page 168. "We were ashamed," author's interview with Tatiana Legat, September 2000.
Page 169. "dramatically nonsense," Mary Clarke, *The Dancing Times*, October 1970, p. 19.
Page 170. "It is impossible," Natalia Makarova, *A Dance Autobiography*, p. 91.

CHAPTER 24

Page 182. "The dancers needed," author's interview with Mai Murdmaa, February 1999.

CHAPTER 26

Page 192. "vociferous hysteria." John Gregory, *Leningrad's Ballet: Maryinsky to Kirov*, p. 142.

CHAPTER 27

Page 195. "I wanted to bring," author's interview with Boris Eifman, April 1998.

CHAPTER 30

Page 217. "Don't worry," author's interview with Veronika Part, January 2011.

CHAPTER 32

Page 142. "class in Petipa variations," author's interview with John Taras, December 1999.

Bibliography

Allbert, Gennady. *Alexander Pushkin: Master Teacher of Dance*. New York: New York Public Library, 2001.

Alexeyeva, Ludmilla and Paul Goldberg. *The Thaw Generation: Coming of Age in the Post-Stalin Era*. Pittsburgh, PA: University of Pittsburgh Press, 1993.

Aliakrinskaya, M. A., ed. *Alla Osipenko*. St. Petersburg: Terpsichore, 2007.

Alovert, Nina. *Baryshnikov in Russia*. New York: Holt, Rinehart & Winston, 1984.

Alovert, Nina. *St. Petersburg Mirrors*. Moscow: Ballet, 2003.

Ardoin, John. *Valery Gergiev and the Kirov: A Story of Survival*. Portland, OR: Amadeus Press, 2001.

Baronova, Irina. *Irina: Ballet, Life and Love*. Gainesville: University Press of Florida, 2005.

Barghoorn, Frederick C. *The Soviet Cultural Offensive: The Role of Cultural Diplomacy in Soviet Foreign Policy*. Princeton, NJ: Princeton University Press, 1960.

Bartig, Kevin. *Composing for the Red Screen: Prokofiev and Soviet Film*. New York: Oxford University Press, 2013.

Beaumont, Cyril. *The Ballet Called Swan Lake*. London: C.W. Beaumont, 1952.

Beaumont, Cyril. *The Ballet Called Giselle*. London: C.W. Beaumont, 1945.

Beaumont, Cyril. *The Diaghilev Ballet in London: A Personal Record*. London: Putnam, 1940.

Beaumont, Cyril. *Michel Fokine and His Ballets*. London: C.W. Beaumont, 1935.

Bellew, Hélène. *Ballet in Moscow Today*. London: Thames and Hudson, 1956.

Benois, Alexandre. *Memoirs*. Translated by Moura Budberg. London: Chatto & Windus, 1960.

Benois, Alexandre. *Reminiscences of the Russian Ballet*. Translated by Maria St. Just. London: Putnam, 1941.

Billington, James. *The Icon and the Axe: An Interpretative History of Russian Culture*. New York: Vintage Books, 1970.

Binyon, Michael. *Life in Russia*. New York: Pantheon Books, 1983.

Blankov, Boris, ed. *Yuri Soloviev: His Life and Work*. St. Petersburg: DEAN Publishers, 2004.

Bremser, Martha, ed. *International Dictionary of Ballet*. Detroit: St. James Press, 1993.

Brown, Archie. *The Gorbachev Factor*. New York: Oxford University Press, 1997.

Buckle, Richard. *Diaghilev*. New York: Atheneum, 1979.

Buckle, Richard. *Nijinsky*. New York: Simon and Schuster, 1971.

Buckle, Richard, with John Taras. *George Balanchine: Ballet Master*. New York: Random House, 1988.

Carter, Huntley. *The New Spirit in the Russian Theatre 1917–1928*. New York: Brentano's, 1929.

Caute, David. *The Dancer Defects: The Struggle For Cultural Supremacy During the Cold War*. New York: Oxford University Press, 2003.

Clark, Katerina. *Petersburg: Crucible of Cultural Revolution*. Cambridge, MA: Harvard University Press, 1995.

Clarke, Mary and Clement Crisp. *Ballerina: The Art of Women in Classical Ballet*. London: BBC Books, 1987.

Cohen, Selma Jeanne, ed. *International Encyclopedia of Dance*. New York: Oxford University Press, 1998.

Cohen, Stephen F. *Soviet Fates and Lost Alternatives: From Stalinism to the New Cold War*. New York: Columbia University Press, 2011.

Cohen, Stephen F. *Failed Crusades: America and the Tragedy of Post-Communist Russia*. New York: W.W. Norton, 2000.

Conyn, Cornelius. *Three Centuries of Ballet*. New York: Elsevier Press, 1953.

Croce, Arlene. *Afterimages*. New York: Alfred A. Knopf, 1977.

Croce, Arlene. *Going to the Dance*. New York: Alfred A. Knopf, 1982.

Croce, Arlene. *Sight Lines*. New York: Alfred A. Knopf, 1987.

D'Amboise, Jacques. *I Was a Dancer*. New York: Alfred A. Knopf, 2010.

Danilova, Alexandra. *Choura*. New York: Alfred A. Knopf, 1986.

Denby, Edwin. *Looking at the Dance*. New York: Pellegrine & Cudahy, 1968.

Denby, Edwin. *Dancers, Buildings and People in the Streets*. New York: Horizon Press, 1965.

Du Plessix Gray, Francine. *Soviet Women: Walking the Tightrope*. New York: Doubleday, 1991.

Edele, Mark. *Stalinist Society, 1928–1953*. New York: Oxford University Press, 2011.

Ezrahi, Christina. *Swans of the Kremlin: Ballet and Power in Soviet Russia*. Pittsburgh: University of Pittsburgh Press, 2013.

Figes, Orlando. *Natasha's Dance: A Cultural History of Russia*. New York: Metropolitan Books, 2002.

Figes, Orlando. *The Whisperers: Private Life in Stalin's Russia*. New York: Metropolitan Books, 2007.

Fitzpatrick, Sheila. *Tear Off the Masks! Identity and Imposture in Twentieth-century Russia*. Princeton, NJ: Princeton University Press, 2005.

Fitzpatrick, Sheila. *Everyday Stalinism: Ordinary Life in Extraordinary Times: Soviet Russia in the 1930s*. New York: Oxford University Press, 2000.

Fokine, Michel. *Memoirs of a Ballet Master*. Translated by Vitale Fokine. Edited by Anatole Chujoy. Boston: Little, Brown, 1961.

Fonteyn, Margot. *Autobiography*. New York: Alfred A. Knopf, 1976.

Fonteyn, Margot. *The Magic of Dance*. New York: Alfred A. Knopf, 1979.

Frame, Murray. *The St. Petersburg Imperial Theaters: Stage and State in Revolutionary Russia 1910–1920*. Jefferson, NC: McFarland, 2000.

Frame, Murray. *School For Citizens: Theatre and Civil Society in Imperial Russia*. New Haven: Yale University Press, 2006.

Furst, Juliane. *Stalin's Last Generation: Soviet Post-war Youth and the Emergence of Mature Socialism*. New York: Oxford University Press, 2010.

Garafola, Lynn. *Diaghilev's Ballets Russes*. New York: Oxford University Press, 1989.

Geva, Tamara. *Split Seconds: A Remembrance*. New York: Harper and Row, 1972.

Glantz, David. *The Siege of Leningrad: 900 Days of Terror*. London: Cassell Military Paperbacks, 2010.

Gottlieb, Robert. *George Balanchine: The Ballet Maker*. New York: Harper Collins, 2004.

Gorsuch, Anne E. *Youth in Revolutionary Russia: Enthusiasts, Bohemians, Delinquents*. Bloomington: Indiana University Press, 2000.

Gorsuch, Anne E. *All This Is Your World: Soviet Tourism at Home and Abroad after Stalin*. New York: Oxford University Press, 2011.

Gregory, John. *The Legat Saga*. London: Javog, 1992.

Gregory, John and Alexander Ukladnikov: *Leningrad Ballet: Maryinsky to Kirov. The Story of the World's Greatest Ballet School*. London: Robson Books, 1980.

Grey, Beryl. *Red Curtain Up*. London: Secker & Warburg, 1958.

Guilbaut, Serge. *How New York Stole the Idea of Modern Art: Abstract Expressionism, Freedom and the Cold War*. Chicago: University of Chicago Press, 1983.

Hall, Coryne. *Imperial Dancer: Mathilde Kschessinskaya and the Romanovs*. Stroud, UK: Sutton, 2005.

Hall, Fernau. *The World of Ballet and Dance*. New York: Hamlyn, 1970.

Haskell, Arnold. *Dancing around the World*. New York: Dodge, 1938.

Haskell, Arnold. *The Russian Genius in Ballet: A Study in Continuity and Growth*. New York: Pergamon Press, 1963.

Homans, Jennifer. *Apollo's Angels: A History of Ballet*. New York: Random House, 2010.

Horwitz, Dawn Lille. *Michel Fokine*. Boston: Twayne, 1985.

Hurok, Sol. *S. Hurok Presents: A Memoir of the Dance World*. New York: Hermitage House, 1953.

Ilyacheva, Marina. *Irina Kolpakova*. Leningrad: Isskustvo, 1986.

Jacobs, Laura. *Landscape with Moving Figures: A Decade on Dance*. New York: Dance & Movement Press, 2006.

Jelagin, Juri. *Taming of the Arts*. Translated by Nicholas Wreden. New York: E.P. Dutton, 1951.

Johnson, Priscilla. *Khrushchev and the Arts: The Politics of Soviet Culture 1962–1964*. Cambridge, MA: M.I.T. Press, 1965.

Johnson, Robert. *Diana Vishneva: Beauty in Motion*. New York: Ardani, 2008.

Johnston, Timothy. *Being Soviet: Identity, Rumour, and Everyday Life under Stalin, 1939–1953*. New York: Oxford University Press, 2011.

Jones, Polly, ed. *The Dilemmas of De-Stalinization: Negotiating Cultural and Social Change in the Khrushchev Era*. London: Routledge, 2006.

Karsavina, Tamara. *Theatre Street*. New York: E. P. Dutton, 1931.

Kavanaugh, Julie. *Nureyev: The Life*. New York: Pantheon Books, 2007.

Kchessinskaya, Mathilde. *Dancing in St. Petersburg*. Garden City, NY: Doubleday, 1961.

Kendall, Elizabeth. *Balanchine and the Lost Muse*. New York: Oxford University Press, 2013.

Keynes, Milo, ed. *Lydia Lopokova*. New York: St. Martin's Press, 1982.

Kozlov, William, Sheila Fitzpatrick, and Sergei V. Mironenko, eds. *Sedition: Everyday Resistance in the Soviet Union under Khrushchev and Brezhnev*. New Haven, CT: Yale University Press, annotated second edition, 2011.

Krasovskaya, Vera. *Nijinsky*. Translated by John E. Bowlt. New York: Schirmer Books, 1979.

Krasovskaya, Vera. Vaganova: *A Dance Journey from Petersburg to Leningrad*. Translated by Vera Siegel. Gainesville: University Press of Florida, 2005.

Kucherenko, Olga. *Little Soldiers: How Soviet Children Went to War, 1941–1945*. New York: Oxford University Press, 2011.

Kyasht, Lydia. *Romantic Recollections*. Edited by Erica Beale. Boston: Da Capo Press, 1978 [reprint of 1929 first edition published by New York: Brentano].

Lawler, Lillian B. *The Dance in Ancient Greece*. Middletown, CT: Wesleyan University Press, 1965.

Lee, Carol. *Ballet in Western Culture: A History of Its Origins and Evolution*. Boston: Allyn and Bacon, 1999.

Lifar, Serge. *History of Russian Ballet from Its Origins to the Present Day*. Translated by Arnold L. Haskell. London: Hutchinson, 1954.

Lopukhov, Fyodor. *Writings on Ballet and Music*. Edited and with an Introduction by Stephanie Jourdan. Madison: University of Wisconsin Press, 2002.

MacDonald, Nesta. *Diaghilev Observed by Critics in England and the United States, 1911–1929*. New York: Dance Horizons, 1975.

Mackrell, Judith. *Bloomsbury Ballerina: Lydia Lopokova, Imperial Dancer and Mrs. John Maynard Keynes*. London: Weidenfeld & Nicolson, 2008.

Makarova, Natalia. *A Dance Autobiography*. New York: Alfred A. Knopf, 1979.

Manchester, P. W. *The Rose and the Star*. New York: Macmillan, 1950.

Mandel, William M. *Soviet Women*. New York: Anchor Books, 1975.

Malia, Martin E. *Russia under Western Eyes: From the Bronze Horseman to the Lenin Mausoleum*. Cambridge, MA: Belknap Press, 1999.

Mason, Francis. *I Remember Balanchine*. New York: Doubleday, 1991.

Massie, Suzanne. *Land of the Firebird: The Beauty of Old Russia*. New York: Simon and Schuster, 1980.

McDaniel, Cadra Peterson. *American-Soviet Cultural Diplomacy: The Bolshoi Ballet's American Premiere.* Lanham, MD: Lexington Books, 2014.

McGowan, Margaret M. *Dance in the Renaissance: European Fashion, French Obsession.* New Haven, CT: Yale University Press, 2008.

Mikes, George: *Leap through the Curtain: The Story of Nora Kovach and Istvan Rabovsky.* London: Weidenfeld and Nicholson, 1955.

Money, Keith. *Anna Pavlova: Her Life and Art.* New York: Alfred A. Knopf, 1982.

Moore, Lillian, ed. *Russian Ballet Master: The Memoirs of Marius Petipa.* London: A & C Black, 1948.

Morley, Iris. *Soviet Ballet.* London: Collins, 1945.

Morrison, Simon. *The People's Artist: Prokofiev's Soviet Years.* New York: Oxford University Press, 2009.

Naroditskaya, Inna. *Bewitching Russian Opera: The Tsarina from State to Stage.* New York: Oxford University Press, 2012.

Newman, Barbara. *Grace under Pressure: Passing Dance through Time.* New York: Proscenium, 2003.

Nice, David. *Prokofiev—A Biography: From Russia to the West, 1891–1935.* New Haven, CT: Yale University Press, 2003.

Nureyev, Rudolf. *Nureyev: An Autobiography.* New York: E.P. Dutton, 1963.

Panov, Valery. *To Dance.* 1978. New York: Alfred A. Knopf, 1978.

Pawlick, Catherine E. *Vaganova Today: The Preservation of Pedagogical Tradition.* Gainesville: University Press of Florida, 2011.

Plisetskaya, Maya. *I, Maya Plisetskaya.* Translated from the Russian by Antonina W. Bouis. New Haven, CT: Yale University Press, 2001.

Prevots, Naima. *Dance for Export: Cultural Diplomacy and the Cold War.* Middletown, CT: Wesleyan University Press, 1999.

Pritchard, Jane and Caroline Hamilton. *Anna Pavlova: Twentieth Century Ballerina.* London: Booth-Clibborn Editions, 2012.

Poznansky, Alexander. *Tchaikovsky: The Quest for the Inner Man.* New York: Schirmer Books, 1991.

Poznansky, Alexander. *Tchaikovsky's Last Days: A Documentary Study.* New York: Oxford University Press, 1996.

Racster, Olga. *The Master of the Russian Ballet: The Memoirs of Cav. Enrico Cechetti.* London: Hutchinson, 1922.

Radzinskii, Ėdvard. *The Life and Death of Nicholas II.* New York: Anchor Books, 1993.

Raleigh, Donald J. *Soviet Baby Boomers: An Oral History of Russia's Cold War Generation.* New York: Oxford University Press, 2013.

Remnick, David. *Lenin's Tomb: The Last Days of the Soviet Empire.* New York: Random House, 1993.

Reynolds, Nancy. *No Fixed Points: Dance in the Twentieth Century.* New Haven, CT: Yale University Press, 2003.

Riasonovsky, Nicholas V. *A History of Russia.* New York: Oxford University Press, 1977.

Risch, Willian J., ed. *Youth and Rock in the Soviet Bloc: Youth Cultures, Music and the State in Russia and Eastern Europe*. Lanham, MD: Lexington Books, 2014.

Robinson, Harlow. *The Last Impresario: The Life, Times and Legacy of Sol Hurok*. New York: Viking Books, 1994.

Roné, Elvira. *Olga Preobrajenska: A Portrait*. Translated, adapted, and introduced by Fernau Hall. New York: Marcel Dekker, 1978.

Roslavleva, Natalia. *Era of the Russian Ballet*. New York: E. P. Dutton, 1966.

Ross, Janice. *Like a Bomb Going Off: Leonid Yakobson and Ballet as Resistance in Soviet Russia*. New Haven, CT: Yale University Press, 2015.

Rudnitsky, Konstantin. *Russian and Soviet Theater, 1905–1932*. New York: Harry N. Abrams, 1988.

Rudolf Nureyev. St. Petersburg: Kult-Inform-Press, 1998.

Salisbury, Harrison. *The 900 Days: The Siege of Leningrad*. New York: Harper and Row, 1969.

Sayler, Oliver. *The Russian Theatre*. New York: Brentano's, 1922.

Scheijen, Sjeng. *Diaghilev: A Life*. New York: Oxford University Press, 2009.

Schmelz, Peter. *Such Freedom, If Only Musical: Unofficial Soviet Music during the Thaw*. New York: Oxford University Press, 2009.

Scholl, Tim. *From Petipa to Balanchine: Classical Revival and the Modernization of Ballet*. New York: Routledge, 1994.

Scholl, Tim. *"Sleeping Beauty": A Legend in Progress*. New Haven, CT: Yale University Press, 2004.

Schwezoff, Igor. *Borzoi*. London: Hodder and Stoughton, 1935.

Slonim, Marc. *Russian Theatre: From the Empire to the Soviets*. Cleveland, OH: World, 1961.

Slonimsky, Yuri, et al. *Soviet Ballet*. New York: Philosophical Library, 1947.

Smakov, Gennady. *Baryshnikov: From Russia to the West*. New York: Farrar, Straus & Giroux, 1981.

Smakov, Gennady. *The Great Russian Dancers*. New York: Alfred A. Knopf, 1984.

Smith, Hedrick. *The Russians*. New York: Random House, 1983.

Smith, Marian Elizabeth. *Ballet and Opera in the Age of Giselle*. Princeton, NJ: Princeton University Press, 2000.

Solway, Diane. *Nureyev: His Life*. New York: William Morrow, 1998.

Sorrell, Walter. *Dance in Its Time*. Garden City, NY: Anchor Press/Doubleday, 1981.

Sorrell, Walter. *The Dance through the Ages*. New York: Grosset & Dunlap, 1967.

Souritz, Elizabeth. *Soviet Choreographers in the 1920s*. Translated by Lynn Visson. Durham, NC: Duke University Press, 1990.

Stites, Richard. *Serfdom, Society and the Arts in Imperial Russia: The Pleasure and the Power*. New Haven, CT: Yale University Press, 2005.

St. Petersburg Artistic Life 1900–1916, Photochronicle. St. Petersburg: Iskusstvo, 2001.

Sullivan, Lawrence. *Elizabeth Anderson-Ivantzova: A Bolshoi Ballerina Abroad*. Xlibrisi, 2006.

Swift, Mary Grace. *The Art of the Dance in the USSR*. Notre Dame, IN: University of Notre Dame Press, 1968.

Taper, Bernard. *Balanchine: A Biography*. Berkeley: University of California Press, 1996.

Taruskin, Richard. *On Russian Music*: Berkeley: University of California Press, 2009.

Tchernichova, Elena, with Joel Lobenthal. *Dancing on Water: A Life in Ballet from the Kirov to the ABT*. Boston: Northeastern University Press, 2013.

Tompson, William J. *The Soviet Union under Brezhnev*. London: Routledge, 2003.

Troyat, Henri. *Daily Life in Russia under the Last Tzar*. New York: Macmillan, 1962.

Vaganova, Agippina. *Basic Principles of Classical Ballet*. Mineola, NY: Dover, 1969.

Volkov, Solomon. *Balanchine's Tchaikovsky: Interviews with George Balanchine*. New York: Simon and Schuster, 1985.

Volkov, Solomon. *St. Petersburg: A Cultural History*. Translated by Antonina W. Bouis. New York: Free Press, 1995.

Volynsky, Akim. *Ballet's Magic Kingdom: Selected Writings on Dance in Russia 1911–1925*. Translated and edited with notes and introduction by Stanley J. Rabinowitz. New Haven, CT: Yale University Press, 2008.

Vishnevskaya, Galina. *Galina: A Russian Story*. San Diego, CA: Harcourt Brace Jovanovich, 1984.

Wiley, Roland John. *A Century of Russian Ballet*. Oxford: Clarendon Press, 1990.

Wiley, Roland John. *The Life and Ballets of Lev Ivanov*. New York: Oxford University Press, 1997.

Wiley, Roland John. *Tchaikovsky's Ballets: Swan Lake, Sleeping Beauty, The Nutcracker*. New York: Oxford University Press, 1985.

Willis-Aarnio, Peggy. *Agrippina Vaganova (1879–1951): Her Place in the History of Ballet and Her Impact on the Future of Classical Dance*. Lewiston, NY: Edwin Mellen Press, 2002.

Woll, Josephine. *Real Images: Soviet Cinema and the Thaw*. London: I. B. Tauris, 2000.

Zeglovsky, Alexander. *Ballet Crusade*. Melbourne, Australia: Reed and Harris, 1944.

Zozulina, Natalia. *Alla Osipenko*. Leningrad, USSR: Isskustvo, 1987.

Yale, Richmond. *Cultural Exchange and the Cold War: Raising the Iron Curtain*. University Park: Pennsylvania State University Press, 2003.

Index